C000199251

MORE THAN
A GAME

MORE THAN A GAME

Saving Football from Itself

MARK GREGORY

YELLOW JERSEY PRESS
LONDON

1 3 5 7 9 10 8 6 4 2

Yellow Jersey, an imprint of Vintage, is part of
the Penguin Random House group of companies whose addresses
can be found at global.penguinrandomhouse.com.

Penguin
Random House
UK

First published by Yellow Jersey in 2021

penguin.co.uk/vintage

A CIP catalogue record for this book is available from the British Library

ISBN 9781787290549

Typeset in 10.75/15.5 pt Mercury Text G1
by Integra Software Services Pvt. Ltd, Pondicherry

Printed and bound in Great Britain by Clays Ltd, Elcograf S.p.A.

The authorised representative in the EEA is Penguin Random House Ireland,
Morrison Chambers, 32 Nassau Street, Dublin D02 YH68

Penguin Random House is committed to a sustainable future for our
business, our readers and our planet. This book is made from
Forest Stewardship Council® certified paper.

For Jax, Joe, Ben and Molly – the only team that matters.

CONTENTS

PREFACE

It is a long way, not just geographically, from the Bet365 Stadium to Wembley. Trudging out of the national stadium on a damp Friday evening after a dull, goalless draw between England and Scotland, I did not expect the journey of this book, which began in the Potteries, would end in northwest London. Yet there I was on 11 July, back in Block 140 watching England play Italy in the Euro 2020 Final. Huge credit to England manager Gareth Southgate, his background staff and the consistently impressive – on and off the pitch – playing squad for lifting the mood of the nation.

As an emotionally drained Wembley crowd came to terms with England running out of steam, I found myself reflecting how ironic it was that the national team was enjoying success only weeks after the proposed creation of a European Super League had threatened to destroy the core of English football.

It was a journey that began when the FA's desire to improve the performance of the England team led them to back the breakaway Premier League. Four decades later, the Three Lions were succeeding *despite* the Premier League, not because of it: the fewest national-team-qualified players in a domestic top division in Europe; a manager who had developed his skills primarily in international rather than domestic football; and with many members of the squad having gained valuable experience in the English Football League. And, after years of the Premier League consistently resisting calls for a meaningful mid-season break to allow England's players to be as rested as those of other countries, it was the rescheduling of fixtures due to Covid-19 that meant all countries turned up in similar shape.

Fantastic experience that it was, in my opinion Euro 2020 was only the second most important activity affecting English football in the summer of 2021. The UK government's Fan-led Review of Football Governance (FLR), which was running in parallel to the tournament, is the main event, offering a once in a generation opportunity to re-shape the national men's game. Having given evidence to the panel driving the process, I have no doubt they are committed to under-standing what fans want.

Ironically, and in complete contrast to the debate in 1992, there was no mention of the national team in the terms of reference given to the expert panel. And although I do propose ways we could improve the performance of the Three Lions, like the FLR my priority is solving the wider problems of the men's game. (I don't have the detailed knowledge to comment on the women's game and, to be honest, it seems to be doing fine under its own steam.)

However, England's success at Euro 2020 is important: firstly, it has left us in no doubt as to how crucial fans in stadiums and supporters around the country are; secondly, the hugely impressive manager and players offer a positive contrast to the disastrous performance of the owners and administrators of the national game in recent times – we can do better.

In 1990 'Nessun Dorma' provided the soundtrack for change in football. Today 'Three Lions' captures the positive sentiment towards football. Just as we shouldn't rest on our laurels with the national team, so we must grasp the opportunity offered by the FLR to create the game we want.

Of course, there is no right answer – we will all to have to com-promise. But, for the first time, fans are at the centre of the debate. Let's bring football home.

1 WHAT IS THE POINT OF STOKE CITY?

The Stoke City boardroom was a sombre place. It was six o'clock on Saturday, 16 December 2017, and the home team had just lost 3–0 to West Ham United in a Premier League relegation 'six-pointer'. Behind me, the West Ham owners, David Gold and David Sullivan, polite and restrained winners, were quietly sipping tea from some of Staffordshire's finest bone china. In the far corner, Stoke chairman Peter Coates and his son and vice-chairman John, supporters first and owners second, were deep in conversation. With the club edging ever closer to the relegation trapdoor, their well-known loyalty and patience was being put to the test by growing pressure from supporters to sack manager Mark Hughes.

That it was the former Stoke player Marko Arnautovic who had delivered such a telling blow to Hughes's tenure had undoubtedly deepened the gloom hanging over the home club's owners. The mercurial forward had been almost unplayable on the day, scoring the second goal to put the match out of Stoke's reach, a fitting epilogue to the soap opera the player had starred in since the summer. After being appointed manager in the summer of 2013, Hughes had recruited Arnautovic, the player's career having stalled at Inter Milan. The Austrian was rejuvenated in the Potteries, his performances earning him a new, lucrative contract in the summer of 2016. A year later, out of the blue, he demanded a transfer.

Every supporter knows how these dramas unfold. The transfer request and the club's steadfast refusal to accept it occupy the first scene. In the second act, after attempts to change the player's mind fail, the club reluctantly allows him to leave. In the finale, the departing player uses social media to thank the club and supporters while the money received is used to buy a new hero.

The story followed the standard plot line and the player was sold to West Ham for a reported £25 million. But events took an unexpected turn – Arnautovic ripped up the script and began to improvise. Interviewed shortly after his move, West Ham's new star questioned the level of Stoke City's ambition and claimed this, rather than money, was the reason for his move.

'I wanted to join West Ham because, for me', he said, 'it's a bigger club and more ambitious. We can see with the signings that we've made and the players that are already at the club.'[1]

Stoke were unhappy. In July 2017 Peter Coates made his feelings clear in the *Sun*:

> We are disappointed in him personally and the people around him. We resurrected his career. Our managers and coaches worked very hard to improve him and made him a name in the game.
>
> Last year we spent so much effort into giving him a long-term contract, and the first thing we get in the summer, he comes back, he wants to leave.[2]

For broadcasters starved of football content in the summer close season, a full-on public spat was manna from heaven. Modern sports radio relies on sensationalism and controversy to engage its audience, so it was no surprise that talkSPORT, the UK's commercial market leader in the genre,[3] took the bait. It quickly put together a programme, 'What is the point of Stoke City?' and, in classic tabloid style, the presenters set out their case: that football is all about winning, and nothing else matters. If mid-table stability in the Premier League was all Stoke City's owners aspired to then they were in the wrong business.

The programme's script could have been lifted from a supporters' online message board. Up and down the country, fans regularly call for their club's owners to 'move to the next level'. It is a not-particularly-subtle demand for increased spending on transfers and wages, to attract better players as the route to success on the pitch.

Superficially, talkSPORT's point seems a compelling one: after all, football *is* about winning. Even if we accept that talk radio is not the natural home of nuanced, rational argument, the radio station's attack was narrow and one-sided, ignoring the lessons from English football's journey to commercialisation, which accelerated in the 1980s and continued after the creation of the Premier League in 1992. The path is littered with clubs that over-reached financially in pursuit of success and fell from grace: Leeds United, Portsmouth and Bolton Wanderers are just some of the highest-profile examples.[4] A strategy of 'win at any cost' rarely ends well.

Making a logical defence, though, wrongly involves accepting talkSPORT's framing of the issue. Not only does it ignore the financial dangers but just as, if not more, importantly, as I know from working with football clubs, we also risk missing so much of the wider contribution made by the game.

In 2014, in my role as Chief Economist of Ernst & Young, one of the world's leading accounting and consulting firms, my team and I began working with the Premier League to measure the competition's economic and social contribution to the UK. Football was ahead of the curve, recognising early the importance of being able to explain the sport's wider impact to a wide range of stakeholders, but over the next five years we also worked with the Rugby Football Union, the English Cricket Board, the National Football League in America and the International Cycling Union, and advised colleagues undertaking similar activities in Canada, France, Brazil, Australia and elsewhere. Much of this work is published and easily accessible.[5]

After several months' work with the Premier League, we shared our report with journalists and the football industry at the Queen Elizabeth Conference Centre in London.[6] After I presented our findings, the Premier League's Executive Chairman Richard Scudamore invited the then business secretary, Sajid Javid, to comment. The

Minister began on traditional ground identifying the links between money and success in the game:

> The Premier League is one of Britain's most recognised and most popular brands. And it's also one of our biggest and most successful businesses both at home and abroad.
>
> It allows us to invest in continued success at the highest level, and develop the talent of the future at the grass roots.

But he went further, recognising that sport is about more than winning and money: 'It's a tragedy when any local business has to close its doors. But when a sports team locks its doors, the community loses something that's more than economic. It loses its centre, its source of civic pride.'[7]

Pleased as they were at having demonstrated how significant football's economic impact was nationally, (prior to our work, no-one had been aware that the Premier League and its clubs supported over 100,000 jobs across the country) the competition's management, suspecting, as the Business Secretary had asserted, that the game's real power to effect change lies in its local impact, now asked us to analyse the impact of football at the community level.

Following a pilot project with Leicester City after their title-winning 2015/16 season, we undertook an in-depth analysis of Stoke City's role in their community. Hence why I was dining in the board-room that December day: I was there as the guest of the club's chief executive Tony Scholes to celebrate the successful conclusion of our project. You have probably spotted already that I am a Stoke supporter. The club had already been on the shortlist for the project before I became involved – Tony and his team were really keen to have an external assessment of the work they do – but I suspect that my not so subtle lobbying may have had a slight influence on the Premier League's final choice of club.

In common with many other clubs, Stoke City spend significant amounts of time and money on programmes for their local community. The club focus on raising education levels, improving the health of the local population and supporting people in finding employment locally. Our research found that the effort is well worth it. Every pound that the club spends on its community programmes generates £11 worth of social benefit in the local area, a significantly higher return than the average charity achieves.[8]

This community benefit is no accident: it is at the core of the club's strategy. Stoke City is owned by a local family, and everyone at the club is aware of their responsibility. When we launched our report at the bet365 Stadium, Tony Scholes made it very clear that in Stoke City's strategy footballing and community impact are afforded equal priority. Having worked closely with the club's community team to mentor local school students as part of the Premier League Enterprise Challenge, I have no doubt the commitment is real.

In addition to their valuable contribution to their community, Stoke City could justifiably argue that they had been very successful on the pitch for a club without the large fan base and commercial appeal of those based in London, Manchester or Liverpool. The 2017/18 season was their tenth successive in the Premiership: the eighth longest spell of any club in the division at the time, behind only the 'Big Six'[9] and Everton (proud owners of the record for the longest unbroken run in the top level of English football). During this decade, they reached their first-ever FA Cup Final, in 2011, and enjoyed a season of European competition.

But this success, on and off the pitch, came at a price – as in any business, balancing multiple objectives is not easy. The Coates family might reasonably ask what level of commitment talkSPORT would re- gard as demonstrating the required level of ambition. By the summer of 2017, the owners had provided nearly £80 million of interest-free funding,[10] money given with no expectation of payback.

I left the bet365 Stadium that dank, December evening to walk back to the railway station, along the canal Josiah Wedgwood used to ship his pottery to market, already questioning myself. The contrasting moods of Stoke's owners – so disconsolate in the corner of the room – and Marko Arnautovic, triumphant as he left the pitch: why had I not been angrier about the whole saga in the previous summer? All the elements for outrage were there: the player's change of mind; his brother acting as his agent; the intense media coverage; the vast sums of money involved. Not to mention the failure to recognise how important the football club is to its community. I realised I, like so many other people, had bought in to the Premier League story.

Commercial success generates the funds to invest in an ever-improving experience for the supporter, both on and off the pitch. Occasionally individual clubs will lose out, as in the Arnautovic case, but this collateral damage, it is argued, is in the pursuit of a greater good.

It's a credible narrative, because in many respects it is true. Measured by match-going and TV audiences worldwide, English football is the most watched in the world.[11] It is also the highest revenue earner: in 2018/19, the turnover of Premier League clubs was over £5 billion – more than thirty times that of the old First Division in its final season, and around £2 billion more than any other major European league generates.[12]

There is no doubt that this huge inflow of money into English football has changed many aspects of the game for the better. It is easy to identify the positives of the modern era: games are staged in spectator-friendly stadia; playing surfaces are unrecognisable from the muddy fields of the previous era; hooliganism is a rare event. On the pitch, finely tuned athletes from all over the world flourish thanks to rule changes that have made it harder for cynical behaviour to suppress talent. Beyond match days, wall-to-wall media and online coverage mean that fans are constantly in touch with the game, able to engage in ways that were unthinkable in the 1980s.

A believable narrative it may be, but it's also a partial one. Just as talkSPORT's simplistic focus on success at all costs skipped over the risks of overstretching financially and ignored football's wider community impact, so comparing today's game with football of thirty-five years ago ignores the fact that the changes in football have come at a cost. Miserable, long day as it was, with weekend maintenance work now meaning my train home was slowed to a snail's pace, it served to remind me of a dispute that had broken out after the Premier League had accepted Sky's request to schedule Liverpool's visit to London to play Arsenal on Christmas Eve. Designed to maximise the TV audience, it would have created enormous challenges for away fans wanting to make it back to Merseyside on a public transport system closing down for the holidays. Only after a determined campaign by supporters was the game moved.[13]

This was not an isolated case. The emotional commitment that drives supporters to follow their teams to the extent of making a 400-mile return journey on Christmas Eve if they had to, drives the Premier League's economic model: the League, clubs, broadcasters and others know they can squeeze fans more than would be the case in most business and consumer relationships. Loyalty is football supporters' nicotine, and however much they try and wean themselves off the game, they keep coming back. If those Liverpool supporters had failed to have the game rescheduled, they would have made the trip irrespective of the personal cost.

As I pondered the state of the national game that long Saturday evening, it was easy to identify other stakeholder groups who have lost out in football's transformation. The ongoing case against the youth coach Barry Bennell (convicted in 2018 of a horrendous set of offences of abusing young boys in his various roles in club academies), the continuing problems of racism in the sport, the woeful state of many grass roots facilities and declining participation in the men's game[14] – all called into question the priorities of the people leading English football.

By the time I eventually got home, I was convinced that English football was out of balance: commercial considerations were being afforded too much importance compared to supporters and the communities football clubs are based in. That was when the idea for this book emerged.

I wanted to understand how great the imbalances were, and what we might do to address them. I hadn't appreciated how large the gap in revenues between the elite and the rest was. At the start of the twenty-first century, Premier League clubs together generated nearly £500 million more in revenues than the combined total of the other seventy-two English League clubs. A decade later, the gap had become close to three times that amount. Ten years on again, and the twenty Premier League clubs generated five times the aggregate income of the other seventy-two professional clubs – a difference of a staggering £4 billion.[15]

But that wasn't the most shocking finding. Despite generating revenues over £2 billion more than any other country, English football is loss-making in total. When probed, the Premier League story doesn't stand up to scrutiny: the top division's clubs have only recorded a collective profit four times this century. Outside of the elite things were even worse, Championship clubs spent 107 per cent of their income on wages in the 2018/19 season.[16]

Beneath the hype and global profile, English football was living on the never-never, dependent on continually growing its income to paper over the cracks in its finances. It was like a Ponzi scheme: once the growth stopped, the weaknesses would be visible to all.

And I quickly realised the tide was turning. The TV rights auction in the spring of 2018 may turn out to have been a watershed moment. The final bids would certainly have caused a stir at Premier League HQ. The amount offered for domestic rights for three seasons – £4.65 billion – was nearly half a billion pounds down on the previous deal. Despite a higher number of games on offer, this represented the largest ever fall in the value of UK rights between auctions.[17]

This was just the tip of the iceberg. With gambling companies as the main shirt sponsors for a majority of clubs in the top two divisions, another of football's main income streams was coming under pressure. Then, in the summer of 2019, major financial problems emerged at both Bolton Wanderers and Bury FC, exposing football's challenges to a wider audience. As evidence of deep-seated problems in the game mounted, politicians recognised the need for reform could no longer be ignored.[18]

Not only was football as out of balance as I feared, but, even more worryingly, it was unsustainable in its current form. I was equally clear there are alternative ways of organising the national game. We have options and we need to take the time to debate to agree on what our preferred vision is and to identify how to drive the change we desire. I may have been annoyed with myself for failing to spot what was in front of me earlier, but I also believed I could contribute. Let me explain why.

I love football: playing, watching, coaching, talking about it – everything. I can still remember 1969: the year I got my first pair of studded football boots and attended my first live game – Stoke City versus Derby County on Boxing Day (a 1–0 win for the Potters, thanks to a penalty by Harry Burrows). In time-honoured fashion, it was a family event. I went with my dad, grandad and uncle.

Like many of my peers, I wanted to be a footballer, and spent a lot of time trying. However, I was wise enough both to listen to the stories about how few boys made it and to evaluate my ability realistically. Reality started to bite the day Wayne Clarke, who was the brother of the then England star Allan Clarke and went on to play for Everton when they won the Football League in 1986/87, led a 5–0 demolition of our District team. Any lingering doubt went when I played for my county alongside Mark Chamberlain – being that close to someone who can do everything so much better than you is hard to ignore. Events proved me right: I received my first job offer days before he played for England in the 2–0 victory against Brazil in the Maracana Stadium, famous for that goal by John Barnes.

In the Seventies Britain where I grew up, as the country struggled to come to terms with its position in the post-war world, it was hard even for someone as obsessed by football as I was to ignore economics and politics. Sterling crises, strikes and rising unemployment dominated the headlines. Keen to understand more, I headed off to university to study economics, emerging, to the surprise of many people, given how much football I played, with a master's degree in business economics.

I joined Coopers & Lybrand, a business consultancy that at the time employed more economists in the UK than anywhere but the government economic service. I found myself sent off to British Telecom's new HQ in Newgate Street as a junior member of the team working out what the new post-privatisation regulatory and competitive environment meant in practice.

In hindsight, I realise what a great apprenticeship it was – the senior members of my team were ahead of the field in spotting the links between telecommunications, broadcasting and technology. My boss, who worked as an adviser to Robert Maxwell, was the first person I heard talking about the opportunities for convergence between the three sectors. Several of my colleagues went on to leadership roles in BT, British Satellite Broadcasting, the BBC and Ofcom, often shaping the events I examine in this book.

Although today the links between football and the communications sector are there for all to see, it was not until I was working for IBM around 2002 that football started to feature in my work in the converged communications world. Cable and satellite TV were established, the Internet was becoming ever more important, and the launch of 3G mobile services now intensified the battle for content. By the time I joined EY in 2006, because the value and viability of clubs were becoming more and more dependent on the level of TV rights and sponsorship deals, knowledge of the communications sector was in heavy demand from teams working on mergers and acquisitions, tax advice and audits in football (and sports generally). With sport having made its way into the business mainstream, I helped set up EY's Sports Industry Group.

When we look at football through the corporate lens, what we see is not what we expect. Football is a relatively small industry. The 100,000 UK jobs supported by the Premier League are around 6,000 fewer than British Telecom alone employed in 2020.[19] Football is a collection of some medium-sized but mainly small businesses with limited resources to look beyond their own activities.

It is not just small, it is also very different to the classic text book industry in several key aspects: While some clubs are run to make a profit, others accept the risk of losing money in pursuit of success on the pitch; the relationship between football clubs and their supporters is different to the transactional relationship a customer normally has with a business; and we have already touched on how integrated into their local communities football clubs are. And think about international football. What other business would allow its highly paid employees to go off several times a year, risking injuries that could stop them doing their job, to work for other people? Football really is different.

The unique nature of the game means we don't need to be constrained by traditional thinking. We have options for how to organise the game. Football's structure today was not pre-ordained, it reflects choices that have been made.

That is where this book fits in. My objective is, to provide a new perspective on English football by looking at it from the outside, albeit informed with inside knowledge. I analyse how the economic, business and social aspects interact and what options this offers for the future of the game. I have drawn wherever possible on the wealth of high quality existing research and extended it with my own analysis to offer new insights into the drivers of the game's finances, the Premier League's ranking on the international stage, the treatment of supporters, the performance of the England team, and more.

So far, so good. On 7 March 2020, just over two years after starting to research this book, I left the bet365 Stadium one sunny Saturday evening in very upbeat mood having watched Hull City put to the sword 5–1. It was not just the unusual feeling of seeing my team win so comfortably that explained my good humour. I had just finished the first draft of my book in advance of a planned launch after Euro 2020. I was in no doubt that English football was out of balance, and more concerned than when I had started writing, but I was confident English football did have the financial resources to change the game for the better. They just needed to be applied differently, with an improved system of governance. The train ride that Saturday evening was one of my more enjoyable journeys home.

I should have known better.

You learn very early as a Stoke City fan that whenever things are going well it is wise to remember a fall is not far away. I had allowed myself to get carried away. Sure enough, within days, it was clear that a very significant outbreak of Covid-19 had taken hold in the UK. On 23 March, the government announced a nationwide lockdown – a forced closure of many parts of the economy – to protect the National Health

Service. The economic consequences would be dramatic: the UK economy would shrink by almost one fifth in the second quarter of the year – an unprecedented economic shock.[20]

Hull was the last Stoke match before all professional games were suspended. The spread of the virus and the impact of lockdown would hit football hard. Suddenly the imbalances, vulnerabilities and structural weaknesses of the game were exposed for all to see.

This, then, is a book of two halves. The whistle to end the first half blew on 23 March 2020. The second half covers a period like nothing we have experienced before.

I was invited to join the government's Covid-19 Recovery Strategy Taskforce, where we discussed the challenges facing a range of sectors and how to help them. Football never featured. Compared to other industries, it was regarded as having the resources to survive. How to deploy them appropriately was left to football to work out for itself. It found it very difficult to.

As smaller clubs continued to struggle, the game needed decisive leadership. It was nowhere to be seen. In the autumn of 2020 with the Premier League and English Football League (EFL) finding it difficult to agree on a comprehensive support package, everything changed.

On 12 October 2020, Project Big Picture was launched.[21] This was a radical manifesto, reportedly led by Liverpool and Manchester United, to change the game, offering more money for the EFL and the wider game for a price: change was conditional on reforms that would give the Big Six and the three clubs with the longest stay in the Premier League effective control over the competition as well as increased influence over the English professional game.

Following negative comments by the government and the FA, the Premier League voted unanimously to reject the proposals and commit to a review of the game.[22] The proposals may have been defeated, but the die had been cast. Splits within the Premier League, between the top divisions and the EFL, and between the leagues, the FA and the government were now out in the open, demonstrating beyond doubt that there was no organisation within the game in charge: English football was leaderless.

It would be easy to conclude that Covid-19 and the response to it had destabilised English football. Easy but incorrect. As in the wider economy, Covid-19 primarily exacerbated weaknesses that already existed rather than created new ones. The problems facing English football have developed over a long period.

On a positive note, lockdown has shown us that there are alternative ways to organise our economic and social activities. Many activities successfully moved online. People found they didn't need to commute on crowded trains to large cities without losing the benefits of agglomeration and local high streets benefitted.

The same was true of football. Empty stadia made everyone realise just how important supporters are. Football club staff reached deep into their local communities, giving money, delivering food and calling vulnerable and lonely people. Grounds were turned into medical testing centres, and some clubs redeployed their staff in the community. English football rediscovered its roots and demonstrated once again how it can be a force for good.

Just as there were signs of normality on the horizon as a small number of fans were allowed into Wembley on FA Cup Semi-Final weekend, a bombshell struck. Twelve of Europe's largest clubs, including England's Big Six, announced their plan to form a breakaway European Super League. I had seen change coming but not on this scale.

What followed was truly extraordinary. I was watching the build up to Manchester United versus Burnley on Sky on Sunday 18th April 2021 when news started to come through of plans to launch a European Super League.[23] Football across Europe, and beyond, came together to condemn the moves. Supporters were first to make their views clear – images of Chelsea fans with a banner stating, "We want our cold nights in Stoke", was my favourite moment – but they were quickly joined by players and managers, commentators and broadcasters. Influenced by the populist mood of the times, politicians could no longer stand on the sidelines – in a complete reversal of the position thirty years earlier, football is too important to ignore. Not only is football not simply a business, it is not just a game, it is much more.

I said this was a book of two halves. In fact, thanks to a massive own goal by the elite clubs, we have gone into extra time. The Government's rushed announcement of its long-delayed 'fan-led review of governance'[24] confirmed momentum is now with football's supporters and communities.

A conversation on the future of football was urgent when I started this book, but it is critical now. It won't be easy. The required changes are far-reaching, from redesigning the overall structure of governance, bringing both government and supporters into formal roles, to a new financial settlement for the professional game and grass roots activities. Above all, this must be done in an integrated way across the whole game. Powerful vested interests will have to be overcome, and we will all need to listen and compromise. We have a unique opportunity to rebalance football and save it from itself. (Note when I say 'football' I am referring to the male game. This is not because I don't value the women's game, it is because I don't feel equipped to comment on and the last thing it needs is to repeat the failures of the men's game).

I hope this book will provide you with the information, analysis and ideas to join the debate. While I draw extensively on recent events, because the last two seasons have been so atypical, I use 2018/19 as the basis for assessing long-term trends. Having set the scene, we can now turn to assess football's journey over the last four decades or so to understand how we got here.

2 A WHOLE NEW BALL GAME

In September 1984, having secured my first full-time job, I crammed all my belongings into my Ford Fiesta and drove to London. Planning a weekend of sightseeing before donning my brand-new three-piece suit for the first time, I was woken up on Friday morning by the phone ringing. On the line was a Chelsea-supporting friend: 'We're playing West Ham tomorrow – do you fancy coming along? Be a chance for you to see some proper football.'

'Perfect', I replied. 'I can go sightseeing anytime.'

The next day, on a damp, dull September afternoon, after successfully navigating the Underground, I found myself mingling with the crowds pouring out of Fulham Broadway station as we all headed to Stamford Bridge.

We paid at the gate and went into the 'Shed' end, the terraces favoured by the most fanatical of Chelsea's supporters. Looking out over the whole stadium from my vantage point near the top of the banking, I was shocked at the state of the place: run-down, stands and pitch separated by the large gap of a running track, and an ugly metal fence at the foot of the terraces – all-standing – to stop fans coming onto the playing surface.

Prematch, the crowd of just over 30,000 built up to kick-off by running through the football songbook of the time. The repertoire included each team's anthem – 'Blue is the Colour' from the home crowd and 'I'm Forever Blowing Bubbles' by the visitors – alongside a set of somewhat more unpleasant tunes. Both clubs had notorious hooligan elements in their fan bases. West Ham's group were known as the

Inter-City Firm (ICF), while the home team's gang called themselves the Chelsea Shed Boys. Their long-standing antagonism added a further edge.

The Shed was soon bouncing as Chelsea raced into a 3–0 lead. After the home team's third goal, pandemonium broke out. A mob of what appeared to be around 200 West Ham supporters poured into the Shed end. (I subsequently came across an article by the investigative journalist Nick Davies revealing that the ICF 'specialises in infiltrating the terraces reserved at grounds for rival fans.'[1] In hindsight, a little preparatory reading would have been useful.)

As hand-to-hand fights broke out, there was a mass surge down to the front of the terraces. Having been carried about 30 yards downhill without my feet touching the ground, calling out for calm while panicking like everyone else, I found myself at the bottom of the steps just below pitch level. I located my friend in the melée and somehow, we managed to scramble over the fence, dodge the police dogs and find a space on the running track.

The police were quick to act, surging into the crowd to quell the trouble. There was never a suggestion that the game would be called off – the accepted approach at that time was to ensure games were finished to avoid creating a precedent that might encourage fans of losing teams to try and force games to be abandoned. The West Ham fans were eventually removed from the Shed and the police directed us all back onto the terraces to watch the rest of the match. The interruption affected the momentum on the pitch, and nothing much happened after the restart. Chelsea ended up comfortable 3–0 winners, and I was left wishing I'd stuck to sightseeing.

Judged against today's norms, a modern-day supporter would probably assume I'd been unlucky: wrong place, wrong time. A logical conclusion, but an incorrect one: in the mid-1980s crowd trouble was widespread. Chelsea and West Ham were just two of many teams with a dangerous hooligan element among their following. Millwall's were probably the most notorious, establishing their infamy through a series of pitch invasions. The highest-profile one broke out during a televised FA Cup game against Luton Town in 1985 – an incident that led the

Prime Minister, Margaret Thatcher, to assemble what the press coverage at the time described as being akin to a 'war cabinet'[2] to address the problem of football hooliganism.

After that frightening Saturday afternoon, I would have taken some persuading that football's problems were going to get worse, but they did. In May 1985, as the season drew to a close, the country was shocked twice. First when fifty-six people died in a horrific fire at Bradford City's Valley Parade ground, and then, only eighteen days later, by another thirty-nine deaths following crowd trouble before the European Cup Final between Liverpool and Juventus at the Heysel Stadium in Brussels. This was the final straw for UEFA: English clubs were banned from European competition until the 1990/91 season.[3]

Having to attend games in run-down stadia and seemingly facing an ever-increasing risk to life and limb, supporters voted with their feet. To no-one's surprise, in the following 1985/86 season, aggregate attendance at English professional football games fell to its lowest level since the league's expansion to four divisions in 1922.[4] Even then we hadn't reached the nadir. Before the end of the decade, in the worst football disaster in the British Isles, ninety-six people would die in the Hillsborough stadium tragedy.[5] For all that the football on the field at that time offered drama, excitement and disappointment, as it always has, the experience for fans going to a game back then was often a dismal, frightening and sometimes dangerous one.

Once I started work at one of the country's leading accounting and consulting firms, I quickly learned that football was not a topic for office conversation. Rugby, yes, and cricket in the summer, but 'the national sport' seemed taboo. A cup of tea in the print room was the only opportunity to chat freely about the game. As I spent my weekends either playing or watching football, the Monday morning 'What did you do at the weekend?' conversation was one I tried to duck. If my attempts at avoidance failed and I was forced to join in, then 'Not much – a quiet one' was my stock response.

Fast-forward to late spring 2019. The season was edging towards its close and four English teams – Tottenham Hotspur and Liverpool in the Champions' League and Arsenal and Chelsea in the Europa League – had made it to the finals of Europe's two most prestigious men's competitions. Football was now firmly on the corporate agenda. As the games drew nearer, small talk at the start of client meetings was dominated by discussions on the challenges of obtaining tickets for the games and the difficulties in securing flights to Madrid or Baku. I know one CEO of a global corporation, who ended his business trip to Brazil by taking a marathon twenty-three-hour flight to Baku.

It was around that time that any lingering doubts I may have had about how much football's image has changed were dispelled for good. On a Thursday evening, I found myself in one of the grand dining rooms in the Houses of Parliament talking to a collection of the great and good – CEOs, politicians and financiers – about the economic and social impact of football. All had one thing in common, they were supporters of Liverpool FC, and were attending the regular meeting of "Business in the Bootroom", an event run by the club to build and maintain its network of potential influencers. I should say I was very much the warm-up act for a question and answer session with two of the club's legendary strikers, Ian Rush and Robbie Fowler.

Football's move from print room to boardroom is just one manifestation of the English game's transformation in three and a half decades. Football has changed all over the world, but the shift in England has been much greater than in any other major footballing country. Nowhere else even comes close. In 2018/19 the Premier League generated over 70 per cent more revenue than its nearest rival, Spain's La Liga, and more than three times the income of France's Ligue 1;[6] attracted the highest number of paying spectators to games; was the most watched football competition on TV worldwide; and outperformed all its peers in attracting commercial and sponsorship income.[7] Everywhere we look, be it the nationality of owners, players and managers, the treatment of supporters, or global reach, the changes to our game are more profound than anywhere else.

What happened in those three and a half decades to change English football from a game the nation had fallen out of love with to one the whole country – the corporate elite, politicians, the Royal Family and schoolkids playing FIFA online – desperately want to be part of? It is an important question, because many of the challenges the game faces today are either the same as in the Eighties or the result of changes since then. If we can understand how we got here, we will be in a good position to discuss the future of our national game.

I am certainly not the first person to seek answers. A number of notable writers have written eye-opening and invaluable books on much of this period of English football.[8] Rather than attempt to go over the same ground, I have sought to learn from these works and advance the analysis to include the most recent developments – the rate of change in football in the last 5 to 10 years has increased significantly.

While all of the writers identify Hillsborough as a major factor in the transformation of the English game, several characterising it as a 'catalyst', they explicitly recognise that other factors, such as the failure of football's authorities to protect the game's traditions, have played a part in the game's shift. In my opinion, this is an important insight. Without wishing to downplay the horrific nature of the tragedy, I don't believe one single cause can explain the scale of the change. It is the interaction of a range of factors – a process that started some time before Hillsborough – that has led us to where we are today.

Football in the mid-1980s reflected the national mood. In *The Rise and Fall of the British Nation,* David Edgerton describes how a sense of 'declinism'[9]captured Britain from the Seventies onwards. The post-war economic boom had run out of steam and surging inflation, rising unemployment, strikes and sterling crises damaged the nation's self-esteem.

Football followed a similar path. The rise in attendances that had characterised the post-war period went into reverse, with an 11 per cent fall in the 1980/81 season alone.[10] The problems of hooliganism and crumbling stadia were there for all to see, and the failure of England to qualify for both the 1974 and 1978 World Cups shook the long-standing and widely held belief about the superiority of the English game. Used as we are today to England coming home empty-handed from major tournaments, in the 1970s failure, with the exploits of the 'Boys of '66' still fresh in our minds, was a huge blow. As the shocks mounted up, the post-mortem seemed to get longer and longer.

Just as the British economy and English football had declined in parallel, so they would change together. Paradoxically, it would be the policies and beliefs of governments led by Margaret Thatcher – a prime minister completely uninterested in football – that would play a crucial role in the transformation of the English game. When I search for reasons why the English game evolved differently and more dramatically compared to Europe, it is impossible to ignore the role of Margaret Thatcher. Just as no other country had a Hillsborough, so no other country had Thatcherism.

As prime minister from 1979, Thatcher oversaw a radical programme of economic reform, moving the UK away from the 'mixed economy' model that had shaped economic policy since the end of the Second World War. It was a radical change of course – *Mrs Thatcher's Economic Experiment*[11] was how the respected commentator William Keegan's book characterised it. The UK and USA were the only two large economies to change course so dramatically; other large Western European countries continued with their social market policies, adopting much more gradual approaches to economic reform.

In common with many people who lived through that time, my over-riding memory is of the surge in unemployment to over three million people in 1983, as an unwavering adherence to monetarist doctrines drove policy. Having surged, unemployment never fell below two million under Mrs Thatcher's leadership.[12] Heavily reliant on the hardest-hit manufacturing and coal industries, traditional football areas of the country such as the North-West, North-East and West Midlands bore the brunt of the job losses (in Lancashire unemployment increased 166 per cent between 1979 and 1982)[13] – another factor alongside hooliganism that contributed to the slump in attendances in the middle of the decade. Even though the rise in unemployment delivered a huge debilitating shock to the economy and to football, two other core tenets of Thatcherism would turn out to have a more significant long-term impact on English football.

First, the belief in the power of markets to drive wealth creation led to policies designed to reduce the role and size of the state, to limit regulation and to encourage private ownership and competition.

The second core belief was that the individual citizen should be free to choose, requiring government to ensure meaningful choices in as many areas of life as possible, and, in return, would be trusted to behave in a responsible manner. In her autobiography, *Margaret Thatcher: The Downing Street Years*, she characterises her thinking as '... the root cause of our contemporary social problems ... was that the state had been doing too much.' Going on to assert, ' ... people must look to themselves first. It is our duty to look after ourselves and then to look after our neighbour'.[14]

Thatcherism was at least as much about beliefs as policy positions. The almost evangelical narrative used to justify the actions being taken was very important in shaping the mood in the country and legitimising courses of action that would previously have been viewed as untenable. Football, or at least its new owners, would be caught up in the mood.

Let's start with policies. A combination of pro-market and pro-individual policies reshaped the UK's financial and corporate sectors. The removal of restrictions on capital flows began in 1977 and was completed by 1979. When the changes to the regulation of the City of London culminated in 1986 in 'Big Bang', ending minimum commissions and the separation between traders and advisers and removing the restrictions on foreign ownership at the London Stock Exchange. As a result, London was now open for business to the globe, and foreign ownership surged as the world's largest investment banks raced to buy up some of the world's most attractive financial services firms.[15] The Thatcher government's laissez-faire attitude to the ownership of UK assets meant investors from around the world were welcomed. For money, open markets meant open borders.

The UK had created a potent cocktail: money looking for a home, unquestioning support for enterprise and entrepreneurship, and a belief in the need to maximise profits above anything else. Business was freer than ever before. 'Financialization' is how Rana Foroohar characterises it: 'the trend by which finance and its way of thinking have come to reign supreme.'[16] Four decades after Margaret Thatcher came into power, the proposals for a European Super League would demonstrate beyond doubt how finance can become completely detached from the real world. No doubt, the proposals looked great in Powerpoint and made sense in Excel, but it seems the proponents of the new competition had no inkling of how strong a reaction they would provoke.

With entrepreneurship and wealth creation the flavour of the moment, football was quick to embrace this new world, enthusiastically working its way through the new menu of ownership options. The starter in the 1980s was the listing of football clubs on the stock market. As financiers became more aware of the opportunities offered, take-overs became the dish of choice as cable television companies bought stakes in football clubs. This phase ended when Sky's bid to buy a share of Manchester United in 1998 was halted by the UK competition authorities.[17] Future courses would see rich foreign investors and private equity businesses secure control of English clubs. Time and again, as we will see, changes in ownership have played and continue to play a central role in shaping English football.

The Thatcher revolution ran through the whole economy, but what today is known as the communications industry – a combination of telecommunications, media and the Internet – was where all the strands of the economic experiment would ultimately combine to have the greatest impact on football. In the early 1980s you would have been hard pressed to find anyone talking about a *communications industry* – the telecommunications and media sectors operated independently, while the Internet didn't exist. Over time, though, technological and market developments would drive convergence between these sectors across the whole of the global economy, not just football.

In the early 1980s, however, with convergence some way off, each sector was managed separately. Broadcasting generally, and the BBC specifically, appeared to represent many of the things Margaret Thatcher found most objectionable in British society. 'Broadcasting', wrote Nigel Lawson, Mrs Thatcher's Chancellor of the Exchequer, in his memoirs, 'was a subject on which Margaret held a great many firm views and prejudices'.[18] With the Prime Minister unconvinced of the value of public service broadcasting, relations between the government and the organisation deteriorated during the Thatcher years. Mark Wheeler, professor of political communications at London Metropolitan University, summed up the situation thus: 'By the middle of the 1980s the British broadcasting and political elite were probably as distant from one another as they have been in the last thirty years.'[19] With this mindset, it is unsurprising that the Prime Minister was attracted to the opportunity technology appeared to offer to introduce more choice and competition into broadcasting and programme production. Change to UK broadcasting was in the air, and Sky would be the major beneficiary.

Having won the 1986 tender for exclusive rights to satellite broadcasting in the UK, British Satellite Broadcasting launched in 1990. The loser in the tender, Sky, had already begun offering services from the Luxembourg-registered SES Astra telecommunications satellite in 1989. (Operating abroad meant Sky was not subject to UK broadcast regulation). Competition between the two providers damaged both businesses, as neither could build a critical mass of subscribers quickly enough. Having started out believing that Hollywood movies were the way to attract customers, both companies shifted relatively quickly to the potential of top-flight football to provide the 'killer content' to ensure market success. However, in 1988 ITV won the competition for the rights to show league football, leaving BSB with the consolation prize of a small number of FA Cup and England matches.[20]

Building these new satellite businesses from scratch was expensive. Faced with mounting financial pressure, the owners of BSB decided in late October 1990 to divest their licence and merge with Sky. Although the Broadcasting Act, passed on 1 November 1990, contained several provisions that could reasonably have been expected to have led to the merger being disallowed, calls for the merger to be referred to the Monopolies and Mergers Commission fell on deaf ears Tempany suggests that Rupert Murdoch's relationship with Margaret Thatcher arguably influenced the process, and looking at events with hindsight, it is surprising that there appears to have been so little detailed scrutiny.[21] 'The government must answer for this,' Anthony Simmonds-Gooding, the former Chief Executive of *BSB*, subsequently reflected. 'They turned a blind eye …This is going to be a fearfully powerful company.'[22] The emergence of Sky in broadcasting would have an immediate, significant and readily identifiable impact on football.

By contrast, changes in the telecommunications sector, driven by the core belief that private ownership was superior to public, would take much longer to affect the national sport. British Telecom (BT) was privatised in 1984 through a sale of 50.2 per cent of its shares, and a limited number of fixed and mobile competitors were licensed. In later phases of liberalisation, more licences were let, and the local cable companies initially licensed in 1984 solely to offer TV services were from 1991 permitted to offer telephony.[23]

Although these policies created the basis for the converged environment that would lead, two decades later, to highly competitive bidding for the rights to broadcast football, working in the sector at the time, I heard little if any discussion of the long-term consequences. The focus was tactical not strategic.

The national economic policy agenda of the 1980s had both immediate and longer-term impacts on football, but what of policy towards football itself? How did the response to Hillsborough influence the agenda? Once again beliefs were to play a key role in shaping outcomes.

Margaret Thatcher was not a fan of football: the shared, almost tribal domain of supporters and the anti-social behaviour of hooligans were each in their own ways utterly at odds with her values. Strikingly, despite the scale of the tragedy, there is no mention of Hillsborough in her memoirs – a single reference to Heysel is the only comment on football.[24] She was not alone: Nigel Lawson[25] and Michael Heseltine, both extremely prominent figures in her governments, made the grand total of one reference to the national game between them in their own reflections. Events off the pitch meant politicians could not ignore football, but their lack of enthusiasm for the game created a reluctance to intervene. However, the tragic death of a spectator at Birmingham City on the same day as the Bradford fire forced their hand. In 1985 the Government established the Popplewell Inquiry into crowd safety at sports grounds.[26] Its progress became bogged down in a debate over membership cards for supporters and the findings were not fully implemented because, as is often the case, events, specifically the tragedy at Hillsborough and the response to it, took over.[27]

When commentators identify the pivotal role of Hillsborough on English football, they are referring to the results of the inquiry into the tragedy that was led by Lord Justice Taylor.[28] His package of proposed reforms, the central feature of which was a requirement for all-seater stadia in the top two divisions of English football by 1994/95, was the catalyst for a programme of modernisation that would transform the match day experience and open the doors to a new group of spectators.

Thirty years on, analysis of the rationale and impact of Lord Taylor's proposals illustrates perfectly both the challenges of balancing the interests of the game with the interests of finance and how integrated the various factors shaping football are.

Aware that the changes would be expensive, Lord Taylor noted that clubs would need help in funding their investment, but he also believed that clubs could generate some of it themselves – paving the way for changes in football's commercial model: 'I would expect the football authorities to extract the highest possible price for TV rights,'[29] he wrote, and 'clubs may well wish to charge somewhat more for seats than standing.'[30]

What is puzzling, given the concern he expressed about how the owners and management of clubs treated their supporters, is that Lord Taylor did not propose any measures to provide at least some protection for supporters in the face of increased commercialisation: 'In some instances it is legitimate to wonder whether the directors are genuinely interested in the welfare of their grass-roots supporters.'[31]

His lack of action is even more surprising as he was also very critical of the game's administrators, the Football Association and Football League:

> One would have hoped that the upper echelons in this hierarchy would have taken a lead in securing reasonable safety and comfort for the spectators and in enforcing good behaviour by precept and example. Unfortunately, these hopes have not generally been realised and indeed at times poor examples have been set.[32]

As a result, the pro-market, anti-interventionist stance of the Thatcher government, coupled with its lack of interest in football, meant supporters were on their own. Although, thanks to Lord Taylor, some public money (via reductions in the levy from the football pools – the medium by which people bet on the game at the time) was allocated to help clubs with the costs of improving grounds, the burden of the new financial model for football would fall on clubs and therefore on supporters. Just how large was left to clubs to determine. In Chapter 6 we will see just how significant it turned out to be.

In Lord Taylor's defence he was dealt a bad hand. First, when clubs undertook detailed work to estimate the costs of modernising their grounds, the required expenditure turned out to be three to four times higher than he had been led to believe.[33] Secondly, he could not have foreseen how unwilling the government would be to allow the Exchequer to provide funding to assist the clubs in their transition to implementing what were after all, new statutory requirements.[34] Thirdly, no-one expected the huge shift in the football labour market initiated by the Bosman Judgement in 1995.[35] With much greater control over their terms of employment, players were able to secure higher wages, while the battle for talent drove up transfer fees. In addition to funding the investment in improved stadia, club owners had to deal with much higher labour costs.

If he had any inkling of how large the increase in costs would be, Lord Taylor might have sought to introduce controls over ticket prices for match-going spectators. What Lord Taylor completely missed was the implications of his proposals for how much fans would have to pay to watch broadcast games. From his comments, it is clear he assumed the free-to-air model in place at the time would continue, albeit with the broadcasters paying a higher price: 'They should be expected to pay a higher price for the rights to relay popular matches.'[36] There was no sense in his proposals that viewers might be asked to pay to watch broadcast matches. Taylor was not alone: as Bose identified, most TV executives at the time had not understood just how significant the impact of pay-TV would be on the traditional broadcasting market.[37]

The investment requirements of the Taylor Report together with the higher costs resulting from the Bosman Judgement created a need to generate higher revenues. Freedom to adopt more commercially driven ticket pricing and to maximise the value of TV rights provided owners with the tools to increase income and the actions of successive Thatcher governments to refashion the UK economy and society while adopting a 'hands off' approach to football, created the opportunity for change.

But it still needed to be taken. When the drive for change started to gather momentum at the end of the 1970s, the five richest clubs were still family-owned businesses. The fortune generated by the pools and Littlewoods stores enabled different parts of the Moores family to control both Everton and Liverpool. The Edwards family were in charge at Manchester United. Arsenal were led by members of the Hill-Wood and Smith families, and the Wale, Bearman and Richardson families provided all of Tottenham Hotspur's chairmen from 1943 to 1984.[38]

By normalising behaviour that would previously have been objected to within football, the pro-market, pro-wealth-creation narrative of the times attracted new owners alert to the commercial potential of the game. In 1981 Ken Bates bought Chelsea for £1, taking on £600,000 of debt. Robert Maxwell paid £120,000 to acquire Oxford United. David Dein secured a 16 per cent share of Arsenal for £292,000 in 1983, the year Irving Scholar, having bought Tottenham Hotspur for £500,000, floated the club on the London Stock Exchange using a holding company structure to get around a supposed FA prohibition.[39]

With the pressure for greater commercialisation and a largely in-
different government, football was crying out for strong leadership to
shape its future and balance the interests of all its stakeholders, rather
than merely allow the new owners to dominate. It is still waiting. Just
as no other country had a Margaret Thatcher or a Hillsborough, so
nowhere else had a national football elite that so abrogated its
responsibility for trying to protect its position in the game.

Competitive professional football in England can trace its origins
back to the nineteenth century. As the game spread from the public
schools to the working class in the industrial cities and towns, a split
emerged between the Football Association, with its roots in the amateur ethos of the south of England, and the professional game supported
by mill and factory owners of the North and Midlands. Wealthy owners
began to seek out talent and pay their players, and crowds started to
grow. The FA resisted for as long as it could, but eventually legalised
professionalism in 1885. Within three years, the Football League was
launched, one division made up of twelve teams drawn exclusively
from the North and Midlands. From its birth, English football was
handicapped with a divided leadership that has consistently hampered
the game's ability to manage itself effectively.[40]

From the 1880s until the end of the 1970s, governance of professional football in England was based on two principles. First, reflecting
the FA's fear of professionalism, football was run as a game, not a business, meaning owners had to be restricted from profiting from the
game too greatly. Secondly, the collective was more important than
any one club, so a competitive balance had to be maintained between
teams of different financial strength. This struggle to balance football
and finance remains at the heart of the game's challenges today.

Constraints on directors' earnings and players' terms and conditions were imposed by the FA, while the Football League introduced
the sharing of gate money, and later the equal distribution of television
money. The result was a level of competitive parity in the Football
League and limited potential for financial speculation.

The first chink in the armour came in the 1960s when Jimmy Hill,
Chairman of the Professional Footballers' Association (the players' trades

union), led a successful campaign to secure the removal of the maximum wage and a relaxation of contractual restrictions.⁴¹ While there was no doubt that the players had right on their side, as would be the case time and time again, the failure of the authorities to anticipate the shift jeopardised the delicate balance between stakeholders. With the other regulations remaining in place, the game was able to adjust to increased player power, but the seeds of change were sown and, as the new, more financially oriented owners came into the game, they sought more control over the game's finances for their own advantage.

The FA bowed to the inevitable. In a radical move, Thatcherite in nature and very much in keeping with the sentiment of the time, the FA liberalised its financial regulations in 1981. The constraint on directors being paid was removed, and the ceiling on the share of annual dividends that could be paid to club shareholders raised from 5 per cent to 15 per cent. In truth, the organisation had lost control of the game's finances some time before: Manchester United had had a new corporate structure to facilitate higher dividends since 1978.⁴² Now, for the first time, there was an authorised way for owners and investors to benefit personally from the commercial possibilities of the game.

Shortly afterwards, the five-year deal the NFL in North America signed in 1982, worth $400 million a season, illustrated beyond doubt the commercial potential of English football, increasing the pressure for reform.⁴³ In this environment, with the FA having given way, it was less of a shock when the Football League's clubs agreed in 1983 to do away with the long-standing agreement to allocate 20 per cent of matchday revenues to the away team,⁴⁴ which had successfully narrowed the extent to which higher attendances at certain clubs translated into greater financial strength. This long-standing cross-subsidy from rich clubs to the rest had been instrumental in preserving competitive balance in the competition.

Two years later, the Posthouse Agreement, so named as it was brokered at Heathrow's Posthouse hotel by the then Professional Footballers' Association (PFA) chief executive Gordon Taylor, shifted the balance of power forever. This deal ended the equal distribution of television and sponsorship money across all teams, in favour of 50 per cent going to the First Division (now the Premier League), 25 per cent to the Second (the Championship today) and the remaining 25 per cent split between the Third and Fourth Divisions (current Leagues 1 and 2).[45] Infused with the mood of the times, football was moving towards a Darwinian regime of survival of the fittest or, more accurately, the richest. In the space of just four years, the FA and Football League had said goodbye to a regime that had lasted almost a century.

Despite the slump in attendances, football did not lose its intrinsic appeal. David Goldblatt is one of many who have argued that, during the difficult early 1980s, football provided a link to a past that in many other areas of life had largely disappeared. For Simon Inglis, for example, football was 'an emotional time machine that took [you] to a working-class industrial city that had been lost.'[46] For the emerging commercial interests, however, the resurgence in football's appeal could not have been better timed: as the 1980s drew to a close, there were signs that public sentiment towards football was changing. Fans wanted to reclaim some of their ownership of the game from the hooligan element that captured the headlines. Grassroots movements emerged: supporters started to organise, and When Saturday Comes, launched a year later, was just one of the fanzines offering supporters an alternative voice, producing their own content, typically on a shoestring.[47]

With the economy recovering, so did the game's popularity over the rest of the decade, but the shift accelerated as the 1980s came to an end. The evocative 'Nessun Dorma' soundtrack and the stylish Italian stadiums created an atmospheric backdrop for the Italia '90 World Cup. England's unexpected success in reaching the semi-finals captured the nation's heart. The agonising semi-final loss on penalties to West Germany and the pictures of Paul Gascoigne in tears cemented the public mood. In the following season close to three quarters of a million more people went to top flight league games.[48]

As the England team returned home triumphant and the game's popularity on the rise, English football was approaching a tipping point. With owners increasingly aware of the true scale of the cost of implementing the Taylor Report's recommendations, maximising the game's commercial potential had become a necessity. The next TV deal, due to start with the 1992/93 season, was make-or-break.

Although the first game, a for-television exhibition between Arsenal and Arsenal Reserves, was broadcast on the BBC as far back as September 1937,[49] football was only occasionally seen on the screen until the 1960s, when ITV started to show highlights. In 1964 the BBC introduced *Match of the Day*, in part to help train cameramen for the upcoming 1966 World Cup in England – an element of England's successful bid to host the tournament was a commitment that every game would be covered by 'electronic cameras'.[50]

Following England's success in winning the World Cup, the popularity of the game surged. Four years later, the first 'in colour' tournament in Mexico 1970 further boosted football's appeal.[51] Soon it was a core component of the broadcast schedule, though mostly fans had to make do with recorded highlights: only the FA and European Cup Finals, end-of-season England internationals and major international tournaments were broadcast live.

Live broadcasting of Football League matches started in earnest in the 1983/84 season. Tottenham Hotspur versus Nottingham Forest on 2 October 1983 was ITV's first broadcast, followed by Spurs again against Manchester United on the BBC a few weeks later. Football was in demand. The three-year deal cost £4.5 million in 1983, but in the subsequent deal the value surged, with ITV securing the exclusive rights to Football League games for four years from 1988 at a cost of £44 million.[52]

With the divided, dysfunctional leadership of English football now struggling to respond to the pressure from club owners, the government, desperate not to have to take the lead, called on the game 'to speak with one voice'[53] as a prerequisite for receiving financial support to address the costs of the Taylor recommendations. The response was not what the government was hoping for: even greater in-fighting and battling for position.

The Football League made the first move, setting out its position on 18 October 1989 in *One Game, One Team, One Voice: Managing*

Football's Future.[54] As Fynn identifies, its proposal of equal status in running the game through a joint committee was probably never going to be acceptable to the FA. In addition, the splits between and within divisions raised real questions about the League's ability to align its clubs behind even the limited reforms it was putting forward.[55]

Just as it still is now, the number of clubs in the top division was a true fault line in the game. Believing a busier schedule was detrimental to the performance of the England team, the FA gained the support for a pared-down First Division from the richer owners, for whom reducing player fatigue was more important than a marginal financial benefit. By contrast, smaller clubs, less likely to be competing in European competition, wanted more games to generate higher gate receipts. In a very public illustration of the schism at the top of the national game, the England team had barely touched down from Italy when, by a majority decision, the top division voted to return from twenty clubs to the twenty-two it had been until the mid-1980s. Chelsea's Chairman Ken Bates, a key advocate, saw it as necessary to limit the power of the rich clubs (Chelsea were a few years away from crossing over into the game's financial elite at this time), dismissing the view that fewer teams would mean less football: 'the most ardent advocates of smaller divisions can't wait to jump on an aeroplane and get jet-lagged on the other side of the world, either because the directors want an all-expenses-paid booze-up or they want to get the money that's on offer.'[56]

Outraged, the richest clubs accelerated their plans for change. Challenged by the Football League's proposals and fearing a breakaway by the largest clubs, in June 1991 the FA published *The Blueprint for the Future of Football.*[57] Reaching into the Football League's territory, the FA proposed an elite league of eighteen teams, claiming that a smaller competition with fewer fixtures would reduce the demands on top players and hence improve the performance of the England team.

It was the prospect of an eighteen-team competition that persuaded the FA to support the proposals by First Division clubs to break away and create a new Premier League. Not only would the new structure reinforce the FA's overall leadership of the English game, but it believed it would also have direct control over three valuable assets: the FA Cup; Wembley Stadium; and the England men's team while retaining its role as England's representative in the international game.[58]

The shallowness of the FA's commitment to the greater good quickly became clear when the breakaway clubs pushed back on the proposed reduction, deciding to stick with twenty-two clubs. The Football League sought to enforce its rule of a three-year notice period for clubs resigning from the competition, but the FA's refusal to back it effectively enabled the breakaway.

Very quickly, the Premier League moved itself outside of direct FA control, the founder members agreeing on 17 July 1991 that 'all decisions would be taken on "a one club, one vote" basis.'[59]

Not only the FA had been completely outmanoeuvred: so had the rich clubs. The new Ken Bates-sponsored agreement gave the smaller clubs an effective veto. Thirty years later, the arrangement is still contentious, as the proposals to reform it in Project Big Picture demonstrate.[60]

The way was now clear for the first Premier League TV deal, and BSkyB outbid ITV to secure five-year exclusive rights to broadcast Premier League football for five seasons, beginning in 1992.[61] Alan Sugar, chairman of Tottenham Hotspur but also owner of Amstrad, satellite dish suppliers to BSkyB, described his conversation with Sam Chisholm, BskyB's Chief Executive, as the battle came to a head: 'ITV had somehow found out the details of BSkyB's bid and wanted to top it [they raised their bid from £205 million to £262 million]. I told Sam, "There's only one way to clinch the deal – you'll have to blow them out of the water!"' Chisholm responded with a bid of £304 million to secure the contract: a sevenfold increase on the winning amount in 1987. 'Little did I know', Sugar went on to note, 'that this call would go down in the annals of football history as "the phone call that irrevocably altered the history of sport and media in Britain".'[62]

When push came to shove, money had talked. By a vote of fourteen to six, with two abstentions, the clubs had voted for change and allied themselves to BSkyB. (Sugar had declared a conflict of interest and offered to not vote, but his offer was declined).[63] Here was the new football economy on full show.

The deal provided the basis for BSkyB's 'A Whole New Ball Game', its strapline for coverage of the Premier League, with sixty live games in the first season and two flagship programmes, *Super Sunday* and *Monday Night Football*, the latter copying the model of the NFL in the USA. News International and Rupert Murdoch had staked their business, no less, on the belief that enough of the footballing public were so committed to the game that they would either install satellite dishes or go to the pub to watch, allowing Sky to create a monopoly on the broadcast of live football into homes and licensed premises. Murdoch described the content as 'a battering ram'[64] Just over three years after Hillsborough, on 15 August 1992, Sheffield United's Brian Deane scored the Premier League's first ever goal in a 2–1 win over Manchester United. The next day, the initial televised game ended in a 1–0 win for Nottingham Forest over Liverpool.

The competition was an immediate success. Innovative programming and technology brought fans much closer to the action. Sky reaped the benefits, subscriber growth surged, and, by end of 1995, the company had five million subscribers: more than three times the total subscriber base of Sky and BSB in 1990, when growth was proving hard to find.[65]

By the time Margaret Thatcher left power in 1992, not only was the first stage in the transformation of English football almost complete, but a number of the key elements that would shape the game in later years, such as the liberalisation of the communications sector and the presumption in favour of a market-led, open economy, were also in place. However, as we have already identified, before the Conservative era ended, there was one other hugely important development. In 1995 the Bosman ruling gave players much more contractual freedom. Bosman was a Belgian footballer who was placed on the transfer list by his club, RC Liège, after he refused to accept a new contract at a lower wage. Bosman wished to move to a French club, US Dunkerque, but RC Liège were unwilling to process the transfer because of doubts over US Dunkerque's ability to pay the agreed fee. The Belgian Football

Association and UEFA both argued that their respective rules requiring transfer fees were lawful.

The European Court of Justice, however, ruled in Bosman's favour, agreeing with the opinion that the transfer system was an unfair restraint of trade and incompatible with the European Union's rules over freedom of movement. Although the case was about player contracts, the judgement also raised questions about the compatibility of EU law and national rules, which imposed quotas on the number of foreign players that could be fielded in a match. In so far as players who were EU nationals were concerned, the European Court ruled that such quota systems were unlawful. The European Union's enforcement of the free movement of labour opened the football labour market across the continent, and eventually across the world.[66] We should not underestimate how significant an event Bosman was. While the response to Hillsborough and the policies of Margaret Thatcher's Governments created the platform for change in the English game, by giving players much greater power over their careers, strengthening their hand relative to owners, the Bosman Judgement changed *world* football.

Creating a market for players across the European Union had a huge impact. In 1992 only eleven foreign players started on the first weekend of the Premier League; two more came on as substitutes.[67] By 2019, on an average Saturday, only around one-third of players starting a Premier League game were qualified to play for England.[68] With a growing war for footloose talent, the balance of power had shifted back from owners to players, and a rise in wages was inevitable and rapid.

In May 1997, a Labour Government under the youthful-looking Tony Blair came to power, and 'Cool Britannia' became the *Zeitgeist*. It embarked on a programme to modernise the British economy and society, combining a series of socially liberal measures with the pro-market, light-touch regulation of the Thatcher years. The new administration would oversee the final act in the first phase of the modern transformation of English football.

With football now back as the country's favourite sport, there was little surprise in 1997 when the TV rights were sold for £670 million,[69] more than double the previous amount. Politicians were desperate to be associated with the game: Blair was filmed playing head tennis with Kevin Keegan; it was widely known that Chancellor Gordon Brown was a keen football fan, supporting his boyhood team, Raith Rovers; and future Ministers like Andy Burnham and Ed Balls were regular players for Demon Eyes, a side formed by Labour Party staff. All this might explain why, despite its pro-market instincts, the new administration sought to establish a larger role for itself in running football.

In opposition, Labour had published its Charter for Football, which called for a restructuring of the FA, a review of the relationship between football and television and an investigation of football's finances. These proposals were accompanied by additional suggestions for better policing, improved minority rights and a new focus on grass roots football.

Labour had identified the right set of issues to address, but once in office, it failed to deliver. A Football Task Force was established, chaired by David Mellor, with Andy Burnham as the administrator. However, the level of ambition was much lower than the Charter had promised: the promised reviews were all omitted. Hopes of significant reform were further stymied by internal Labour Party politics and wrangling with stakeholders, especially the Premier League.[70]

At the same time, the Office of Fair Trading (OFT)'s investigation into the Premier League's approach to selling TV rights found that the Premier League operated an unlawful, anti-competitive cartel by negotiating as one block, rather than giving clubs the individual right to negotiate their own deals. The case went to the Restrictive Practices Court (RPC).

In 1999, the court duly rejected the OFT's case, arguing that although it accepted there was a restriction on the number of matches that could be broadcast, this was in the public interest and therefore not illegal. A key piece of the rationale for the decision was the view that football was a part of a wider TV market rather than a separate one. Several years later, as we will see, the European Commission would adopt a very different view of the market when considering the bidding for, as opposed to selling of, rights.[71]

Exactly what happened is difficult to determine: the process was very politicised. That the government chose not to push harder further reflected successful lobbying by the Premier League, and an unwillingness to go out on a limb over football. The final settlement over the Premier League's contribution was a vague commitment to 5 per cent of some of its revenue to good causes, significantly less than the 10 per cent David Mellor believed he had secured when he reportedly agreed to give evidence to the RPC on the Premier League's behalf.[72]

Football was not important enough for politicians to be willing to take the risk of disrupting the status quo. The Government's retreat removed the final obstacle to the full commercialisation of the Premier League. With the FA sidelined, the Football League divided and the PFA focused on the interests of its members, the game was now free to move into the twenty-first century and the second phase of its transformation – one in an economy where private companies were licensed to operate free from day-to-day state control, constrained only by independent regulators seeking to ensure conduct met with the statutory objectives. As would regularly be the case across the wider economy, the public bodies generally found themselves playing catch up. Supporters were not even consulted.

With the game's popularity still growing, the relationship between television and football dominated. Although Sky's improved performance encouraged other companies to enter the market, none established a foothold. NTL, a cable operator formed by mergers of the local franchises, won the rights to show forty-four games on a pay-per-view basis from 2001 but the deal collapsed.[73] According to the BBC, NTL was unable to agree on the packaging of its offer to customers with the Premier League. Breaking into the market is about more than winning the TV rights: with a commercial partnership as well-established as it was with Sky, it was unsurprising the Premier League was keen to retain control.[74] With no support from politicians or the footballing authorities, NTL was forced to step away.

When the Football League's deal with Carlton and ITV Digital for £315 million over three years also collapsed it was replaced by a £96 million agreement over four years with Sky from 2002,[75] confirming Sky alongside the Premier League as the dominant commercial forces in English football, and illustrating the importance of competition in determining the price paid for TV rights. With no alternative to Sky, the value slumped dramatically.[76]

The 2001 deal was for 110 games a season, fifty more than previously available, supporting a further increase in the value of rights to £1.2 billion. Without a serious competitor for the 2004–7 deal, the trend for ever higher prices came to an end, with Sky securing 138 live games a season for £1.024 billion.[77] By contrast, in a sign that the competition's global appeal was growing, the Premier League also generated £325 million from the sale of its international rights for the three-year period from 2004/5 to 2006/7.[78]

Sky's success in securing more games for less money from 2004 suggested it had seen off the various competitive and regulatory challenges. Certainly, there seemed little prospect of either the Football Association or the government intervening. However, the landscape was about to change dramatically.

In 2005, the European Commission (EC), filling the vacuum left by the government, independent regulator and domestic football authorities, made the first significant intervention in the market for football TV rights in the UK. In 2003 it had investigated the process for selling European Champions' League rights and negotiated several important changes. These principles were now applied to the Premier League, with the most important being the 'no-single-buyer rule'.[79] As the name suggests, this is a requirement that no single bidder could win exclusive rights for live broadcasts of tournaments – a radical shake up of the market, disrupting the calm that had existed since the decision of the UK's Restrictive Practices Court in 1997.

Change was immediate and dramatic. Able to bid for a share of the action, and with the Premier League now obliged to be supportive, in contrast to NTL's experience, the Irish company Setanta Sports secured forty-two games in two packages in the auction of TV rights for 2007 to 2010. The impact of competition was there for all to see: the value of the rights increased from £341 million to £569 million a season. (The average price per broadcast game rose from £2.5 million to £4.1 million.)[80]

However, Setanta's success was short-lived. The company found the economics of entering an established market challenging. In late June 2009, the company failed to make a payment of £30 million to the Premier League. The American sports broadcaster ESPN stepped in and took over the two packages for the 2009–10 season. The new broadcasting deal from 2010–13, however, saw ESPN's coverage reduced to just one package or twenty-three games. Sky had fought back to secure five out of the six – but its dominance had been brought into question for the first time.[81]

The pattern of external regulatory intervention continued in 2010 when Ofcom, the UK communications regulator, finally entered the fray in an effective manner, concluding the investigation into the UK pay-TV market it had opened in 2007. (Sky had emerged relatively unscathed from two earlier UK reviews). Unlike the previous investigations by the OFT into Sky's dominance, Ofcom did find decisively against Sky, determining that the broadcaster had 'market power in the wholesale provision of premium channels' and 'exploits this market power by restricting the distribution of its premium channels to rival pay TV providers'.[82]

With more than one company guaranteed to win TV rights in each cycle due to the single buyer rule, Ofcom's aim now was to protect consumer interests, by ensuring that customers of companies that won packages of TV rights for Premier League games could gain access on fair terms to the packages won by other companies – in other words, to watch all the games they wanted without having to buy each supplier's proprietary technology, such as a Sky dish or a cable television set-top box. The case didn't end until 2014, but an interim order meant that suppliers agreed to cooperate and sell each other content. At the time, it appeared that the platform for truly competitive bidding for TV rights had finally been established. Gradually though it became clear that more cooperation reduced the incentives to bid aggressively to own all the content. After an initial surge in the prices paid, the market has settled at a more collaborative equilibrium, suggesting less intensive competition, and hence less upward pressure on prices, can be expected in future.[83]

There was one more legacy from the Thatcher era that would increase the difference between the Premier League and its European peers. The UK was now the most open major, developed economy, welcoming to individuals and finance from around the world. With the value of TV rights having soared, globalisation and an increasing number of international players boosting the Premier League's international profile, and gambling and e-gaming presenting new commercial opportunities, a new wave of investors, this time from abroad, emerged – little did we know at the time how significant this would turn out to be.

The Thatcher era reforms had moved football from its niche to the mainstream economy turning clubs into attractive assets. This was a shift that many of the traditional owners had failed to spot. When David Dein moved to acquire an interest in Arsenal, the then Chairman, Peter Hill-Wood, more accustomed to a world where owners had to put money into clubs, expressed his surprise: 'I told him it was dead money.'[84] Although he was correct that running a football club is often an unattractive proposition, selling one turned out to be a very different one. Many of the owners who had driven the initial phases of football's journey to commercialisation, took the opportunity to cash in, John Hall at Newcastle United, Doug Ellis at Aston Villa and David Dein at Arsenal were among the investors who realised significant value through selling some or all of their shares.[85]

As it became apparent through the 1990s that professional football's economic model was too volatile for the stock market, ownership moved first from public capital markets to corporates and then towards wealthy individuals and investors. The UK's open, light-touch regime attracted a mixed bag of oligarchs and private equity and hedge fund owners. So limited was the screening of potential suitors it seemed a prospective buyer would have to be either totally unacceptable or inept to fail the Premier League's owner fitness test.

Two years after Bosman came the first high-profile foreign owner: Mohamed Al-Fayed, the owner of Harrods. In 1997 he acquired Fulham and, despite some eccentric moves – he is still remembered for installing a statue of Michael Jackson at Craven Cottage – his was a successful stewardship, establishing Fulham as a Premier League Club.

Not long after, Milan Mandarić acquired Portsmouth, but his tenure was somewhat more volatile and ended in difficult circumstances.[86]

Roman Abramovich's purchase of Chelsea in summer 2003 was a game changer. It quickly became clear he was serious about winning, hiring Jose Mourinho (who had somewhat miraculously just won the Champions League with highly unfancied Porto) as manager and sanctioning spending on an unprecedented scale. Chelsea's wage bill doubled in a single season and was 35 per cent higher than next highest spenders Manchester United during Mourinho's first two title-winning campaigns and it wasn't just wages that soared: Chelsea's total transfer spending in that period was £200 million.[87]

The next significant market entry, with a totally different business model, was by the Glazer family from the USA. Buoyed by the eventual success of their then record $192 million purchase of the Tampa Bay Buccaneers in 1995, in 2003 they began building a stake in Manchester United. It was the dispute between the manager Alex Ferguson and shareholders John Magnier and J. P. McManus over the ownership of a racehorse, Rock of Gibraltar, that gave the Glazers the chance to acquire a substantial stake and launch a debt-financed takeover.[88]

This was financial engineering writ large. The initial deal valued Manchester United at around £790 million, and was funded with over £540 million of debt, partly secured on the club's assets and partly through £275 million of payment-in-kind notes with an interest rate of 14.5 per cent. In 2005, however, the global economy was building up the debt bubble that ultimately led to 2008's financial crisis, and football was not exempt. In the *Guardian* in 2019, David Conn estimated that 'the Glazers' takeover … has since cost more than £1 billion in interest, fees, refinancing penalties and other dead money.'[89]

The contrast with Chelsea is striking. Research by the football financial expert Swiss Ramble estimated that in the five seasons ending with the 2018/19 campaign, Roman Abramovich has put £440 million into Chelsea; in the same period, the Glazers have extracted over £80 million in dividends from Manchester United.[90]

These two deals illustrate the full width of the range of objectives owners may have when investing in football: the success driven approach of Abramovich compared to the Glazer's financially driven model. For some investors, football is not a business, for others it is nothing more than a transaction. Few industries have such a range of objectives which goes a long way to explaining why the footballing authorities find managing the balance between the game and money so challenging.

When they arrived, the Glazers were the fourth foreign owners in the Premier League. In another two seasons by 2007/8, the number had doubled to eight.[91] It was a classic case of supply and demand working together. The financial boom in the global economy meant that there was money actively seeking investment opportunities, while existing club owners increasingly realised new capital was needed to compete with the likes of Chelsea and Manchester United. That there were more transactions in England than in other major footballing countries is due to Mrs Thatcher's legacy: an open economy and sophisticated financial markets.

A major source of new money was the United States. The Glazers were not the only people to believe that introducing US sports management knowledge could create value. Aston Villa, Arsenal, Liverpool, and Sunderland all attracted new transatlantic owners or investors. But English football was attracting money from all over the world. Portsmouth had already changed ownership, with the French/Israeli Alexandre Gaydamak joining Milan Mandarić before taking over from him in 2008, Thaksin Shinawatra, a controversial Thai businessman and politician, bought Manchester City and Markus Liebherr, a Dutch businessman, took control of Southampton. There was also a wave of investment from Asia: Malaysian businessmen bought Cardiff and QPR; Leicester City were acquired by Thailand's King Power; Chinese investors, responding to President Xi's desire to improve China's standing in world football, also emerged on the scene, leading to investment in Southampton, West Bromwich Albion, Aston Villa, Birmingham City and Wolverhampton Wanderers.[92]

Together with the entry of Roman Abramovich, the purchases of Manchester City led by Sheikh Mansour and the acquisition of Liverpool by John Henry, the owner of the Boston Red Sox baseball team, may ultimately turn out to be the transactions that most significantly impact the competitive balance in the Premier League. With both groups bringing professional management and financial resources to bear on their investments, they created two teams extremely well equipped to compete for trophies and the important places in European competition.[93]

It took over a decade for the Premier League to reach three foreign-owned clubs. Within another four years the numbers had trebled. By 2012/13, there were eleven international owners anticipating the benefits of the new TV deal and, as this duly delivered increased profitability, more foreign owners were attracted through the decade. With promotion and relegation, the numbers have remained in the teens but fluctuated season to season. The total was back up to fourteen majority non-British-owned clubs at the start of the 2020/21 campaign, increasing to 15 midway through when Burnley were acquired by a private equity fund from the USA.[94]

The interventions by the two regulators, the European Commission and Ofcom, changed the landscape and created the platform for the next period of change in the second decade of the twenty-first century. With new owners in place, the English game now moved into its third phase of its modern transformation. After the Thatcher era and the regulated market period, the converged communications revolution would shape the landscape. Football was about to boom, but would it end in bust?

BT's entry into the bidding for Premier League TV rights in 2012 was the most significant development since Sky won the first set of rights in 1992. This was the moment when the Thatcher Government's reforms from three decades properly crystallised.

In 2012, Sky, BT, Virgin Media and other companies were all looking to develop their 'bundled' offers, comprising telecommunications, broadband and Internet services and, in many cases, mobile. Such companies spoke about wanting to 'own the customer'. Partly this reflected a desire to keep competitors out of their space, but it was also based on evidence that the more services a customer took from one company, the less likely they were to switch to another provider.

With a proven history of being the best content to attract subscribers, the Premier League found itself in the sweet spot – the source of competitive advantage in the battle for household broadband. Research by Ofcom in 2016 found that 74 per cent of Sky Sports and 63 per cent of BT Sports subscribers agreed that Premier League football was 'essential' and would not subscribe if it was not available. No other sport came close, confirming what Rupert Murdoch spotted all those years earlier.[95]

Starting from scratch in the TV market and wanting to push its own boxes into homes to create a longer-term customer relationship, BT wanted its own rights to Premier League football, not to be just a re-seller of Sky's content. The impact of its entry into the market was both immediate and dramatic. The auction of 154 games, up from 138 in the previous three deals, raised just over £1 billion a season for 2013 to 2016: an increase of over £400 million on the £594 million paid for 2010–13. The average price per game leapt from £4.3 million to £6.5 million.[96]

Sky now found itself facing a real competitor with ambition and deep pockets. Because it couldn't afford to lose too much ground, while BT needed to build on its initial achievement, the result of the 2016 to 2019 auction was staggering. BT paid £960 million for forty-two games – four more than its previous deal – but Sky bid £4.176 billion for 126 games: almost double the £2.3 billion it had paid for 116 matches under the previous deal.

When the final bids were opened at Premier League headquarters, no-one could quite believe what had happened. The average price paid per game had increased from £2.47 million in 2004–6 to £10.2 million from 2016 onwards, and Sky had paid £11 million per game, compared to £7.6 million by BT.[97] When the dust had settled, the lesson was clear: owning the content that provides the key source of differentiation in a competitive market is a quick route to making money. It seemed that everything the Premier League touched turned to gold. Almost everything that could have gone right had done so – football led a charmed life.

But 2018/19 was the end of an era. Cracks in the façade were emerging and football was entering the fourth stage of the journey that began in the 1980s: the first one likely to take place in an environment of events working against rather than for the game.

Most notably, football may no longer be able to bank on ever higher income from TV rights. Ofcom's interventions after 2010 created the opportunity for a more collaborative approach to competition that eventually allowed both Sky and BT to bid less aggressively, the first sign of a shift in approach reflective of other changes in their corporate circumstances and strategies. As a result, the domestic TV deal for 2019 to 2022 was worth less than the previous deal, despite more matches being available.[98] An agreement to change the approach to sharing foreign TV revenues – the first since the Premier League was established – signalled a pivot by the richest clubs towards the global market, but a changing geopolitical landscape may also have a role to play here.[99]

There were also signs of a change in the government's attitude towards football. As I identified in Chapter 1, the child abuse scandal, the failure to improve diversity, growing concerns over the relationship between football and gambling and the evident failure of governance in the crises at Bury and Bolton Wanderers, meant politicians could no longer ignore the game. In its manifesto for the 2019 General Election, the Conservative Party made a commitment to a 'fan-led review of governance' – an opportunity to reset its governance that the game must embrace.[100]

While it may appear that Covid-19 changed the landscape, football was entering a new era before the pandemic struck – the lockdown only exacerbated existing trends. In the same way as it exposed the fragilities of the UK's pro-market, individualistic, unregulated economy in the health sector and labour market, the Covid-19 pandemic exposed the fragile nature of the game's finances. Despite the headline grabbing TV and sponsorship deals, English football has lost money through the Premier League era and 2018/19 saw the top division's clubs record a collective loss after 2 years of profits. The rest of the English game was loss-making.[101]

As the most Thatcherite of economies, with so many stakeholders driven by their own interests, football struggled to put together a coherent collective response to the pandemic – a failure which opened up the game's secrets to a wider audience and accelerated the drive for reform.

As the UK faced up to a second wave of the virus, Liverpool and Manchester United launched Project Big Picture: a proposal to change the commercial structure and governance of the whole English game. What was striking was how many themes were the same as those that dominated the debate in the 1980s and 1990s: an eighteen-club top division; the approach to selling TV rights; revenue sharing across the divisions; the governance of the game. This at a time when the communications market was going through another major evolution.[102]

Although Project Big Picture was rejected by the Premier League's clubs, the momentum for change continued to grow. Frustrated by their failure to wrest more control of the Champions League from UEFA, twelve European clubs, including six from the Premier League, announced a breakaway European Super League in April 2021. Suddenly it was clear to everyone: we were in the next phase of the game's transformation, but this was now a battle for survival.

Change in English football on the scale we have seen was not inevitable. Time does not stand still, and the game would have evolved anyway, but we should be clear that choices were made, especially on the balance between the game and money, that have shaped English football as we know today.

What is striking looking back over the period, especially after the failed proposals for a European Super League, is how little challenging or questioning there was to the changes in the game, most obviously about the growing influence of television, the financial stress across the pyramid and the reasons foreign owners were so attracted to English football. While it was pleasing to see the football community rise up to protect the game's traditions in 2021, it is worth remembering the majority of those people and organisations had been silent for the previous thirty plus years – like me they had let themselves believe the narrative.

Football's challenges are not new. The struggle to balance, money, competition and community have dominated football's governance for over 150 years. We are at a critical point: a once in a generation oppor-tunity to rebalance the game. The choices we make in future could have similar or greater consequences than those made in the last four decades. We need to be clear on the trade-offs.

Informed by history, it is now time to start to think about the fu-ture, beginning by opening the lid on English football's economic model. Understanding how money flows through the game is the only place to start.

3 SHOW ME THE MONEY

The capacity of Old Trafford, Manchester United's stadium, is 74,879, only slightly less than seven times that of AFC Bournemouth's 11,329-seat Vitality Stadium. The population of Bournemouth in 2019 was around 200,000. Every season Manchester United attract crowds more than six times the size of the South Coast town.[1]

And there is an audience available to Manchester United that AFC Bournemouth can only dream of. In a survey conducted by Kantar Media in 2019,[2] 467 million people self-identified as Manchester United fans, and an additional 635 million as followers. Of the total of almost 1.1 billion people, 253 million were from China. These are truly staggering numbers. I can't decide if I am more shocked that one in every seven people on the planet is a fan or follower of Manchester United or that the total has increased by 400 million people since a similar survey in 2012.

Despite the efforts of the Premier League to ensure a reasonably equitable distribution of revenues between clubs, such disparities in popularity lead to very different financial results. In 2018/19, Manchester United's turnover of £627 million dwarfed Bournemouth's £131 million. While broadcast revenues of £241 million for United and £116 million for the South Coast team were not as far out of line, those billion global fans and followers powered Manchester United's commercial income to £275 million, a world removed from the £10 million achieved by Bournemouth. But it is the difference in match day income that creates the chasm between the two clubs. Across the season, Old Trafford's huge capacity and the global appeal of the Red Devils drove match day revenues of £111 million, twenty-two times the £5 million generated at the Vitality Stadium – Manchester United earn almost as much in one game as AFC Bournemouth take in a season.[3]

Inevitably, an imbalance in income translates into an imbalance in expenditure. Manchester United spent £582 million on transfers during the same five-year period that Bournemouth spent £122 million. It was a similar story on wage bills in 2018/19: £332 million for the team from Old Trafford and £111 million for the Cherries. However, due to their much greater revenue, the spending was more affordable for the richer club – wages represented 56 per cent of Manchester United's turnover but 85 per cent of income for the South Coast team in 2018/19.[4] This is where the economic model really bites: not only were Bournemouth completely outspent, but they also had to accept a much higher level of financial risk to support what they could only hope would be competitive wages. Starting at such a disadvantage, surviving for five seasons in the Premier League was a huge achievement.

The comparison shows how money and sport are uneasy bedfellows. Understandably, supporters focus on the performance of their own team, but leagues are collective in nature. Since the dawn of professional football, governing bodies have sought to achieve a reasonable balance between teams, so as to create a degree of uncertainty about both the outcome of individual matches and the overall standings. The worry is that if a mismatch in financial strength leads to one or more teams buying up the best talent and becoming too strong relative to the rest, then the competition itself may become boring and, crucially, lose its commercial appeal. Sport is unlike normal business. Corporates aim to become better than their competitors to dominate their markets. Do this in football and you might destroy the market.

Understanding the interaction between off-the-pitch finances and on-the-pitch outcomes is therefore key to identifying the options for the English game in future: Money shapes the game. I will start by analysing where the money comes from and where it goes before going on to explore the consequences for the structure and balance of competition across English football in the next two Chapters. As it generates

85 to 90 per cent of the total revenue in the game from season to season, the Premier League is the only place to start.[5]

Revenue is generated from match days, selling the rights to broadcast games and commercial and sponsorship income. A share of the TV and sponsorship income attracted by the major competitions, both domestic and international, is awarded for success, measured by league position or progress in a cup. Player wages and the transfer fees paid to sign them and the investment in facilities such as grounds and training complexes, are the major sources of expenditure, generally dwarfing the other costs incurred in running a club. Taken together, the revenues and costs generate profits or losses and the potential need for extra financing. As we will see, when costs exceed revenues, owners often step in to bridge the gap – sometimes voluntarily, sometimes not.

By any measure, the Premier League has been phenomenally successful in generating revenue. According to the consultancy Deloitte, pre-pandemic, the highest recorded Premier League revenues of €5.85 billion were achieved in 2018/19, way ahead of the nearest challengers, Spain's La Liga, with €3.38 billion in income, and the Bundesliga with €3.35 billion. It is a remarkable success story: by my calculations, England accounts for less than 3 per cent of the world economy but nearly 20 per cent of global football revenue. To put this into context, it is a similar proportion to Saudi Arabia in the world market for oil.[6]

With strong growth in all European countries, payments for television broadcast rights dominate football finances. They are the major source of revenues in the five largest European leagues, accounting for 59 per cent of total income in England and Italy and 54 per cent in Spain in the 2018/19 season. The Premier League's ability to generate much higher revenues from broadcasters than its peers is the major reason for the differences in total revenues across the five leagues. In 2018/19, the Premier League generated TV revenues of almost €3.5 billion, way ahead of the €1.8 billion achieved in Spain and the €1.5 billion received by the top division clubs in Germany, the second and third most valuable leagues. The Premier League generates the highest amount both from its home market and from selling the foreign rights to other countries.[7]

Because they are sold in a less visible way, foreign rights have tended to slip under the radar, yet they are increasingly significant. In the most recent cycle, starting with the 2019/20 season, the foreign rights went for an estimated £1.4 billion a season. With domestic rights being sold for £1.55 billion a year, this represented the highest share of total broadcast income ever accounted for by non-UK sales. The scale of foreign revenues is what sets the English competition apart from its peers.[8]

This success is no accident: Premier League broadcasts are hugely popular around the world. Securing the TV rights to the Premier League had an immediate impact on Sky's subscriber base in the UK, and it is a similar story internationally with viewing figures estimated at 3.2 billion viewers a season. Indeed, international Premier League TV rights are worth more than the total of *all other exports of UK television programmes*. This includes sales of shows like *Top Gear* and *Doctor Who* and formats for popular programmes like *Strictly Come Dancing* and *Who Wants to be a Millionaire?*[9]

The other major sources of income are commercial (including sponsorship) and match day receipts. Even though clubs in Germany (40 per cent) and France (42 per cent) generate a higher share of their total income from commercial and sponsorship activities, the Premier League's is the highest in cash terms: €1.6 billion in 2018/19, almost €300 billion more than the next highest, Germany.[10] Commercial and sponsorship revenues derive both from international and domestic businesses, reflecting the brand and reach of individual clubs in the global and national markets, and local businesses keen to be associated with their hometown team. It is a virtuous circle: greater broadcast reach leads to more exposure, which in turn increases the value to businesses of being associated with the Premier League.

While TV viewers drive broadcast revenues, attendance size and spectator profile drive match day revenues. On average, the larger the crowd the greater the revenue, and the higher the share of corporate and VIP spectators, the more money per head. Even though clubs have raised ticket prices over time, physical capacity limits in stadia set a ceiling on match day income. Across the five major leagues, these revenues account for between 11 per cent and 16 per cent of total receipts, with the Premier League at around 13 per cent. Nevertheless, once again, in absolute terms, the £683 million earned by Premier League teams in 2018/19 was the highest in Europe – the impact of Germany's larger average crowds is offset by a shorter thirty-four-game season and lower ticket prices.[11]

A club's location, profile and size of fan base all affect its potential to generate revenues. Aware that there would be wide differences in revenue across teams, the Premier League's clubs, especially the smaller ones, were keen to ensure a degree of equity in the distribution be maintained. Under the formula agreed when the competition launched in 1992, half of the value of domestic TV rights and central sponsorship was to be shared equally between clubs, a quarter allocated based on final league position, and the remainder divided up in proportion to number of times a club featured in a live TV broadcast. As foreign TV rights were insignificant at the time, they attracted much less attention, and a simple approach was adopted with every team receiving an equal share.[12]

The Premier League makes a great deal of its desire to ensure balanced competition, and as far as the income from its TV rights is concerned, it has been true to its word, consistently achieving the most equitable balance of the richest five leagues in Europe. A project I led for the Premier League compared the allocation of television revenues in the five competitions in 2013/14.[13] At that time, the Premier League's ratio of 1 to 1.6 between the top and bottom earners was the most balanced, compared to 1 to 2 in Germany, 1 to 3.4 in France, 1 to 5.3 in Italy and 1 to 6.9 in Spain. The must-read football analyst, Swiss Ramble, published an updated analysis for the 2018/19 season. The ratios were still 1 to 1.6 in England, but had moved to 1 to 3.3 in Germany, 3.1 in France, 1 to 2.3 in Italy and 1 to 3.6 in Spain. (The significant change in the Spanish ratio over time resulted from a change in approach. In 2013/14, Real Madrid and Barcelona were taking 38 per cent of total revenues through their own deals. Since the introduction of a collective selling model in 2016/17 their share has fallen to 23 per cent).[14]

Laudable though the efforts to ensure a balance in financial strength in the Premier League are, they have a limited effect. First, television rights payments for Premier League games are only one part of total broadcast income. Over the five seasons up to 2018/19, European TV rights payments accounted for 26 per cent of the TV rights income of the six richest teams in England. As a result, the Premier League's revenue sharing only covered 51 per cent of the competition's total income in 2018/19, and less than one quarter of the revenue generated by the seven clubs engaged in European competitions.[15]

Secondly, as TV revenues have grown rapidly, even though the allocation ratios have remained the same, the gap in the absolute value of money being allocated has increased. In 2015/16, the last year of the three-year TV deal, the gap between top earners Arsenal, with £101 million in TV receipts, and the lowest earners Aston Villa, was £35 million. By 2018/19, the last year of the subsequent deal, the gap between Liverpool and Huddersfield on Premier League rights alone, before taking European monies into account, was £56 million.[16] Measured in cash terms, the difference is growing, and disproportionately increasing the spending power of the highest earners.

Although income from TV rights is the most important single source of money, clubs have limited ability to influence it, as the process and negotiations are handled by the Premier League. Paradoxically, because it is managed centrally, the largest income stream requires the least amount of effort from clubs to achieve. They therefore devote their resources to generating the commercial and sponsorship and match day income they can directly influence.

The gap in TV income, even after accounting for the increase due to European competition rights, is relatively small. When you look at the split of total income, very quickly, the gap becomes a chasm. Quite simply, size and reputation matter. The 'Big Six', the six largest clubs with the highest turnover in the top division (Arsenal, Chelsea, Liverpool, Manchester City, Manchester United and Tottenham Hotspur) generated 57 per cent of total Premier League revenue in the five seasons to 2018/19 but only 42 per cent of all television income.[17] The larger grounds and higher global profiles of the Big Six enable them to generate higher match day incomes and attract more valuable sponsorship and commercial deals than their smaller rivals. For example, 42 per cent of 2018/19 champions Manchester City's income came from commercial sources and 47 per cent from television. This is very different from relegated Huddersfield's revenue, with 88 per cent coming from television, 8 per cent from commercial sources and only 4 per cent from match days.[18]

In recent years, with signs that TV income for domestic rights was reaching a peak, the richest clubs intensified their efforts to generate commercial and matchday revenue, recruiting business talent from around the world to drive their efforts. From the time Ed Woodward took over as CEO in 2012/13 until 2018/19, Manchester United's commercial revenues grew from £152 million to £275 million, according to the *Financial Times*.[19] As we might expect from the Kantar research mentioned previously, the club has led the Premier League in securing sponsorship partners, famously being rumoured to deploy a grid divided into sectors and countries, supported by a sponsorship team of over 100 people. In 2018/19 alone, the club announced ten new partnership deals. The *FT* highlighted the jewels in the crown as the £750 million, decade-long kit sponsorship deal with Adidas and a US$559 million, seven-year partnership with Chevrolet to be the club's main shirt sponsor. For sponsorships and partnerships with the world's largest companies Manchester United are competing with other footballing giants like Paris Saint-Germain, Real Madrid, Barcelona and Bayern Munich, rather than the smaller teams in the Premier League.

Following the recent changes to the distribution of money from foreign TV rights in the Premier League, broadcast revenues are increasingly driven by results on the pitch. By contrast, commercial and sponsorship revenues for clubs like Manchester United are at least partly driven by the strength of the club's brand. As Ed Woodward put it on an analyst call in 2018, 'Playing performance doesn't really have a meaningful impact on what we can do on the commercial side of the business.'[20]

Reflect for a moment, on the message: on-the-pitch and off-the-pitch success are not related. Is this true? If so, it would turn all our thinking on the economic drivers of the game upside down. Why invest in expensive players to win matches if there is a better return from brand building and marketing? Should Manchester United adopt the model of the Harlem Globetrotters and travel the world playing exhibition games? Taken to its logical conclusion, Woodward's assertion would imply that the footballing authorities don't need to concern themselves with competitive balance.

United's strong commercial performance, despite relatively poor performance on the pitch after Sir Alex's Ferguson's departure in 2013, provides some limited support for the claim. However, it is always wise to be sceptical of good news stories delivered to the financial markets – Woodward was over-simplifying, ignoring the likely effect on income of an extended period of disappointing on-the-pitch performance. Delve a little deeper and it's clear on- and off-the-field success are directly linked.

First, as the *Financial Times* reported, if the club fails to qualify for the Champions' League for two consecutive seasons, then in the subsequent campaign the payment for sponsorship by Adidas falls by £21 million. And secondly, it is becoming clear that with no return to the levels of success achieved under Sir Alex Ferguson, since 2016/17 commercial revenues have flatlined, allowing more successful domestic rivals to close the gap.[21] What Woodward was explaining was that, just as it takes time to build a global brand, so it erodes slowly – even during the pandemic, the club signed a five-year deal for shirt sponsorship worth £235 million with Teamview, a software company.[22]

Manchester United still generated over £40 million more in commercial revenue than Manchester City in 2018/19, despite their Mancunian rivals winning the Premier League, and almost 50 per cent more than Champions' League winners and Premier League runners-up, Liverpool.[23] Their closest rivals in England are struggling to catch up. But, outside of the elite, Manchester United's performance is a thing of wonder, completely out of reach.

As match day income depends directly on the size and mix of crowds attracted to games, stadia have become a new competitive battleground. With over £3 billion invested in stadia in England during the Premier League era,[24] there is no doubt that the clubs have delivered an enormous transformation in the quality of the spectator experience.

Entering Tottenham Hotspur's new state-of-the-art stadium takes your breath away. Go to watch a traditional football match there and the grass pitch looks immaculate, surrounded by shiny new, rising terraces. But this is also 'the home of American Football in England'. Visit on one of the days when the arena is transformed into a venue for gridiron and you will be amazed at how different it feels: the Astroturf pitch shining under the floodlights. Inside, the facilities include a microbrewery, the longest bar in Europe and a 'Dare Skywalk' offering visitors the chance to explore the roof of the stadium. It is truly a twenty-first- century venue, out of keeping with both the last-century London suburb that surrounds it and the crumbling public transport infrastructure it relies on.

It was not cheap. Interviewed prior to the opening, Spurs' Chairman Daniel Levy suggested the whole project had cost over £1 billion, and the club took on debt of £627 million to help fund the construction.[25] When the Covid-19 pandemic hit and events had to be cancelled, the club was forced to take out an additional emergency loan from the government of £175 million.[26] In the high-stakes Premier League, balancing risk and reward is not for the faint-hearted.

Tottenham's ambitious project, the expansion of Old Trafford to 75,000, Liverpool's plan to increase Anfield's capacity to over 60,000 and recent moves to new, larger stadia by Arsenal and Manchester City, all confirm the growing importance of the stadium as a commercial asset in top-flight football. The more people that can be accommodated on a match day, the more events that can be staged and the more the stadium can be used for other purposes, the greater the potential revenue improvement.

From 1997/98 to 2019/20, the average capacity of stadia in the Premier League increased from around 35,000 to just over 40,000, helping to contribute to the steady rise in match day income. This was not a competition-wide development though: more an arms race among the richest clubs. Over 80 per cent of the growth in the average was down to increases in capacity at the four clubs with the largest grounds.[27] The message to ambitious clubs is clear: if you want to compete for the highest rewards you need a large stadium. It is no surprise that West Ham left Upton Park to move to the London Stadium and Everton, constrained by the location of their long-term home, have announced ambitious plans to develop a new ground.[28]

Generally, smaller clubs are reluctant to commit money to expanding their capacity by any significant amount. The evidence supports their reticence. Research in 2007 by Santos and others found a reasonably strong relationship between the population and income of a city and the performance of its football clubs. At the time, they concluded that a population of just under 600,000 was required to provide a city with a reasonable chance of having clubs in Europe's elite. Interestingly in their analysis, Liverpool and Newcastle overperformed on the pitch, while Birmingham underperformed. With smaller catchment areas the benefits of investment in larger stadia are unlikely to make the risk of incurring higher capital spend worth it.[29] As we have seen in other areas, left unchecked by regulation, the gap between the richest and the rest will only grow wider.

For match day income, size matters. Although a good season with success in cup competitions does generate additional games and hence more income – Liverpool's success in the Champions' League in 2018/19 saw their match day income rise to £84 million – stadium size limits total income growth. Even after a stellar season, Liverpool's match day receipts out of their 53,000-seater stadium were some way behind Manchester United's £111 million from a capacity of just shy of 75,000, and Arsenal's £96 million from their 60,000 seats, with Premier League champions Manchester City's 55,000-person arena only leading to £55 million from match day activity that campaign.[30]

With a greater focus by the largest teams on match day and commercial revenue, the gap between the largest teams and the rest on additional income streams is widening. In 2018/19, according to Swiss Ramble, the top six earners captured almost £850 million more than the other fourteen clubs. Across the categories, the Big Six earned £822 million more in commercial income, £308 million more on match days and £427 million of European TV income. TV income was the exception. The agreed sharing formula resulting in the fourteen earning £290 million more than the Big Six.[31]

While the ratio for the share of TV revenue was 1 to 1.6 between the highest and lowest earners, the equivalent figure for total revenue was 1 to 5.1. Suddenly the disparity with other leagues is less. In 2017/18 in Germany the ratio for total revenues, by my estimates, was 1 to 7.5, still 50 per cent higher than the Premier League, but a significantly smaller multiple than on TV revenues alone.[32]

It is not just about how much money. Where it comes from matters too. As in any business, as the relative share of revenue generated by different segments of the market changes, so the priority afforded to those different stakeholder groups will shift. In rational companies, resources will normally be directed to where they can generate the highest return.

In the 1980s, supporters attending matches were the primary source of income and were treated as such. As domestic TV income grew, match day supporters were forced to accept shifts in the timing of matches to maximise the TV audience. More recently, the growth in corporate sponsors around the world, together with the increasing importance of foreign TV income, have led to further shifts in scheduling and the emergence of the global pre-season tour. (With more Premier League games televised during the pandemic, a weekend 11.30 a.m. kick-off has crept into the schedule – even a slightly earlier start increases the chances of fans in Asia tuning in).

Today, English football's income derives from distinct groups, the most significant of which are: supporters who attend matches; domestic TV viewers; foreign TV viewers; overseas fans who attend exhibition or international competition games; and sponsors. As each of these groups engages with football in their own way, what they want from football differs. For clubs and administrators, as the game has commercialised, identifying how to balance the interests of different stakeholders has become increasingly challenging. In my experience, chasing new customers tends to excite businesses more than retaining their existing base – we see it regularly in commentary on the utilities and insurance sectors for example. As we will see in Chapter 6, football's traditional base – match going supporters have been victims of this approach as more and more effort has gone into chasing global TV viewers and corporate sponsors.

The priority afforded to traditional supporters was exposed at the launch of the proposed European Super League in April 2021. Dan Roan, a BBC Sport's Reporter tweeted: "According to source, some of those involved in ESL call traditional supporters of clubs 'legacy fans' while they are focused instead on the 'fans of the future' who want superstar names."[33]

This is football as finance – decision by focus group. I can't think of a clearer illustration of the difference between viewing football as a business and valuing the game in its widest sense.

The Premier League has been incredibly successful at building up interest and turning this into revenue growth. Football needs money as urgently as at any time in its history. As we seek to reshape the game, we must bear in mind that any proposals for change will have to take into account the potential risk of damaging this successful model, but it needs to be tempered by consideration for the wider game and football's community.

Generating income is the first stage of the battle for success. Once Premier League clubs have built up their firepower, the next step is to fire those financial weapons. It is important to remember that revenue is not the same as profit or value – how wisely they deploy their income determines how successful they are. Let's turn to look at the expenditure side of football's financial model.

Payments to secure, retain and reward talent dominate the spending of all English football clubs. In 2018/19, of total Premier League revenues of around £5.2 billion, £3.2 billion – 62 per cent of income – was spent on wages and nearly £1.3 billion on transfers.[34] In total, 87 per cent of Premier League revenue in 2018/19 was spent on transfers and wages. It is hard to think of another industry with such an extreme economic model; even investment banking at the height of the financial boom would have baulked at such a high labour cost-to-revenue ratio.[35]

It was the landmark, so-called Bosman ruling[36] that opened the floodgates. It changed the football talent market in three ways. First, it created, as we have seen, a Europe-wide market for footballers. Secondly, by removing the limits on the number of foreign players generally, it effectively opened up the global market, subject only to restrictions from national employment regimes. And thirdly, it removed the remaining contractual restrictions on players, including those remaining in their home market.

Bosman transformed the economics of the game. Just as it was in 1888, having the best players is still seen as the way to achieve success on the pitch. While it was once just a belief, there is now a large body of research supporting the view that wages are the primary driver of success on the pitch.[37] (It is not just the academic research: listen to managers talk and there is no doubt how important having the best players is to them.) Teams that have the highest wage bills will, other things being equal, be the most successful.

Although transfer fees measure the value of talent brought into clubs, the research suggests that spending to acquire talent is a little less strongly correlated with success, probably in part because not all transfers turn out as planned. Every supporter will be able to name at least one hugely expensive acquisition who flopped. It is also the case that clubs devote significant resources to maximising their acquisition of talent at the lowest cost, using approaches such as those underpinning 'Moneyball', an analytic approach developed in North American baseball that seeks to identify undervalued talent.[38] (It came to wider attention after its use by the Oakland Athletics was captured in print and then on film). Add in the development of local talent in academies, and clubs may be able to assemble talent competitively, but ultimately they will have to pay the going rate to retain it.

In recent seasons clubs with the highest wage bills have dominated the Premier League. Consistent with the accepted wisdom, my own analysis of wages and performance over the last twenty seasons found total pay to be strongly correlated with final position in the Premier League table, and even slightly more so with points earned (points may be a better guide to relative strength as there is more scope for divergence in points than league positions). In the recent seasons up to 2018/19, the correlation became even stronger, driven by the growing gap in revenues, and hence wages, between the Big Six and the rest.

When I considered spending on transfers over three, four and five seasons rather than a single campaign, the correlation to success was higher, albeit still weaker than the relationship with wages. These findings fit with how the game operates – it usually takes several seasons to either assemble or reshape a squad, hence one year's data is unlikely to capture the full picture. It is also worth pointing out that the analysis based on wages alone may overstate the strength of the relationship as bonus payments can distort the analysis, almost by definition, successful teams will pay out more. Whatever the limitations of the analysis, I and many others are in little doubt that spending more on acquiring and retaining talent is the most likely way to achieve success on the pitch over time.

With clubs desperate to secure the best talent, and that talent, post-Bosman, having more power in the market, it was no surprise that spending soared in the Premier League era. Whatever the nuances in what the economics tells us about the impact of wages, the intense competition for players that plays out in the transfer market is what captures the attention of fans and headline writers alike. Fans want big money spent to move their club to 'the next level'. The two transfer windows every season now attract saturation media coverage, with every move analysed in ever increasing detail.

Historically, the English transfer deadline – the last day in the season on which players could be bought and sold – was in late March. (A deadline was imposed in the first place to ensure an orderly end to the season by stopping panic purchases.) Subsequently, concern over the disruption caused by incessant transfer speculation during the season led to the introduction of two transfer windows, one near the start of the season and one in January (with some local variations), across European football.

For Sky Sports, the transfer window has become a drama box set. The deadline day clock is launched on screen early in the summer and late in December, counting down the days, hours and minutes until the window opens. Immediately the window opens, the clock switches to a countdown to the close. Programmes throughout the day update the viewers, repeating, incessantly it seems, the slightest piece of gossip, while a stream of experts share their views on what is happening, what could happen and what should happen.

As deadline day approaches, preparations step up a notch. All the presenters will be seen wearing some yellow on their clothing (a trend that started, according to lead presenter Jim White, when he wore a yellow tie to match the 'Breaking News' banner on the bottom of the screen)[39] and Sky reporters are dispatched to stadia and training grounds around the country in the hope of capturing an exclusive. Who could forget the pictures showing the joy of Manchester City supporters when Robinho, the first trophy signing of the regime under their owners from Abu Dhabi, arrived; or the excitement as Sky filmed Dimitar Berbatov completing a last-gasp signing at Manchester United's training ground? Tony Pulis's stint at Stoke was characterised by a penchant for moving late in the window, and time after time Rob Dorset was the reporter saddled with trying to keep a boisterous bunch of the club's supporters from shocking the nation with their songs. Back in the studio, yellow tie brightening up the screen, Jim White would slide into the presenter's chair for the last slot of the evening, driving the rhetoric to fever pitch as we all hoped for a helicopter bringing a mystery player to our club. It is football as theatre, often more comedy than drama, but the sums of money involved are anything but a joke. With revenue having soared, the transfer market is where success can be won and lost, where football gambles with its finances.

Fans had a glimpse of the future even before the first Premier League game kicked off. The British transfer record was broken in the pre-season of July 1992 as Blackburn Rovers moved to sign Alan

Shearer for a reported £3.6 million, breaking the record of £2.9 million that Liverpool had paid to buy Dean Saunders in 1991. When Shearer moved again, this time to Newcastle in July 1996, the fee was £15 million, smashing the then record of £8.5 million that had been paid for Stan Collymore the previous summer.[40]

By the turn of the century, the market had grown further, total Premier League spending in 2001/02 was £323 million. As spending soared, concerns at the rate of increase emerged. In its 2002 *Annual Review of Football Finance*, with Premier League clubs recording their highest ever loss to date of £137 million, Deloitte stressed the financial challenges facing English football, especially for clubs outside the Premier League with the collapse the previous season of the TV deal with OnDigital. 'The evidence suggests that the 2001/02 season will prove a watershed for the transfer market,' said Deloitte's Dan Jones, 'and we will never see again the levels of transfer spending seen over the last five years.'[41] Jones's colleague Paul Rawnsley was of the opinion that the balance of power in transfer negotiations was shifting from players back to clubs: 'The future for the majority of players is one of short-term contracts ... more sophisticated [financial and football] performance-related pay; and signings for clubs as an unattached free agent or on one-season loan deals.'[42]

Nothing could have been further from the truth. Within a couple of years, Premier League wages had taken off once again and, with the 2004–7 TV deal being lower in terms of domestic rights than the previous deal, salaries increased faster than revenues. In the first few years of the twenty-first century the ratio of wages to turnover had edged downwards, but now it started to edge upwards again, going from around 60 per cent to over 70 per cent by the end of the decade. Even a significant boost in the value of domestic TV rights to £570 million a season from 2007/08 did not stem the rise in the wages-to-turnover ratio. The Premier League was entering a new era that would separate it from other leagues around Europe. According to Deloitte, in 2001, English and Italian top division wage bills were broadly equivalent. By 2005, total wages in England were around 50 per cent higher than Italy's.[43]

A surge on this scale was unexpected. What happened to change the situation so dramatically? Why did wages suddenly take off even though a lack of a competitor to Sky in the auction for TV rights for 2004 to 2007 meant the value paid fell, and hence the early years of the twenty-first century saw some of the slowest rates of growth in Premier League clubs' incomes?

There was an obvious catalyst: Roman Abramovich. Seemingly out of nowhere, the Russian billionaire arrived to buy Chelsea from Ken Bates in the summer of 2003 in a deal valued at £140 million. The Russian businessman, said Bates, would move Chelsea onto the 'next level'. He was half right. Abramovich moved the whole English game.[44]

In the first season of new ownership, Chelsea's wage bill increased from £54 million, joint third in the league, to £115 million – £38 million more than the next highest spenders, Manchester United. The increase in Chelsea's wage bill accounted for 80 per cent of the total increase in top-flight wages that season. The following season the total wage bill fell as clubs adjusted to the disappointing new TV deal, but it rose by £53 million the following season, with almost 70 per cent of the increase accounted for by the 'Big Four': Arsenal, Chelsea, Liverpool and Manchester United.[45]

Wages were just part of the story. Chelsea were taking no chances. Abramovich underwrote transfer spending of £110 million in his first summer and another £90 million a year later. He was rewarded with Chelsea's first title since 1955, but it was an expensive process – in the first five seasons of his ownership Chelsea recorded operating losses of £449 million. Chelsea's successful manager, Jose Mourinho, has often been accused of referring to himself as "the Special One" (though he actually said 'a' rather than 'the').[46] In truth, with the resources available to him, 'the Fortunate One' would have been more appropriate.

Just as we identified how there is a range of segments generating revenues, each with specific demands of the game, so there is more than one type of owner. Roman Abramovich is a classic example of what economists call a 'win-maximiser': willing to lose money to achieve success. At the other extreme is the 'profit-maximiser', wanting to run their club as a business. In the game today, there is a spectrum of people with objectives between these extremes – the Coates family for example, owners not seeking necessarily to win the Premier League but aiming for some level of on the pitch achievement alongside a contribution to the local community.

As identified in the previous Chapter, the FA's initial regulatory approach back in 1888 was based around ensuring competition on the pitch, limiting the ability of owners to overspend and ensuring the financial sustainability of clubs. Football has changed hugely, yet many of the fundamentals remain the same.

The FA was right to be concerned. Ignoring financial constraints, Abramovich transformed the game, and the battle to stay in touch accelerated. With the game's elite players having significant power in the labour market, cost control is only possible if clubs are restrained in their spending. When an owner comes along willing to underwrite high wages and transfer fees, competitive pressures are likely to drive up outgoings. Even if you are a profit-maximising owner, when you control a Big Six club and your competitors are spending aggressively, there is pressure to match them, so as not to fall behind and potentially reduce your appeal to supporters and commercial partners. Unless you strike lucky with a few transfer deals or bring through some academy players, then there is little option but to spend as required and hope your competitors will stop chasing success at any cost before you run out of money.

This scenario accurately captures what happened. By 2008/9, the sixth season after Abramovich arrived, Arsenal, Liverpool and Manchester United had joined Chelsea in spending over £100 million a year on wages. Having been bought by Sheikh Mansour bin Zayed al-Nahyan in 2008, another win-maximising owner, Manchester City vastly increased its wage bill to £83 million, a hint of things to come, and when Fenway Sports acquired Liverpool FC in autumn 2010, the new competitive landscape was complete.[47]

The ambition and competitive dynamics of owners, together with a new and much more lucrative TV deal after Sky upped its efforts to regain its dominance, drove transfer spending in England over £1 billion for the first time in 2013/14. Spending continued to rise. By 2014/15, gross transfer spending (excluding the income from selling players) by Premier League clubs alone was £1.25 billion, as clubs continued to chase the best talent. The unexpected, to put it mildly, success of Leicester in 2016/17 saw expenditure leap to £1.9 billion in 2017/18, as the richest clubs responded to Leicester's extraordinary title win. Gross transfer spending soared again in the following year to £2.7 billion, with the January window alone seeing record spending of £430 million, almost double the previous January record of £225 million set in 2011. With Manchester City well clear at the top of the table, the teams battling for Champions' League slots splashed out on Pierre-Emerick Aubameyang, Ross Barkley, Olivier Giroud, Virgil Van Dijk and Lucas Moura. And this total does not include the swap deal between Arsenal and Manchester United involving Alexis Sanchez and Henrikh Mkhitaryan.[48]

Spending on this scale to acquire talent inevitably impacts the wage bill – if you tell a player he is worth £50 million to you, he is likely to have high expectations on pay (and his agent certainly will!). Between the 2001/2 and 2003/4 seasons, the total Premier League wage bill increased by roughly £150 million, and in the next three years to 2006/7, the increase was just under £160 million. The next two three-year TV deals were hotly contested and hence much larger; this translated directly into wage rises of just over £360 million in the first three-year period, and almost £450 million in the second period to 2012/13.[49]

The transfer market is not just about buying players. Selling them is an important line of business. With such an intense battle for talent, the ability to spot future stars and develop them offers clubs the opportunity to generate additional income. Player trading is a high-risk activity: players can get injured; form can dip or even disappear; and the players have market power that can disrupt careful planning. While mindful of the risks, clubs outside the Big Six engage in the market as it offers the opportunity to bolster their finances.

Since the 2014/15 season, with the richest clubs intensifying their search for talent, the transfer market has grown significantly, allowing the fourteen clubs outside the Premier League's Big Six to increase their profits from player trading by a large amount. Trading profit of around £100 million a season in the four campaigns ending in 2015 grew to £165 million in 2015/16, before more than doubling to £347 million in 2016/17 and £349 million the year after. Even after a decline to £241 million, 2018/19 was the third most valuable trading season ever for clubs outside of the Big Six.[50]

Player trading helps compensate for the ever-increasing expenditure on wages and transfer fees, but only goes so far. The sheer scale and speed of the financial transformation of the Premier League, and its huge growth relative to its peer leagues, mean it is very easy to find headline statistics to surprise people. And yet what to me is the most amazing finding of all gets very little attention – mainly, I suspect, because it is so hard to believe. Despite having the highest revenue of any football competition in the world, the Premier League, the competition that was established to improve the commercial performance of English football, was *unprofitable* in aggregate between 1992/93 and 2018/19. After generating an overall pre-tax profit in 1998/99, in every one of the next fourteen seasons the Premier League was *loss-making* in total.[51]

It is a puzzle we can solve. The basis for the competition's success in generating revenue goes a long way to explaining its failure to turn a profit: very light-touch financial governance. The removal or relaxation of nearly all the constraints on owners, clubs and players in the decade or so leading up to the launch of the Premier League created a competition largely unregulated in commercial terms. On one hand, this allowed clubs, supported by the League itself, to maximise their market opportunities to grow their revenues. On the other, it meant there were no constraints on their spending. Once the Bosman ruling had opened the European labour market, the arrival of owners, starting with Roman Abramovich, willing to spend whatever it took to achieve success and facing few constraints, caused spending to surge.

Compared to the past, we tend to view football today as a business. In terms of generating revenues this is an accurate characterisation: clubs are very effective at maximising their income even if this increases the burden on their most loyal followers. However, on the expenditure side, the situation is less clear-cut with a significant number of owners willing to spend in excess of their club's income in pursuit of on the pitch success. Not only does this behaviour risk destabilising the game's finances, it also risks unbalancing the game on the pitch.

Worries over exactly these types of behaviours explain the approach adopted by the FA in the late nineteenth century. The underlying assumption is that owners cannot be trusted to act in the interests of the sport – they must be restrained from damaging the sport either by milking their assets or speculating recklessly. Unlike the tightly managed business model in North American sports, just one single commitment – to share domestic TV revenues equally – was initially adopted by the Premier league. On its own it has had a limited impact on either financial performance or competitive balance.

This difference in approach is very surprising. The closed North American leagues, have neither promotion nor relegation, while the English game is open. Not only does every division in the English pyramid below the Premier League have promotion and relegation, but the top division also offers the opportunity to earn a place in the highly lucrative European competition. It is fair to say English football is hyper-competitive: as well as being engaged in a domestic battle, the top clubs are competing against European giants with significant financial resources. The investment by the state of Qatar in Paris Saint-Germain, the corporate backing of clubs like Juventus and the vast resources of Real Madrid and Barcelona, able to draw on direct or indirect state support[52], all serve to increase the pressure to spend in pursuit of success. Comparing the structure of the English game with that typically found in North American sports, economists would expect to find a higher degree of regulation of behaviour in the more complex environment in England.

Recognising the risks to financial stability at the European level, UEFA introduced its own Financial Fair Play (FFP) regulations to govern the spending of clubs in Europe-wide competitions. Although Manchester City became embroiled in a lengthy case with UEFA, it is difficult to find evidence that the European regime has had any significant impact on limiting spending across the Premier League.[53] The lesson is clear: to change the behaviour of owners significantly requires a regulatory approach on the lines of those adopted in the USA than the 'light touch' model historically deployed in the Premier League.

We can see how the trends identified above have played out in the Premier League, especially at the top end. Manchester United's early domination of the Premier League turned into a battle with Arsenal around the turn of the century, and then into a three-way battle after Roman Abramovich's purchase of Chelsea. This relatively stable oligopoly allowed the three clubs to budget for top-level European football every season and the associated additional income. Alongside the changes in ownership at Manchester City and Liverpool, the renewed ambition of Tottenham Hotspur under Daniel Levy's leadership further heightened the competitive intensity at the peak of the English football pyramid: six teams were battling it out for just four places in the Champions' League. Even more significantly for financial performance, two of them – Manchester City and Chelsea – appeared willing to spend whatever it took to succeed.

The consequences were immediately apparent. An arms race in spending broke out among the elite. Despite significant increases in the value of the TV deals for 2007–10 and 2010–13, as wages and transfer spending accelerated the Premier League collectively registered a pre-tax loss of over £1.3 billion in the four seasons from 2009/10 to 2012/13.[54] For the Big 6, securing a position in the Champions' League went from aspiration to necessity. The richest clubs required the international exposure to increase their TV income, fill their ground more often and boost their brand profile to fund the spending on wages and transfers required to secure the European slot in the first place. It was like being a hamster on a wheel. Falling off was not an option, but not everyone could win.

The light-touch regulatory model of the Premier League was failing. Action was needed to allow clubs to regain some degree of control over their finances and the league introduced a series of measures, the most significant of which was short-run cost control (SRCC). In the first phase, from 2013/14 to 2015/16, each club could only increase wages by £4 million a season over a base value plus any incremental commercial income, excluding television rights. In the second phase, 2016/17 to 2018/19, the allowable annual wage increase was £7 million.[55]

By stopping the immediate and direct flow of higher TV income through to wages, the consequences on financial performance were immediate and dramatic. In 2013/14 total Premier League operating profits increased by 650 per cent to £618 million and remained over half a billion pounds throughout the six years to 2018/19, peaking at just over £1 billion in 2016/17. Even with higher transfer spending, the clubs managed to earn a collective pre-tax profit after all outgoings in four of the six seasons – a major improvement on fourteen seasons of straight losses before SRCC was adopted.[56]

Despite these constraints, the growing commercial success of the Big Six meant wages continued to rise, but at a slower pace than previously. Nevertheless, by the 2018/19 season the gap to Italy had stretched further, and Premier League wages at £3.6 billion in total were £1.6 billion higher than in any other country. The average Premier League wage was double that of the average across the other four main European leagues.[57]

Just consider that for a moment: the average English Premier League player earns *twice as much* as his peers in Europe. Is the English competition twice as good? It is a question we will return to. What it does tell us is that the clear winners from football's transformation have been players, to be precise the elite players (and managers to an extent), particularly, given the relative wage levels, those who spent at least some of their career in the Premier League. How players react to future proposals for change will have a major influence on the future shape of the game.

SRCC was a fascinating experiment. As we'll see in more detail in the next chapter, financial regulation had, as the academic research predicted and the FA foresaw 150 years ago, a significant impact on both behaviour and competitive outcomes in the Premier League: the changed financial situation translated into results on the pitch. The correlation between wages and league position strengthened. In the six seasons that SRCC was in place, the Big Six took the top six places in the competition in every season except 2015/16, when Leicester disrupted the established order and 2013/14 when Manchester United's horror show saw them slump to seventh place.

If we were in any doubt about how powerful regulation can be, the experiment with SRCC provides confirmation. An approach that most supporters had probably not heard of, and that did not receive widespread media coverage, had a significant impact on both the nature of competition in the Premier League, the make-up of playing staffs and the profitability of the competition. It shows that we do have choices about how we organise English football.

However, while SRCC demonstrated that we can use regulation to impact competitive performance, it also showed us that we need to be very clear in defining the outcomes we want, as the balance between on- and off-the-pitch success is a delicate one. While the SRCC regime was successful in influencing spending of clubs outside of the Big 6, by failing to reign in the richest clubs, it both increased the competitiveness of the elite relative to the rest while not completely alleviating the financial pressures on the fourteen – leading to losses in the final year of each three-year cycle of the SRCC regulations. The lesson is regulation is a potentially useful tool, but we must be very clear on what we are trying to use it to achieve.

Premier League clubs chose not to renew the SRCC regime to cover the TV deal starting in the 2019/20 season, arguing that the principles of cost management were embedded in the competition, and hence formal regulation was not required. It is a bold assertion. The history of the Premier League is one of ever-increasing spending – even with SRCC in place, expenditure continued to rise. Do clubs really believe their peers will not take that extra risk in pursuit of success?

With wage constraints now removed, how will things evolve? At the end of the 2018/19 season, the dominance of the richest six teams appeared more entrenched than ever, with the gap in points between sixth and seventh place the highest it had ever been. Unable to generate additional revenues of the scale required to allow them to break away from the pack, the clubs outside the elite became ever more tightly bunched during the SRCC era. It was starting to look like two leagues in one. Or maybe three leagues would be more accurate – Manchester City and Liverpool appeared to be playing a different game altogether.

2019/20 was not a normal season – we may never see the like of it again, with a lockdown causing an unprecedented break in the schedule. Nevertheless, without SRCC to constrain spending, there were signs of change in the competitive balance in the Premier League. The dominance of Manchester City and Liverpool continued, albeit with roles reversed: Liverpool finished way out in front, 18 points ahead of City, who were 15 points ahead of third-placed Manchester United, and only Arsenal of the traditional Big Six finished outside of the top six. But the competitive dynamic was different. The points gap between sixth and seventh places was the lowest for over a decade, and the gap between third and seventh the smallest in the competition's history.

The shift continued to gather momentum in 2020/21. Although Manchester City finished way out in front, albeit after an early season wobble, the rest of the top 6 places were hotly contested with Leicester City again disrupting the so-called 'Big Six', West Ham United asserting themselves and sleeping giants Everton, Aston Villa and Leeds United confirming their potential. By contrast, for the second season in a row, Arsenal struggled to stay with the leading pack. Exactly how much these results reflect either the unique nature of the 2020/21 season or are the first signs of an emerging trend remains to be seen. It is prudent to wait for more evidence. 2020/21 was atypical: In addition to the rapid decline in Liverpool's results, elite clubs across Europe struggled – Bayern Munich were the only champions in the five major leagues to retain their title, suggesting injuries, fatigue and less time to prepare may have impacted performances in spectator free stadia.

Seeking to gatecrash the exclusive Big 6 group and challenge for the lucrative European places is a high stakes game – Everton recorded a loss of £140 million in 2019/20. While the impact of the pandemic was identified as accounting for £67 million of the deficit, the club's total loss over 3 seasons was £265 million, accounting for the lion's share of the £350 million in loans provided by relatively new owner Fahrad Moshiri.[58] Aston Villa were not far behind, posting a loss of £99 million in their first season back in the top flight as well as spending £156 million to acquire new players.

Increasing domestic pressure is only part of the story: The Big Six are under threat from all sides. The acquisition of Paris Saint-Germain by Qatar Sports Investments in 2011 created another club largely unconstrained in their spending[59]. Across the continent, the other European leagues had all unveiled plans to close the financial gap with the Premier League before Covid-19 hit. La Liga's chairman has made clear that its strategy is to match the Premier League, and pre-pandemic proposals for a thirty-ninth game in the USA and the staging of the Spanish Super Cup in Saudi Arabia in 2020 showed this was not just talk.[60] During the pandemic, Italy's Serie A found itself the subject of a bid from a US private equity house and both the German and Spanish leagues considered selling off stakes in their TV operations – investors clearly believe there is scope to boost the competition's commercial performance, possibly securing access at a very attractive price due to the financial stress caused by the pandemic.[61] How these strategies evolve post-pandemic remains to be seen, but the Premier League is undoubtedly facing more competition for revenues, possibly in a world where, as we will assess later, football's income is static or even falling as the world economy adjusts to the effects of Covid-19.

Since the arrival of Roman Abramovich, the profile of owners in the Premier League has changed. Most significantly, the Big Six are controlled by international groups, with Chelsea and Manchester City having owners who have prioritised success, while the other four operate with more balance between financial and competitive objectives. Yet, as we have seen, even for the more financially motivated owners, success on the pitch is necessary to underpin their off-the-pitch performance. Missing out on the top four is a huge issue. Despite what Ed Woodward claimed, on the pitch success is vital: by the 2018/19 season, Manchester United had spent over £39 million on compensation for managers fired since Sir Alex Ferguson retired.[62] The stakes are very high.

Recognising the changing landscape, the Big Six have decided to reshape the financial model in their favour. Their first move was to seek to maximise their share of the available revenues. Towards the end of Richard Scudamore's time in charge of the Premier League a dispute broke out over the distribution of foreign TV rights and,[63] with ominous echoes of past disputes, Tottenham Chairman Daniel Levy claimed, 'We only want what's fair. . .'[64] At least it was less threatening than when, in the early 1980s, Martin Edwards of Manchester United made no attempt to hide his views: 'The smaller clubs are bleeding the game dry. For the sake of the game, they should be put to sleep.'[65]

Finally, in 2018, after a fraught process, the dispute was resolved: the clubs voted to adjust the distribution of foreign TV revenues. From the 2019/20 season, any increase in foreign TV revenues over the level in the 2016 to 2019 deal will be allocated by position in the league table. The team in first place will get twenty times the amount of the team in twentieth position. As a result, the target ratio for the distribution of TV ratios between the highest and lowest earners will be allowed to increase to 1:1.8 up from the 1:1.6 ratio established in 1992/93. This will most likely increase the share of revenues flowing to the richest teams, further challenging the equitable sharing model.

Announcing the deal on 7 June 2018, the then Executive Chairman, Richard Scudamore, sought to play down the impact. 'When the Premier League was formed in 1992', he said,

> nobody could have envisaged the scale of international growth in the competition which exists now. Back then the clubs put in place a revenue-sharing system that was right for the time and has served the League well, enabling them to invest and improve in all areas. This new agreement will continue that trend with a subtle change that further incentivises on-pitch achievement and maintains the Premier League's position as the most equitable in Europe in terms of sharing central revenues.[66]

Despite his words, the first ever change to the Founder Members' Agreement in the twenty-six years of the competition is a major shift. While a crisis was ultimately averted, the difference in objectives and ambitions between the Big Six and the rest of the division put the balance between rewarding success and protecting the collective interest under real pressure.

Not long after the dust had settled, rumours began circulating of proposals to create a European Super League. A number of proposals began to emerge from Europe's richest clubs and from outside investors, possibly even imagining a world league. UEFA was forced to enter the fray with proposals to revamp its European competitions in the next cycle from 2024, offering a model with much less uncertainty for the top teams over their participation in the elite (richest) tournament.[67]

The financial shock by Covid-19 increased the pressure. With no spectators allowed in grounds, matchday revenues fell and both commercial and TV income streams came under pressure. With seasons being extended beyond the typical financial reporting years used by clubs, the data became hard to interpret and compare as it was more influenced by accounting policies than normal. As a result, the exact impact of the pandemic won't be clear until 2022 at the earliest. Nevertheless, based on published accounts and commentary to date, I estimate Premier League clubs will lose 5 per cent or more of their revenue in 2019/20 and possibly upwards of 15 per cent in 2020/21. The other English divisions are likely to be hit harder – a fall in revenues of 30 to 40 per cent seems a reasonable view over the period. It is similarly tough across Europe – the then Chair of the European Clubs Association, Andrea Agnelli, forecast the loss across UEFA's footprint could be over €8 billion.[68]

In addition to having to deal with a fall in its own revenues, the Premier League faced calls from the FA, the EFL and the government to bail out the rest of the English game. In Autumn 2020, with discussions seemingly deadlocked, Liverpool and Manchester United launched Project Big Picture. Although it purported to be a solution to the issues caused by Covid-19, it appears to have been in preparation for some time, and was more the next stage in the strategic response of the richest clubs to the changing economics of the game.[69]

The economic rationale is straightforward. With the scope for growth in domestic TV, commercial and match day revenues appearing limited for the largest clubs, maximising their income from Europe and beyond is a priority. The pressure is especially intense on the clubs owned by investors who aim to make a profit from football. Operating alongside clubs such as Chelsea and Manchester City in England and battling with state-owned teams such as Paris Saint-Germain and indirectly state supported ones such as Real Madrid and Barcelona traditionally willing to spend big, their business model requires: guaranteed participation in European competition; more control over foreign TV rights; and the freedom to play matches all over the world. However, more European and international matches will put a greater strain on playing resources, hence a need to reduce the volume of matches and the competitive pressure at home – just as Ken Bates predicted three decades ago.

Alive to these challenges, Project Big Picture offered a greater sharing of revenue across the wider English football pyramid in return for agreement on a model that would have squeezed the Premier League clubs outside the Big Six . Weakening the rest of the Premier League, through a shift in revenue sharing rather than cost controls, would reduce the competitive pressure on the Big Six, while the reduction from twenty to eighteen clubs would ease the physical stress on players. Taken together, these changes would make it easier for the richer clubs both to guarantee themselves European competition season after season and increase their chances of being successful abroad and at home.

Although Project Big Picture was quickly rejected by the Premier League's clubs, the proposals confirmed that pressure for change was building. Only a week or so after the vote, rumours of a European Super League resurfaced.[70] Six months later, the rumours became reality as twelve of Europe's largest clubs announced their plans for a twenty-team competition. Just as with Project Big Picture, limiting competition and taking control away from governing bodies were the central features of the plan.

Although both initiatives collapsed, change is on the way. Our challenge is to identify what is best for the game in the widest sense. How should the interests of different parties be balanced?

Undeniably, the game's income is unevenly distributed. Yes, there are ways to redistribute income, but some clubs will be larger and more successful at generating revenue than the rest, and, in addition, their owners may provide further resources. An uneven distribution matters because talent drives success on the pitch. Therefore, the more revenue you have, or more accurately, because of the behaviour of success chasing owners, the more you spend, the higher your chances of success. With elite players having significant market power and some owners unwilling to face them down, spending consistently runs out of control.

The game will need as much revenue as possible as it adjusts to life after the pandemic, so any changes must be designed to avoid damaging the game's appeal. However, as has been the case ever since the advent of professionalism, the challenge is to find the balance between money and the game, especially now that the game has become much more complex to manage. Owners and players have much greater power and resources; the sources of income have multiplied, originating from a range of segments all with potentially different preferences for how the game is organised; and the competitive landscape has widened to Europe and potentially beyond. Change one area and it's possible the balance will be disturbed in another.

We now know for sure the football community does not want to pursue money at all costs – the reaction to the European Super League was unequivocal, competition is the heart of the game. Our challenge is to find the right balance.

Armed with our understanding of how the money flows in and around the English game, let's now explore the other side of the relationship at the heart of football's economics: how finance shapes outcomes on the pitch.

4 THE BEST LEAGUE IN THE WORLD?

The bet365 Stadium stands on a hill of reclaimed industrial land in the centre of a soulless business park on the edge of Stoke-on-Trent. Nestling below the arena, the Trent and Mersey Canal, championed by Josiah Wedgwood[1] to allow him to avoid transporting his fine pottery on cobbled roads, offers a reminder of the city's proud industrial heritage. On cold, misty days, supporters approaching the ground on foot along the towpath are greeted by pungent, white smoke rising out of the imposing waste incinerator. Once you have passed through the turnstiles, there is little to please the eye; a functional stadium that, until a new corner was built in the summer of 2017, had three sides open to the elements. Even on the sunniest of days, a wind whistles through the ground, and if the rain comes, no spectator can be sure of remaining dry. A snowstorm during an evening League Cup tie between the home team and Manchester United in December 2013 was so intense that the referee took the teams off the pitch until the worst had passed.

Known as the Britannia Stadium until club owners bet365 became sponsors in 2016, the ground achieved notoriety during Stoke City's early years in the Premiership, as the stark environment combined with the uncompromising attitude of Tony Pulis's team and the noisiest crowd in the division to create an environment almost unmatched for its lack of hospitality. During his time as Arsenal's manager, Arsène Wenger never worked out the challenge and, after referring to Stoke as a 'rugby team', found himself being serenaded with renditions of 'Swing Low, Sweet Chariot', the England rugby anthem. Whenever a new high-profile signing by a top Premier League club was rumoured, it became customary to ask, 'But can he do it on a wet Tuesday night in Stoke?'

On Wednesday, 31 January 2018 a freezing mist shrouded the bet365. The icy, plastic seats sent a chill up the spine, and even two pairs of socks were not enough to avoid your feet freezing on the concrete floors. Nevertheless, 27,458 supporters endured the inhospitable evening to watch Stoke and Watford play out a dull 0–0 draw. Xherdan Shaqiri missed the home team's only real opportunity, and the best chance of the game fell to the visitors' Abdoulaye Doucouré midway through the second half, Stoke's captain Ryan Shawcross denying him with some last-ditch heroics. These were odd flashes of excitement in an evening of tediousness, aptly summarised by Goal.com as a game that 'looked destined for eternal goallessness'.[2]

Tedious as the game was, it was a record breaker – the ball was only in play for 42 of the 96 minutes and 41 seconds between the first and final whistles: the lowest ever in the history of the Premier League.[3] Conscious that avoiding defeat would be a significant boost in avoiding relegation, Watford took every opportunity to slow down the game – even the kick-off was delayed as Watford's pre-match huddle overran. Goal kicks and throw-ins took an age and, although no player had to be substituted due to injury, every Watford outfield player received treatment at some point in the game. While this was an extreme example, time-wasting is not unusual in the Premier League and, frustrated as Stoke fans were that evening, they would grudgingly have to admit that their team were no strangers to a bit of time-wasting. Earlier in the season, Stoke's away game to Watford ended in a fracas that saw the Watford captain Troy Deeney sent off for violent conduct after he reacted badly to Stoke's attempts to preserve their 1–0 lead by running down the clock.

Tune in to Sky Sports on a typical weekend and the chances are that an excited pundit will react to a moment of high skill by asserting that the Premier League is 'the best league in the world'[4] It is a relatively new occurrence. When the Premier League launched in 1992, Italy's Serie A was unquestionably the elite competition in Europe.

And with good reason: footballing legends Roberto Baggio, Marco Van Basten, Gianfranco Zola and Gabriel Batistuta all featured in the chart of leading goal scorers that year, and in the decade from 1988 Italian teams featured in nine of the ten Champions' League finals. In a reminder of how things can change, as revenues grew rapidly in English football, Serie A was gripped by *'Calciopoli'* (Footballgate), a match-fixing scandal hitting four of its leading teams. Italian football slipped from grace, and the Premier League claimed commercial leadership.[5]

We have seen England's highest division outperforms every other soccer competition on the planet in terms of revenue generation and even though the German Bundesliga attracts more spectators into its stadia on an average matchday, by virtue of its huge broadcast reach the Premier League can fairly claim to be the most watched football league in the world. But is it the 'best league in the world'? Given even a spin doctor with the skills of Alastair Campbell would have struggled to convince the 27,458 frozen people leaving the bet365 that January evening that they had been watching the best world football has to offer, what does drive the phenomenal success of the Premier League?

An obvious place to start is the quality on show. Since the Bosman judgement Premier League clubs have been extremely successful in capturing talent in the global market. The FIFA World Cup in Russia in 2018 highlighted the depth and breadth of talent in the English game. There were 108 players on show from the Premier League, significantly more than Spain's 78 and Germany's 62, and higher than the total number of players from Serie A and France's Ligue 1 combined.[6] However, only five Premier League players featured in the final, compared to seven from Germany and Italy, nine from France and eleven from La Liga.[7] Is the absolute level of quality in the Premier league lower than the quantity of international players might suggest?

That quality is not easy to measure in such a subjective team sport like football has never deterred fans and pundits. In 1965 the Sportswriter Gabriel Hanot launched the Ballon d'Or, for which football journalists vote to choose the best male player over the previous year. Originally an award for players from Europe, it was expanded in 1995 to include all players from any origin that had been active at European clubs, and then again in 2007 to become a global award.

During the Premier League era players from La Liga have dominated the award, taking first place on sixteen occasions out of twenty-seven and securing half the second and third place slots. This largely reflects the extraordinary feats of Lionel Messi and Cristiano Ronaldo, with five first places and six minor awards each. With seven winners compared to two from England and one each for France and Germany, Serie A is comfortably in second place.

Before the Premier League launched in 1992 four players from the English First Division won the Ballon d'Or: Stanley Matthews, Bobby Charlton, Denis Law and George Best. (Kevin Keegan won twice during his time at Hamburg in Germany). Since 1992, Michael Owen in 2001 and Cristiano Ronaldo in 2008 are the only players to win when playing in English football.[8]

Alongside Cristiano Ronaldo and Lionel Messi, Real Madrid's Luca Modric is the other recent winner from La Liga. The Croat underlined his excellence in the way he seized control of England's World Cup semi-final in 2018. As all of the trio have spent the peak years of their careers in La Liga, it is difficult to claim that the Premier League is where the absolute elite of the game can be found.

Comparing the performance of their clubs in international competitions is another way of assessing the relative quality of domestic leagues. Although European club football competitions started in the 1950s, English clubs were slow to enter – Chelsea were stopped from participating in the inaugural European Cup by Alan Hardaker, the Football League secretary, who believed it would detract from domestic competition. This allowed Manchester United to have the honour of being the first English team to play in the European Cup. After a London XI lost 8–2 in the first final of the Inter City Fairs Cup (a tournament created to help promote trade fairs that became the UEFA Cup), Tottenham Hotspur were the first English team to taste success in Europe, winning the Cup Winners' Cup in 1962/3.[9]

Following the tragedy of the Munich air crash in 1958, Manchester United's pursuit of the European Cup under crash survivor Matt

Busby's leadership captured the national imagination. The club made it back into Europe's top tournament in 1965/6. After George Best made headlines with a stellar individual performance in a 5–1 away win against Benfica of Portugal, earning himself the nickname 'El Beetle', the campaign came to a disappointing end against Partizan Belgrade in the semi-finals.

Two years later, 100,000 people crammed into Wembley Stadium on a balmy evening for a European Cup Final against Benfica. This was almost certainly the last chance for the Munich survivors Bobby Charlton and Bill Foulkes to help deliver Busby's dream. United raced into the lead, but were pegged back by an equaliser from Graca in the seventy-ninth minute and then required a fantastic save from keeper Alex Stepney to deny Eusebio and take the game into extra time. With 250 million viewers on TV, the tension was unbearable until a piece of magic by George Best secured the first of three United goals in seven minutes, the last fittingly scored by Charlton.

With the victory coming a year after Celtic became the first British team to lift the trophy, expectations were for a period of dominance. It was not to be. United lost to AC Milan in the semi-final the following season and spent seven years out of European competition. Although English clubs had regular success in the lesser two competitions, the UEFA Cup and Cup Winners' Cup, it was not until Liverpool's success in 1977 that the top trophy returned to England. With Liverpool winning four trophies, Nottingham Forest succeeding twice and Aston Villa taking the trophy in 1981, English clubs won seven of the eight European titles played for between the 1976/7 and 1983/4 seasons. At the time the Premier League was launched, English clubs had won more European cups than teams from any other nation's league.

The Heysel Stadium disaster at the 1985 final was the moment UEFA's patience with England's hooligan problem ran out. A five-year ban was imposed on English clubs competing in Europe.[10] Since being allowed back into the tournament, English clubs have never come close to matching their previous dominance of the competition. Just as with the Ballon d'Or, La Liga has surged ahead since 1992 with eleven successes to 2021, equal to the sum of England's six wins and Italy's five, with Germany just behind on four. It is the same story with the Europa League, the successor initially to the UEFA Cup and, since 1998/9, to the Cup Winners' Cup as well.

The dominance of Spanish clubs during this period peaked when Barcelona delivered what the BBC described as a 'masterclass' with their 3–1 victory against Manchester United in the 2011 Champions' League Final at Wembley.[11] Lionel Messi won the Man of the Match award, but Xavi's dominance of midfield was of the highest order as United struggled to get a foothold in the game, rarely able to control possession long enough to put their opponents under pressure. The game was effectively done before David Villa's clinching goal in the sixty-ninth minute, and the final score didn't do justice to Barcelona's dominance: 63 per cent possession, nineteen attempts on goal and twelve on target, compared to Manchester United's four, with their goal coming from their solitary shot on target. According to Xavi, United's Wayne Rooney asked him to go easy as the game drew to a close: 'It must have been around the eighty-minute mark, Wayne Rooney said to me: "That's enough. You've won. You can stop playing the ball around now."'[12]

This victory came during a decade of Spanish dominance that seemed unprecedented, beginning with Spain's 2008 European Championship victory, when their starting XI comprised seven Barcelona and three Real Madrid Players, followed by success at the 2010 World Cup as the first European country to win the title outside Europe. Retaining the European title in 2012 saw the country's footballing prowess at its peak. In similar fashion to Barcelona's success in 2011, Spain completely outplayed Italy in the European Championship final, winning by four goals to none, becoming the only European country to win three major international titles in a row.

In the decade after the 2008 successes, Spanish clubs won seven of the ten Champions' Leagues on offer; six out of ten Europa League titles (three each for Sevilla and Atlético Madrid), provided two losing finalists in the former competition and one in the latter – altogether taking sixteen of the forty final spots on offer. Sevilla's record of six

European titles in fifteen seasons up to 2019/20 is remarkable, and way ahead of any club from a similar-sized provincial city in Europe.

UEFA analyses clubs' performance in its competitions to develop its own benchmarks. Known as the 'UEFA coefficients', these are based on points awarded for how far clubs progress each season and are used to allocate the places in the next tournament. In the five seasons up to and including 2020/21, the results are consistent with the findings so far: England and Spain are the countries with the greatest number of high-performing clubs. Although Spain was in first place at the end of 2019/20, there is nothing between the two – the lead has switched regularly during the last five years. With three English teams reaching the finals of European competitions in 2020/21, England has regained the lead in 2020/21. Nevertheless, up to and including 2020/21, Spain has a much higher share of the top performing teams, with three (Barcelona, Real Madrid and Atlético) of the top six with Manchester City, the only English club in this group.[13]

It is a consistent theme: for a long period, Spain has been the home of quality in European football, the Rolls Royce or Bentley of the game. The Premier League has adopted an upper mid-market position below Spain: more a BMW or Mercedes above the mass-market Fiat, Renault or Volkswagen marques. In other words, a *higher number* of international players and managers, rather than the absolute best, appears to be part of the reason for its broader appeal compared to other European leagues.

The quality on show at Stoke versus Watford was hard to find, but it was still an important match: both teams were battling to avoid relegation. There has always been a desire by the footballing authorities, and in other sports around the world, to ensure competitive balance in the game, driven by the belief that a degree of unpredictability is necessary to retain and grow spectator interest and hence revenue. During the 2017/18 season, the Everton and former England manager Sam Allardyce illustrated the thinking perfectly:

> We don't want somebody winning the League by twenty points – it's not good for our brand. The League loses its power, loses its product, loses its ability to get the worldwide audience excited.[14]

When commentators talk about excitement in the Premier League, they are usually referring to the edge that the unpredictability of results generates. For as long as I can remember, there has been a firmly held view that the English top division is a more open competition than the other main European leagues with shock results more likely.

Although people regularly say that football is a simple game, analysing it is often very complicated. That is certainly the case with competitive balance. It is easy to talk about, but much harder to define and measure. Much of the research on competitive balance originates from the USA – a consequence of both its sports leagues traditionally being 'closed', with no promotion and relegation, and sport there becoming commercialised earlier. In recent years, however, European football has attracted more interest, and the findings are very relevant.[15]

In 2018, two Norwegian academics, Kjetil Haugen and Knut Heen, published a comprehensive research paper, *The competitive evolution of European top football – signs of danger.*[16] They set out to measure competitiveness by analysing the uncertainty of outcome from 1993 to 2017 in the Premier League, La Liga, Bundesliga and Serie A. ('Uncertainty of outcome' is measured by comparing the profile of actual results with that for a perfectly predictable competition – one in which the top team wins all its games, the second-best team beats every club except the top team, and so on.) The more equal teams are, the more balanced a competition is, hence the more uncertain outcomes should be.

Haugen and Heen concluded that since 1993 the uncertainty of outcome (and hence competitiveness) has reduced in all four competitions. With competition for playing talent having increased in the period, we shouldn't really be surprised that top-level European football has become more predictable as it has become richer. The research revealed Germany to be the most unpredictable league. When I extended the analysis for the Premier League to 2019/20 I found the trend has continued: 2018/19 was one of the two most predictable seasons in the history of the Premier League, and both of those have been in the last five seasons. The Premier League is not the most unpredictable major league in Europe, and it has become less competitive over time. Over the last decade the growth in its predictability has accelerated.

These findings fly in the face of the widely held view that the Premier League is attractive because it is unpredictable. Are they telling us that competitive balance doesn't matter for the Premier League?

No. What the research has highlighted is that there is no real agreement on what people mean when they talk about 'competitive balance'. The researchers measured balance in terms of uncertainty of outcome across the whole competition. In North American sports such as the NFL, the balance sought is the opposite: different winners of the competition year on year. How we define what we take competitive balance to mean will have significant implications for what we conclude.

I decided to explore the evidence, first of all taking the North American perspective of focus on the winners of the competition. During the Premier League era up to 2021, Juventus have won fourteen Italian Scudettos, there have been fourteen titles for Barcelona in Spain and Bayern Munich have been Bundesliga champions nineteen times. France has tended to have a more open competition, interspersed with periods of one club dominating, with Lyon winning seven straight titles in the first decade of this century and Paris Saint-Germain coming out on top in seven of the last eight campaigns.

On the surface, England doesn't seem any different: Manchester United won eight of the first eleven Premier League competitions and thirteen of the first twenty-one. Similarly, in terms of the number of teams winning the title, only six have secured top spot in England, the same number of different champions as Germany and one less than Italy and Spain over the first twenty-eight-seasons of the Premier League era. Measured by the identity of the champion club, there seems little variation in the competitive intensity of the major European football competitions.

There is, though, one crucial difference: the number of consecutive titles won. Manchester United have twice achieved three in a row, but this is a short period of repeated success compared to the runs of nine successive wins for Juventus and Bayern Munich. The position is similar elsewhere: In addition to Paris Saint-Germain's success outlined above, Barcelona have come out on top in eight of the last thirteen campaigns in Spain.

We appear to be on to something. Digging a little deeper, beyond the top spot, we find that the Premier League is the most competitive for the top three places and second-most contested, just below Italy, when we include fourth place. Spain is the least open, reflecting the fact that Barcelona and Real Madrid finished in the top three in every season in the decade up to 2019/20 and Atlético Madrid and Valencia achieved this feat in eight and six respectively of those ten seasons. No other competition has six teams with a realistic chance of taking the top spot, or such an intense battle for the Champions' League places.

Perceptions are formed over time, and the history of the top of the Premier League is a dynamic one, driven in large part by changes in the ownership of clubs. A battle between Manchester United and Blackburn Rovers, unlikely challengers funded by the steel magnate Jack Walker's money, defined the early years of the competition. This was followed by the emergence of Arsenal as the main competitor to the Red Devils – the Gunners took the title in 1997/98, then United won four and Arsenal the remaining two of the next six competitions. It was a period of intense rivalry that often erupted on *and* off the pitch.

This second duopoly was broken when Roman Abramovich bought Chelsea in 2003 and embarked on a spending spree that led to back-to-back titles in 2004/5 and 2005/6. Chelsea went from having the fourth-highest wage bill in 2002/3 – £54 million, well behind Manchester United's £80 million – to by some distance the highest – £115 million – in 2003/4. United and Arsenal responded by increasing their spending, and then Liverpool joined in, more than doubling their wage bill from £54 million in 2002/3 to £121 million by the end of the decade.[17] All the talk was of 'the Big Four', a group pulling away from the rest and looking to monopolise the Champions' League places each season. They were extremely successful, filling the four slots from 2005/6 to 2009/10, when Spurs gatecrashed the party, pushing Liverpool into seventh place.

The changes did not slip by unnoticed. In May 2008, early in his second stint as manager of Newcastle, Kevin Keegan identified the risk of a split league emerging. 'This league is in danger of becoming one of the most boring but great leagues in the world,' he declared:

The top four next year will be the same top four as this year. What I can say to the Newcastle fans is that we will be trying to get fifth, and we will be trying to win the other league that's going on within the Premier League.[18]

Keegan had identified a phenomenon, but hadn't appreciated that it was still evolving. Although Tottenham breaking into the Champions' League places stole the headlines by disrupting the so-called Big Four, with hindsight, Manchester City finishing in the top five of the Premier League for the first time was the true harbinger of what was to come. Just as Chelsea surged after being bought by Roman Abramovich, so, following their purchase for £150 million by Sheik Mansour in 2008, would Manchester City.[19]

Since 2010, the Premier League has been unique among the major European leagues in having six teams battling at the top, and their emergence has totally changed the competition. In the first seventeen seasons of the league, the six most successful sides over the period occupied places in the top six on seventy-five occasions: two thirds of all the available slots. In the next decade this increased to over 80 per cent, before rising again up to 2018/19 with the Big Six taking 90 per cent of the top six places. Liverpool missed out on a slot four times in ten years, Chelsea in 2015/16 for the first time since 1995/96 and, in what was not David Moyes' finest hour, Manchester United for the first time ever in 2013/14. Over the period the Big Six went from moderate to almost total domination of the top of the table.[20]

As so often, the exception proves the rule or, in this case, confirms our suspicions. For Leicester City, the 2015/16 season will forever be one of the most memorable in Premier League history. In the previous season, their first back in the Premier League for a decade, they spent four and a half months at the bottom of the table, going into April with just four league wins to their name. From then on, after a 2–1 home win over West Ham, they didn't look back, winning six of their last eight matches to complete the greatest escape from relegation the Premier League has ever witnessed, collecting 19 points from the last 24 on offer.

After a scandal on a pre-season tour of Thailand led to the club sacking manager Nigel Pearson's son, relations between Pearson and the owners broke down, and in July he was sacked and replaced by Claudio Ranieri. Unsurprisingly given the chaos, and despite the great escape, the club were 5,000-to-1 with bookmakers to win the title.

Leicester's start to the campaign was solid, but a 5–2 home defeat by Arsenal in late September hinted at a challenging season ahead. The club then went on a run of eight wins and two draws before narrowly losing 1–0 away to Liverpool in December, leaving them top of the table at Christmas. During the run, Jamie Vardy set a new Premier League record of scoring in eleven consecutive games. After two scoreless draws, the team embarked on a sequence of ten wins, two draws and one defeat in their next thirteen games, all accompanied by Claudio Ranieri denying that the club had any chance of winning a trophy. Ranieri's press conferences became events in themselves – he amused the press with a range of stories such as ordering pizza for the players after they achieved their first clean sheet.

And the unbelievable happened, Leicester City were crowned Premier League champions, an achievement Richard Scudamore, the Premier League's Executive Chairman described: 'I can't think of a comparison in any sport ever, I certainly can't think of one in football, which is the biggest sport, so I think it's the greatest story in sport'.[21] Completely in tune with the mood, Italian opera singer, Andrea Bocelli, turned up to perform *Nessun Dorma,* Leicester fan and BBC pundit Gary Lineker presented a show dressed only in his underpants and the club's owner gave each of the squad a new BMW.

Ranieri's signing of N'Golo Kante from Caen for £5.6 million in early August had almost slipped by unnoticed – a low-key entrance for a low-key individual who has since become one of the outstanding per-formers in the Premier League. Kante and fellow bargain signings, winger Riyad Mahrez and striker Jamie Vardy, were to emerge as stars during the 2015/16 season, earning the top three places in the prestigious Football Writers' Player of the Year award. Ranieri was voted Manager of the Year and Leicester's journeyman captain, Wes Morgan, joined his three teammates in the Premier League Team of the Season.[22]

The Foxes had hit upon a way to counter the impact of the financial dominance of the elite: search out extremely high-quality players at bargain prices. Not only did Mahrez and Kante help Leicester City win the league, but a combined profit of over £80 million from their subsequent sales, together with the higher income from competing in the Champions' League, allowed the club to invest more in talent than their on-going revenue would have allowed. Harry Maguire came and went for a profit of £60 million to keep the model turning over.[23]

It sounds like a simple enough approach, but in practice it is extremely difficult. With top clubs across Europe all operating large academy systems and wide scouting networks, identifying a hidden gem that no other club is aware of is like searching for a needle in a haystack. Consequently, such a competitive market has seen innovative business models. I remember a few years ago, the under-15 team I was coaching was approached by an organisation that specialised in talent spotting. From an initial training session, several of the boys found themselves on a coach to Manchester, where they played against a team from Manchester City. All that was required was for the parents to sign up to a deal guaranteeing the company commission should their child be signed up.

While the triumph of an unfashionable team from the Midlands appeared to support the view that the Premier League is the most open and unpredictable major league, the response it provoked would have the opposite effect. It was the perfect illustration of how financial and footballing outcomes are inextricably linked.

Concerned about losing their perceived right to access the riches of Champions' League places, the Big Six responded to Leicester's success by going on an unprecedented spending spree. According to Transfermarkt, the value of the squads of the six largest clubs increased between

2015/16 and 2017/18 by over 16 per cent a season, double the average annual increase of less than 8 per cent over the previous three seasons.[24]

Since Leicester's triumph, the results are there for all to see: two of the three highest points totals by the champion club in the Premier League's history; the top three points totals in history for the first- and second-place teams combined; the two highest goal differences for the top two teams; and three of the four highest goal differences in total for the top six teams in the classification. In the twenty seasons prior to Leicester's championship, the average goal difference of the top two teams was 89. In 2015/16, Leicester City and second-placed Arsenal had a combined goal difference of 61. In the following three seasons, the comparable figure was 123 on average. Add in the highest ever points gap between sixth and seventh in the table in 2017/18 and 2018/19, and it is hard to avoid concluding that a major divide opened up in the Premier League.

Along with their higher spending, the Big 6 benefitted from the regulatory changes we previously identified. The battle to compete, especially among the Big 6, with owners willing to fund the ever-higher costs of wages and transfers an unregulated labour market created, had created a cycle in which any new money generated was quickly passed on either to players through higher wages, or to selling clubs via transfer fees, or to agents. To create a more stable financial environment, therefore, short-term cost control (SRCC) had been introduced in the 2013/14 season. During the three years of the TV deal wage increases were limited to £4 million per club a season plus any increase in commercial income. (This was increased to £7 million for the second three-year period starting with the 2016/17 campaign). Importantly, although the commercial income included increases in sponsorship and other activities and profits from player trading, it crucially excluded TV income – for clubs outside of the Big Six with limited scope to grow their commercial income, this was a very effective cap on wage rises.

Interviewed when SRCC was first adopted, West Ham's co-owner David Gold said that the proposals had received the backing of the majority of chairmen.

We have all voted and it was overwhelmingly supported, not by all the clubs – some are a little concerned – but the vast majority of the clubs voted in favour. It's not a salary cap, it's a restraint on over-spending. If clubs increase their revenues then they can increase their spending.[25]

Whatever David Gold said, though, the reality was that, for the first time in the history of the Premier League, the ability of smaller clubs to increase wages was constrained by regulation. Even though there was no restriction on transfer spending, the cap on the wage bill meant clubs now had limited scope to pay new signings.

The clubs had voted to increase financial regulation, adopting what was a salary cap in all but name. But since the richest clubs had already embarked on a major push to increase their commercial revenues before SRCC, the new regulations had little impact on their activities. In combination with the spending constraints on the other 14 teams in the division resulting from SRCC, the Big Six's subsequent spending spree to ensure Leicester's success was a one-off left the rest of the competition trailing in their wake.

Adopting a constraint on wage rises achieved the objective of improving the financial performance by significantly reducing the total losses of Premier League clubs and leading to profits in four of the six seasons the regime applied. However, there was a cost too. With smaller clubs having much less opportunity to increase their non-TV income, between 2012/13 and 2018/19, the six seasons SRCC was in place, the average wage bill of the Big Six clubs increased by £115 million, more than double the average increase of the other fourteen clubs.[26] As a result, SRCC had a much more significant impact on the competitive balance than both the Premier League's own and UEFA's Financial Fair Play rules increasing the dominance of the six richest clubs – it did achieve its aim of providing more financial stability but the improved competitive position of the Big Six was more by accident than design.

It was a similar story in terms of the relative gap on transfer spending. With clubs able to use their TV money to fund transfers but not wages, the annual cost of the former soared, measured by amortisation in the accounts, almost tripling for the division, growing from £472 million annually to just under £1.3 billion. Big Six clubs were spending at an annual rate of £112 million in 2018/19, compared to £44 million on average by the other fourteen.[27]

It was a brutal struggle as the teams outside the elite continued to seek to maximise their competitiveness. Crystal Palace increased their wage bill of £46 million in the 2013/14 season, their return to the top flight, to £119 million by 2018/19. With SRCC limiting unfunded wage rises, the club turned to generating profits on player trading to support the increase.

A wage bill of £119 million and revenues of £154 million it is a risky strategy: if transfers don't happen, the finances are very exposed. For the 2017/18 season Palace reported losses of £36 million, as their profits on buying and selling players amounted to only £3 million.[28] They were not alone in finding the going tough. Overall, the other fourteen clubs increased their profits on player trading almost three times as fast as the Big Six over the six seasons of SRCC. Despite this, the fourteen recorded a collective pre-tax loss of £188 million in the final year.[29]

This shows the daunting challenge for smaller clubs of remaining competitive: not only did they have to compete on a lower wage bill, but they also had to sell their better players to richer clubs to stay afloat. The salary cap had little if any effect on the Big Six, but did slow the rate of increase in salaries for the other clubs. Even so, such is the market power of elite players, the smaller clubs did everything they could to stretch their wage budgets within the rules. Alongside a widening gap in wages and transfer spending between the Big Six and the rest, lower-income clubs were forced to sell players to fund the wage increases they were pushed to make to stay in touch. Steve Parish, Chairman of Crystal Palace explained the dilemma: 'We would prefer to hold on to our best players but compliance with Financial Fair Play is a major consideration.'[30]

We now know why competition between the top six of the Premier League became more intense and less predictable at the same time as the performance of the rest of the clubs in the division became more predictable. The adoption of spending controls linked to commercial income growth caused differences in wage levels between teams outside the Big Six to narrow, while allowing the Big Six to widen the gap to the rest. In contrast, the relationship between wage levels and both position and points weakened for the rest of the division. This was because the gaps in wage spending between teams narrowed as clubs without the commercial revenue generation power of the top clubs could not freely increase their wage bills and often had to sell star players.

Promoted teams were more able to erode the wage advantage of clubs that had been in the division longer because of the constraints SRCC imposed, weakening the value of incumbency. Within only a few seasons of being promoted, Newcastle United, Watford and Burnley significantly narrowed the wage gap to the three teams that were eventually relegated in 2017/18, while the wage bills of AFC Bournemouth, Crystal Palace, Leicester City, Southampton, and West Ham United all passed those of the clubs with longer time in the division.[31]

By the end of the 2018/19 season, the Premier League was well on the way to becoming two divisions in one: an elite of six teams, and fourteen other clubs battling first and foremost to avoid relegation. This shift impacted tactics in two major ways.

For the first, cast your mind back to the explanation of why North American sports are heavily regulated: an unbalanced competition risks impacting the game's appeal on television. Sky TV's main expert analysts, ex-players Gary Neville and Jamie Carragher, both commented on how poor the spectacle had been in the 2017/18 and 2018/19 seasons, when weaker teams had shown no ambition other than to defend. In beating Newcastle United in January 2018, Manchester City had 80.5 per cent possession of the ball.[32]

Facing an increased risk of relegation teams outside the Big Six became more cautious in games against the elite, risking lowering the quality of football and diminishing the excitement for spectators. Jonathan Wilson, author of 'Inverting the Pyramid',[33] one of the best books I have read on football tactics, identified exactly this point in his review of the 2019/20 season. Between 2013 and 2016, football data company Opta identified only 3 games in which one team had over 70 per cent possession. In the 2016/17 season there were 36 such games, then 63 and 67 in the following two seasons with a peak of 67 games in 2018/19. Post SRCC, the number fell to 51 in 2019/20.[34]

The Stoke–Watford game was a perfect illustration of the second effect. With picking up points against the Big Six having become much harder, games against the other teams in the remaining fourteen all became must-not-lose games, leading teams outside the elite to play cautiously, reducing the amount of expansive play. If matches become either too predictable, because of the strength of the elite, or uninteresting, because of excessive caution, then the game's appeal to television viewers is likely to suffer, threatening the game's core source of income.

For all the focus on competitive balance, there is no consensus on the optimal level. Do fans prefer a league where the top slots are tightly contested by six teams, or is a two-team struggle more engaging? SRCC was far from a perfect solution – it did initially reduce the pressure on spending but by strengthening the relative position of the Big 6 it ultimately heightened competitive pressure across the rest of the division. Nevertheless, the SRCC era demonstrates that regulation can shape both finances and performance in English football: the state of the game at any point in time is not pre-determined, but reflects choices made.

Haugen and Heen's work, based on the predictability of *all* positions in the competition, found the Premier League to be the second least competitive. But it is a good reminder of how statistics always need to be treated with care. With six teams consistently vying for the top positions in England in recent years, compared to three in Germany and Spain, the predictability throughout the *whole* league in England is indeed higher, because there is a larger number of strong teams more regularly beating the weaker clubs, therefore more results are as predicted. However, because of a more intense competition among the six top clubs in England than elsewhere, the unpredictability of who wins the title and qualifies for European competition is also higher.

The SRCC experience showed us it is possible to influence the competitive balance and that the design of the system will influence the outcome. What then is the desired balance? It's a crucial question. Any proposals for change need to be based on an understanding of what their impact could be, on and off the pitch.

At least as far as the domestic TV market is concerned, recent research by the Centre for Sports Business at the University of Liverpool strongly suggests that the Premier League has evolved into a model that maximises its appeal to viewers. Both the quality of players on show and the competition at the top and bottom of the table were found to influence viewer numbers. But there was more. The study, published in late 2020, found that matches that impact the battle for the title and relegation are the most appealing to viewers, with the struggle for Champions' League places some way behind. 'Everyone assumes people want competitive balance,' said Ian McHale, one of the report's authors.

> In American sports the leagues attempt to keep teams equal by using the draft, revenue sharing and salary caps. It's hard to find evidence of a desire for a similar situation here. The Premier League has developed so that there is intense competition at the top and the bottom. People talk about the division being three separate leagues, but that has worked to the Premier League's advantage.[35]

The study, covering TV viewing of every minute of 790 matches between 2013 and 2019, provides a detailed perspective on what drives interest. 'At the bottom you need at least four sides fighting relegation. After that, there seems to be little interest in parity. People don't want Liverpool and United to be handicapped and become like Crystal Palace and West Ham.' A game likely to affect the destination of the title was forecast to attract 96 per cent more viewers than a match with no impact, and for a relegation battle a 54 per cent increase was expected.

After a game that determined outcomes for the season, the quality of players on offer was the next most significant driver of interest, but it was some way behind. In what may well be a shock to advocates of absolute competitive balance, uncertainty about the outcome of an individual game was not an important factor in influencing viewer interest. Fans want to watch games that matter.

What I wasn't expecting was how significant the impact of individual clubs was found to be on audience size. According to the research, if Liverpool or Manchester United replaced Bournemouth in a televised match, this was predicted to lead to a 75 per cent increase in the audience. (The researchers weren't picking on Bournemouth: the club's low ground capacity and population made them the ideal base case to compare against). This was described as a 'brand effect' and, although it quickly weakens even within the Big Six, with Manchester City and Tottenham in the third tier behind Arsenal and Chelsea, both of which still lag the top two by some margin, the gap between the elite and the rest was significant.

I am not aware of any equivalent research for the global market for TV viewers – it would be fiendishly difficult to do. However, we do know that the Premier League has been more successful than its peers in growing its international viewer base, and international commercial incomes have followed a similar trend. As the previously mentioned Kantar study of Manchester United demonstrated, global interest in the game is strong, and has grown in recent years. There have been various attempts to estimate the follower base of Europe's top clubs, typically using social media reach or replica shirt sales as the basis. On all these measures Manchester United rank in the European elite alongside Real Madrid, Barcelona, Juventus and Bayern Munich, with the rest of the Big 6 comfortably in the top 15 across Europe.[36] When we reflect on the TV viewing figures and the information hinting at global brand strength, the moves to capture a greater share of the Premier League's income and to create a European Super League are easy to understand. The most watched and followed clubs believe they create more value than the rest and hence have a right to be rewarded for this.

The University of Liverpool report's findings were striking. The results of matches matter when they have a potentially significant effect on the outcome of the season, especially the title or relegation; the predictability or otherwise of a match with no bearing on the season does not have huge viewer appeal; quality of players matters; and the brand of teams is a very important influence on viewer numbers. While I was initially shocked, mainly by the brand findings, I shouldn't have been – the results are very consistent with the growth in revenues, spectator numbers and TV viewers over the Premier League's history. When Leicester and Tottenham were battling for the title in 2016/17, viewer numbers were lower than expected for such a close race. By contrast, audiences surged when Liverpool and Manchester City battled it out in 2018/19. Now we know why: the latter was a perfect combination of brand and every point counting.[37]

It is a different story with match-going supporters. Premier League stadia are filled close to capacity every week: 97 per cent utilisation is the norm, higher than other major leagues and, together with EFL crowds, representing the greatest share of population attending matches.[38] This is not surprising: going to a game is an event in itself. Fans love the atmosphere and the opportunity to spend time with family and friends in a familiar setting. When you are inside the ground, *every* game matters. For us Stoke supporters, games against our peers were likely to influence our risk of relegation, matches versus the Big Six offered a chance of an upset, and there were other factors – games against fellow Midlands-based teams were important for local pride. Away games offer a day out with the prospect of a celebratory trip home, and even sharing despair after defeats can be a true bonding experience.

The huge difference between match day supporters and domestic and global TV viewers further helps to explain the thinking behind Project Big Picture and the European Super League. There is little potential growth from domestic supporters and viewers. Possibly higher audiences could be attracted if the competition was more intense, but this is the last thing the Big Six want. Therefore, growth has to come from maximising the brand value and that requires more games between teams with the largest brands. On paper, the logic is clear. It was spelt out in briefings on the proposed new league. According to documents seen by Sean Ingle of the *Guardian*, the thinking behind the breakaway included this view that supporters want to see: 'the best players and the world's top clubs competing with each other throughout the year.'[39]

My view of football is the nostalgic one of a season ticket holder, formed in an era when it was feasible for teams to emerge from nowhere and win the Football League title, and confirmed in the period when the game started to emerge from the depths in the late 1980s and early 1990s: the world of fanzines, 'World in Motion' and Gazza. I remember my excitement when I updated my league ladders (made out of card), an annual free gift from *Shoot* magazine, to find Carlisle United top of the pyramid after three games of the 1974/5 season.

If I am honest, I started out writing this book hoping to find a way back to that era. As I have researched and analysed the state of the game and its finances, I've come to realise the game has changed too much to recapture all of that past. A new balance is possible, but it has to be one fit for the twenty-first century.

It is hard to dispute that the Premier League appears to have arrived at a model that generates a particular level of competitive balance (both at the top and bottom of the table), attracts a reasonable top-end quality of player and supports a brand story, especially for its elite clubs, that constitutes a winning formula in generating revenue.

Without a strong appeal to domestic match goers, national and global TV viewers and business partners, the Premier League would not have achieved the growth it has. That the competition has landed on a successful model for revenue generation shouldn't surprise us. Capable people in clubs have access to their own data to allow them to develop their own simulations of what will maximise their income. Outcomes suggest they have done so.

However, the outcomes have been achieved at significant cost. Despite the world-leading revenue generation, the Premier League has been loss-making throughout most of its existence and the rest of the English football pyramid is extremely challenged financially. We should not be surprised: A hands off approach to regulation in an environment where some owners, faced by talent with significant market power, are willing to spend whatever it takes, only ends in one way.

English football will need significant amounts of money to address its challenges. Moving forward, proposals for change must reflect the existing model, and try to minimise any negative impact on income while identifying where change, especially on managing expenditure, is required. As has been the case since the game became professional, trade-offs will be required to balance the interests of the strong and the rest, both on and off the pitch.

Football's response to Covid-19 and the launch of Project Big Picture, the Top Six's moves first, to try to create for a less challenging, more predictable Premier League to guarantee their participation in an extended European competition and allow them to play more matches elsewhere in the world, and second their backing of a European Super League, have thrust the future governance of the game into the spotlight. The proposals by the Big Six are extreme, especially around the future governance of the game and the future distribution of TV income, but they also reflect the economic realities of the current game, most obviously what drives *their* revenue. It is a self-interested perspective, however, proposing as it does a reduction in the total income of the majority in the Premier League to boost that of the Top Six.

Concerns were being raised even when the breakaway Super League was only a rumour. 'I suppose it's for the big six clubs to really have a careful think,' said Julian Aquilina of Enders Analysis, a media, telecoms and entertainment research agency, 'about whether that's going to benefit them long term or damage the Premier League over all, and therefore harm them in the long term.'[40]

In *Off the Pitch*, James Corbett quoted several 'Premier League' sources arguing on similar lines:

This notion that you have a static mass of clubs at the elite of football is erroneous ... If you had a European or even Premier League 'elite' twenty years ago there's no way Manchester City or Chelsea would be anywhere near that. Cast back twenty years before that, Aston Villa and Nottingham Forest would be part of it. Why should any club have their position enshrined at the top?[41]

Aquilina also raised the risk that a European Super League may lead to money being diverted away from the Premier League rather than increasing the pot – a view Simon Green, the head of BT Sport, speaking at the *FT* Business of Football Summit 2021, endorsed:

It would be undoing the value that already exists and reinventing something that is worth less. It wouldn't be as appealing to the consumers. You wouldn't have the kind of contest that you get in the Premier League and the Champions League if you undid the strength of the leagues as they exist now.[42]

The tension in the game is there for all to see. The pandemic has intensified the financial crisis in football, destabilising the landscape and fragmenting the leadership. For the first time since its creation, the Premier League is no longer in control of the debate: the big clubs have asserted themselves. The reaction of Corbett's Premier League source reflected their concerns over a European Super League: 'How can you qualify for a league of champions having come eighth? How can you justify rewarding Arsenal's worst season in a generation with tens of millions of Champions' League money?'[43]

Having seen the power of the brands of Liverpool and Manchester United, it is easy to understand why they want to maximise the value of them. Equally, it is no surprise that the other members of the Big Six want to remain competitive, or that the other clubs in the Premier League and EFL want to protect themselves too.

When push came to shove, traditional football spoke with one voice drowning out the noise from the elite. There appears limited appetite across Europe for domestic competition subservient to a European Super League. Football's intrinsic appeal continues to rest on providing reasonably fair competition creating the possibility of more rags-to-riches stories like Leicester? Football is a game first and foremost.

We should see the current situation as an opportunity. For the first time in a generation, we have a chance to reshape the game's structure and governance. And this a time when the power of the elite clubs and the Premier League, institutions that have consistently protected their own self-interest, is the lowest it has been for four decades. Now is the time to have a conversation about the type of competition we want and the potential financial consequences of our choices?

To answer these questions, we need to define our objectives and then find the competitive and commercial balance to achieve them. There is no doubt that, especially post-Covid, maximising the amount of money coming into the game will be vitally important, but this needs to be done in a manner consistent with ensuring a balanced and sustainable competition. The SRCC regime has shown that measures to control expenditure exist and do shape outcomes on the pitch. We need to be clear what we want to achieve.

However, before we do this, we need to extend our analysis. It is easy to be sucked into focusing on the top division but if we constrain ourselves to this narrow perspective. we risk missing the wood for the trees. There is one area where England has consistently led the football world: the *pyramid* – the top-to-bottom structure of professional through to amateur football that provides the link to communities up and down the country. I believe it is England's four divisions that are truly *the best league in the world*. Providing as they do the link to communities up and down the country. It is time therefore to look beyond the Premier League to analyse how English football's economic model impacts the rest of the pyramid.

5 WE SHALL NOT BE MOVED

The futuristic arch of Wembley Stadium dominates the North-west London skyline, towering above the drab 1970s concrete offices and light industrial buildings that surround it. On match days, the complex comes to life as spectators pour into the surrounding streets, filling the bars, retail spaces and car parks. Post-match, chaos breaks out. Crowds flood out into the local streets, traffic gridlocks the entire area and the queue for public transport runs from the rear of Wembley Central Station all the way back to the high street. It is a metaphor for English football: an apparently world-class figurehead surrounded by disorganisation and lack of structure.

Befitting one of the world's most iconic sporting venues, Wembley is open all year round. The stadium's guided tours are a popular choice for domestic and foreign football fans alike. Visit on most days and the arena will be eerily quiet. Schedule your trip for the Friday before the second May bank holiday, though, and you will find yourself surrounded by camera crews, journalists and ex-players-turned-pundit. A glance at the football calendar and all would become clear. The media flock to Wembley over that weekend to film and record themselves talking about the Championship play-off – the 'most valuable game in football', as the headline writers describe it.[1] This is where the relationship between football and finance is crystallised.

For once the hype is not misplaced. It is a crucial game: the winners earn promotion to the Premier League and the opportunity to share in the vast revenue streams available to that exclusive group. Success guarantees a minimum of one year's Premiership revenue plus parachute payments: the money paid to relegated teams to help smooth the transition back to, well, less money. Aston Villa, the play-off winners in 2019, knew they would earn at least £170 million (made up of £100 million from TV rights in the first season and parachute payments for at least two more seasons after relegation) even if their stay in the top flight only lasted one campaign.[2]

Here we have it. That such a staggering amount of money rests on one game, unparalleled in the sporting world, perfectly demonstrates the casino-like finances of English football. And the money involved keeps growing. In 2002, a decade after the Premier League was launched, Gerry Boon, the then head of the football team at Deloitte, estimated that 'Promotion means going from a £7 million to a £15 to 20 million business.'[3]

Yet this was a fraction of the amount Aston Villa were counting on a decade later. In two decades, the prize for winning promotion to the Premier League has increased about tenfold. The amounts of money involved in the game continue to increase, and the gaps between the elite and the rest continue to widen.

Supporters inevitably focus on the changes on the pitch that promotion brings: the chance to see the country's top players in the flesh; the prospect of high-profile new signings for their club; and the opportunity to visit the country's largest stadia. For the owners and management of clubs, though, their emotions will be a mixture of anticipation and trepidation. The transition from the Championship to the Premier League is an enormous business challenge.

In 2017 Huddersfield Town won the play-off game, and saw their revenues rise from £15.8 million in the 2016/17 season to £125.2 million. Costs increased too: wages rose from £21.7 million to £62.6 million; and the club invested £58 million in transfer fees. Despite the high increase in outgoings, Huddersfield turned their operating loss of £21.9 million in their promotion season into an operating profit of £23.2 million.[4]

But it is a rollercoaster ride. Teams go down as well as up. 'All that glitters is not gold,'[5] Deloitte's Gerry Boon was warning even about the transition in 2002, when the stakes were much lower. After two seasons, Huddersfield were relegated. If they fail to win promotion within three campaigns, they will be back to revenues of around £25 million a season. This is a tough transition to manage. It is hard to think of a business in any industry for which the economic prospects change so dramatically, so suddenly. Overnight, revenues can increase by 700 per cent, but return to the previous level within three years. At the start of the Covid pandemic, UK hospitality sector revenues fell by 85 per cent in a month:[6] the shock of relegation is potentially as financially challenging as lockdown.

The boost in income is so transient because it comes almost exclusively from TV rights. In Huddersfield's case, TV broadcast rights accounted for £110 million (88 per cent) of the £125 million the club earned in its first Premiership season. It is a far cry from when the BBC first started *Match of the Day* in the 1960s. Then the £5,000 paid for the rights in total was shared, each of the ninety-two clubs in the Football League receiving about £50.[7] In the 2017/8 season, Huddersfield earned more from TV rights than the £91 million combined income of all twenty-four professional clubs in League 1.[8] While promotion offers short-term opportunities to boost revenues through more sponsorship or higher ticket prices, it is very difficult for an individual club to create a large, permanent increase in its income not linked to Premier League status – it would require a larger stadium or an enduring, significant increase in overseas followers, for example. With such a limited ability to mitigate a future loss of TV money, the financial model is extremely volatile.

Not only does the gap in revenues between the Premier League and the Championship create volatility, but it also incentivises risk-taking. So great are the rewards on offer that owners are tempted to throw resources at achieving promotion. When Aston Villa won promotion to the top-flight at the end of the 2018/19 season, it literally was all or nothing – the numbers are staggering. In the three seasons after they were relegated from the Premier League in 2015/16, according to football finance guru Swiss Ramble,[9] Aston Villa had three of the five highest-ever recorded wage bills in the Championship, running up operating losses of over £50 million in the two seasons before achieving promotion in 2018/19.

Delving into the accounts for the successful campaign really lays bare the risks the club were willing to take. Wages for the season were £83 million, 154 per cent of turnover of £53 million, leading to the club making a pre-tax loss of £69 million. While the deficit partly reflected promotion bonus payments of over £40 million, including a £30 million payment to previous owner Randy Lerner, the loss came despite the club receiving £14.5 million from the HS2 high-speed rail project, £36.4 million for a sale-and-leaseback deal on the stadium and over £10 million of profit on player sales. Without these one-off payments, the club would have lost around £130 million, two and a half times their revenue. This was high-stakes roulette: all in on claret and blue. If the club had not been promoted, a fire sale of players and a bonfire of contracts would have been inevitable. Aston Villa were literally betting the club. It was high stakes – Villa finished fifth in the table and had to secure promotion via the play-offs.

Football ownership is not for the faint-hearted. Villa's promotion expenditure was only the start. In the club's first season back in the Premier League, Aston Villa recorded a loss of £112 million despite their revenue more than doubling and spent £156 million on buying new players.[10]

The financial consequences of the play-off game are just one example of how the staggering success of the Premier League and its clubs in generating higher and higher revenues impacts English football more widely. The top flight dominates the domestic game financially – in an average season, not much short of 90 per cent of all the money flowing into the English professional leagues is generated by the top division. In 2018/19, parachute payments to clubs relegated from the Premier League in the previous three seasons and solidarity payments for all other clubs in the English Football League totalled £371 million, 36 per cent of the total income of clubs in the Championship, League 1 and League 2.[11]

Solidarity payments are the modern-day version of the sharing mechanisms that have existed in some form ever since the Football league was established, being similar in design to the Post House Agreement in 1985. In 2018/19 they were just over £100 million in value, with every club in the Championship receiving £4.65 million, while teams in League 1 and 2 collected £690,000 and £460,000 respectively.[12] These payments shape the finances of the whole of English football. Payments to the other divisions accounted for around two fifths of Championship revenues, 11 per cent of League 1 income and 12 per cent of the League 2 total.[13] It is no exaggeration to say that the fragile state of the finances of a large share of football clubs in England means the game is dependent on the Premier League for its continuing existence.

It is positive that the principle of sharing remains in place, however, the current model is much less generous than the pre-Premier League one in terms of the value of total Premier League revenues redistributed. The £371 million paid in 2018/19 represents 12 per cent of TV rights' revenue. If the Post House Agreement was still in force, the payments in 2017/18 would have been around £1.5 billion if total TV income had been distributed using the historic formula.

No other country has a structure with the strength and diversity of the English game. All the other major leagues have smaller numbers of teams in their top three levels, and all divide into regional competitions earlier than is the case in the English pyramid. This depth translates directly into spectator interest. In 2016/17, the Championship attracted the third-highest aggregate attendances of any league in Europe, bettered only by the Premier League and the Bundesliga. In other words, the second level of English football is watched by more people than Serie A and La Liga. And that's not all: the third tier, League 1 was the ninth most watched league in Europe that year, with a higher aggregate attendance than the top division in every country except France, Germany, Italy, Spain and the Netherlands.

Football truly is the national sport, and it is not just in England in the United Kingdom: in 2016/17 Scotland was the country in Europe with the highest share of the population going to football matches.

The spirit and history of English football that drive these attendances are embodied in the pyramid. From the beginnings of the professional game in the industrial towns of the North and Midlands, a national structure grew, with teams embedded in local communities.

If English football has a claim to have 'the best league in the world', it is this structure that supports the top: a unique and precious asset that often appears under- or even unappreciated.

The tension between the interests of individual clubs and the sharing required to support the pyramid is enduring. Until the 1980s a system of cross-subsidy based on transferring revenue from the richest, more popular teams to the rest of the competition was used to retain competitive balance and limit the impact of money on the pitch. Similar approaches were common in many industries before Thatcherite liberalisation – business users subsidised domestic telecoms customers, for example. Such approaches are much harder in unfettered competitive markets, where competitors exploit the distortions caused by cross-subsidy.

Alongside the reduction of the cross-subsidy, the creation of the Premier League further fragmented the game, introducing a one club, one vote system in the Premiership with no effective independent oversight. It is an artificial divide – as long as clubs move up and down through the divisions, it remains an integrated competition and should be managed as such.

With the prevailing revenue sharing approach, the bulk of the pyramid was already at the mercy of the elite clubs, but the challenges over agreeing Covid-19 bailouts have exposed just how unsuited to effective, enlightened, whole-game governance this model is.

Unsurprisingly given the competitive intensity in the top flight, clubs are reluctant to share more revenue than they can get away with. As the Premier League's offer to Championship clubs during the second lockdown in autumn 2020 illustrated, the clubs outside the Big Six are the most reluctant sharers – because they regard strong clubs in the division below as direct competitors. With hindsight, the rush of these clubs to condemn the Big Six for their plans to join a European Super League was hard to swallow – "do as I say not as I do" sprung to mind.

The creation of the Premiership was the final step in a process that divided the English football league system in two. Money was always important in football, but the scale of the inflows and the more unequal distribution mean that financial strength is now a much more important driver of success on the field.

The story of the last three decades is not just of a widening gap within the Premier League but also of a growing chasm between the top division and the EFL. Following the recent surge in both TV and commercial income in the top division over the last decade, by my estimation the ratio, before parachute and solidarity payments, between Premier League revenues and those of the rest of the pyramid is now more than five times.[14] The staggering rewards for making it into the top division and the increasing disparity between divisions have created an inherently unstable environment that is now putting the future of the pyramid itself at risk.

Striking the right balance between ambition and prudent stewardship is difficult in the face of supporters clamouring for their teams to do everything they can to break into the elite and ambitious owners and managers keen to test themselves at the highest levels. Wage bills show us how intense the pressure is. In the 2018/19 season, Championship clubs spent 107 per cent of their income on wages. This means clubs are borrowing money or owners providing cash to pay players' wages before all the other costs of running a club are provided for. The numbers are scarcely believable – in the 2017/18 season, Birmingham City's wage bill was 194 per cent of revenues, Wolverhampton Wanderers just a little lower at 192 per cent and Reading slightly further behind at 186 per cent in 2017/18.[15] Just as in the Premier League, we can observe the tensions between win-maximising and profit maximising owners, with the latter pressurised into spending more by the actions of their competitors.

It is difficult to imagine any other industry operating on this basis. Indeed, it adds further support to the argument that football is not a business, or at least not a conventional one. Deloitte expressed the same view in 2008, suggesting English football clubs could be characterised as 'not for profit businesses.'

The consequences are as we would expect. Championship clubs recorded pre-tax losses of £309 million in the 2018/19 season. On a turnover of £785 million, that is a loss of 40 per cent of revenue or, even more shockingly, more than 60 per cent of revenue excluding transfer payments from the Premier League. Without these transfers, the third most watched league in European football would be close to bankrupt. This in a season when Premier League clubs generated over £5 billion in revenues, spent over £3 billion on wages and managed to rack up a pre-tax loss of £165 million.[16] Out of balance doesn't get close to describing the state of English football's finances.

The financial challenges do not stop at the Championship. In 2018/19, turnover of all the clubs in League 1 together was £191 million, and the equivalent measure for League 2 was £91 million. Resources are clearly stretched all the way down the English football pyramid, with League 1 clubs spending 80 per cent of their 2018/19 turnover on wages and League 2 clubs 78 per cent.[17] This despite both divisions having salary caps in place.

Recall the distinction between profit- and win-maximising owners. From the financial performance of clubs in the EFL, it appears that owners have prioritised success over earning a return on their investment – spending more than your total income on wages is not profit-maximising in any sense. Unquestionably, there are owners in the EFL who are desperate for success and willing to risk a great deal to achieve it. However, there are many owners just battling to survive (often owning clubs at least in part out of a sense of loyalty to their community) in the face of the challenging economics they face, a challenge exacerbated because when some owners take risks the extra spending drives up the wages and transfer fees for all.

From the outside, as the 2018/19 season moved towards its conclusion, English football appeared to be financially secure. The introduction of controls had led to a period of relative financial calm in the EFL, with no club becoming insolvent in the five seasons since Aldershot FC's problems at the end of the 2012/13 season.

It seemed too good to be true and it was. Alarm bells should have started ringing when Birmingham City were forced to accept a deduction of 9 points for breaching the financial management protocols.[18] The football finance expert Kieran Maguire told offthepitch.com that in 2017/18 sixty-one of the professional clubs in English football were loss-making. Although clubs had avoided insolvency for almost a decade, forty-three had entered administration since Maidstone's demise in 1992, hardly a sign of financial health. Yes, all the clubs had survived, but more by luck than skilful management.[19]

Later in 2019, while clubs such as Middlesbrough and Bristol City were publicly expressing their unhappiness about the EFL's stewardship, a much greater problem emerged.[20] Over the course of the summer, the scale of the financial problems faced by Bolton Wanderers and Bury FC became apparent. The two-way pressures in the pyramid were fully exposed. Bolton's problems had developed over time as a result of a failure to restructure their finances sufficiently after their relegation from the Premier League, while Bury had run into difficulties moving in the opposite direction. In both cases, financial stress led to changes in ownership that ultimately made the situation worse.

Bolton were relegated from the Premier League at the end of the 2011/12 season after eleven seasons in the top-flight. Financial pressures had been mounting, and the club had become increasingly reliant on financial support from owner Eddie Davies. This continued over the next few seasons as the club's finances continued to deteriorate in the Championship. Following a failure to pay players' wages prior to Christmas 2015, HMRC filed a winding-up petition for more than £2.2 million of unpaid VAT and income taxes. If you are still unconvinced of the unsustainability of football's current economic model, consider this: at that time, Bolton Wanderers FC was estimated to have a debt to Eddie Davies of £183 million.

In 2016 the club was sold to a consortium for £1, but continued to struggle, limping through until the end of the 2018/19 season, at one point receiving a financial injection from the previous owner. With limited resources, it was no surprise the team struggled on the pitch, and the club was relegated before the end of the season. With the prospect of lower finances in League 1, things came to a head: wages went unpaid and the EFL cancelled the club's last home game of the season after the players, supported by the PFA, refused to play. The club entered administration on 13 May 2019.

Problems continued over the summer, and Bolton played their first match of the new season with only three contracted senior outfield players. This was football far removed from the riches of the Premier League. It was reported that there was no drinking water or hot showers at the training ground, and non-playing staff, having not been paid their wages, were forced to use food banks. Bolton scraped a 0–0 draw with Coventry, but then suffered heavy defeats, conceding 21 goals in their next four games, leading to the EFL to postpone the home game against Doncaster Rovers in the interests of the welfare of the younger players.[21]

At the same time, things were happening at Bury. The journey that would eventually lead to the club going out of business after 125 years in the English Football League started when it was acquired by Stewart Day in May 2013; a transaction the Football Supporters Association claim should have led to much closer scrutiny of Day's fitness to be an owner. Day subsequently embarked on a series of financial manoeuvres, including taking out a loan of around £1.5 million at 138 per cent annual interest; creating a scheme to lease car parking spaces at Gigg Lane, Bury's ground; offering investors a 9 per cent guaranteed return; and in 2017 using Gigg Lane as security for a £2.3 million loan.[22] Day used some of the finance generated to fund the club's push for promotion, signing players that the ex-Port Vale manager Michael Brown, interviewed by Radio 5 Live, described as being at a level Bury could clearly not afford.[23]

Under mounting financial pressure, Day sold the club for £1 to Steve Dale in October 2018. Dale's attempts to turn around the club were unsuccessful.[24] After he was unable to secure the necessary financial support or sell the club, Bury went out of business in August 2019. Bolton were sold and survived after a very close call but with points deducted, but the season ended with the club relegated to League 2.

English Football's financial challenges were there for all to see. So shocking was the situation that even politicians felt it necessary to address the issue. After years of steering clear of football, all three major UK parties highlighted reform to football governance in their 2019 General Election manifestos. The new government has since confirmed that it wishes to move ahead with its 'fan-led review of governance'.[25]

Faced with mounting political and financial pressure, most businesses would recognise the need to act urgently. Not football. It stuck with its preferred head-in-the-sand approach. No proposals for reform were advanced during the 2019/20 season. Only when the Covid-19 pandemic hit, and all football was suspended did the debate restart. With match day income accounting for 30 per cent or more of revenues for clubs in Leagues 1 and 2, and not much less for Championship clubs without parachute payments[26], smaller clubs were hit disproportionately hard. With support eventually provided through a combination of EFL and Premier League funding, loans and advance payments, clubs weathered the initial storm.

Wigan Athletic FC was a catastrophic exception. The club went into administration during the first Covid-19 related lockdown in England, with the obligatory deduction of 12 points resulting in relegation. Local MP, Lisa Nandy, described it as possibly 'a global scandal.' Just when you think nothing in English football would shock you, along comes a new development.

According to Adrian Goldberg, 'Wigan's finances were underwritten by Stanley Choi, a professional poker player based in Hong Kong, whose business interests also included a casino and hotel. Choi made an initial outlay of £17.5 million to buy the club, then invested a further £24 million in 18 months.' Although Choi never attended a game, his financial support kept them going. Goldberg goes on to report that the club was transferred to another business controlled by Choi in the Cayman Islands, the ownership of which then passed to Au Yeung, a Hong Kong businessman, who subsequently placed the club into administration.[27]

In 2017/18, Wigan Athletic recorded a pre-tax loss in excess of £17 million on turnover of just over £9 million. With wages alone accounting for 146 per cent of income. While we all want to believe the English game is loved around the world, surely more attention should go into understanding the motivation of prospective owners. Wigan Athletic being owned by companies based in Hong Kong or the Cayman Islands doesn't feel like the natural order of things.

With the return of fans to stadia delayed after the summer, the financial pressures in the game continued to mount. The failure of the authorities to come together to create a rescue package, despite government urging, exposed the frailties and dysfunctionality of English football's finances and leadership to the whole world. Project Big Picture may have been an attempt by a small number of the richest clubs to take control of the governance of English football, but the proposed increase in the cross-subsidy to teams in Leagues 1 and 2 in particular did at least indicate an awareness of the importance of the pyramid and the responsibility Premier League clubs have to support it. It was, of course, partly self-interest at work.

However, the offer within PBP came at a high price: the effective international takeover of top-flight English football by six clubs, five of which were majority foreign-owned at the time. While history was in many ways repeating itself from the 1980s, the proposed solutions were very different, as was the complete lack of any discussion of the future of the England team. If PBP had been approved or the European Super League had won support it is possible that the interests of maybe seven or eight European clubs would have been shaping the future of European, and possibly world, club football.[28]

Why did it come to this? How does the country with the most experience in running football competitions, and home to the richest, most popular league in the world, find itself threatened with losing control of its professional game? And why did none of the bodies involved feel the need to consult with supporters? That the pyramid is currently financially dependent on the Premier League is not in dispute, but do the richest clubs really believe they are independent of the rest of English football?

If they do, it is a brave position to take. The top flight depends on the leagues below more than it seems willing to admit. As the research undertaken at Liverpool University demonstrated, the struggle at the bottom end of the table creates a set of stories that draw viewers in.[29] Changes of clubs provides additional dynamism to the Premier League, helping keep the competition fresh. In the ten seasons up to 2018/19, a total of thirty-seven teams competed in the top division and forty-nine, more than half the professional clubs in the top four English divisions, have featured in the competition in its first twenty-eight years. Even the elite changes. In the 1980s, the 'Big Five' included Everton but not Manchester City and Chelsea, while the early 2020/21 table looks very different again, making a case for a Big Six hard to defend.

There seems little desire on the part of any stakeholder, even the Big Six clubs backing such a model in Europe, for the Premier League to move to a closed model on the lines of the NFL, with no promotion and relegation. Rightly so. As the former FA Chairman and current Chairman of Tranmere Rovers, Mark Palios, puts it, the pyramid 'allows ambition to thrive'.[30]

English followers of the game, brought up on end-of-season drama, which ultimately supports the dream that any club can rise to the top, are not likely to be enthused by such a model. (Presumably the different approach proposed for the European Super League is based on a belief that such would be the brand power of the teams in the competition that their combined appeal would more than offset the absence of relegation).

What, though, of the relationship between the top division and the rest of the game? Just how tense became clear well before Covid found its way into the language, when the Accrington Stanley chairman Andy Holt took to Twitter in May 2017, following reports that the agent Mino Raiola had received payments of £40 million for his work on Paul Pogba's transfer to Manchester United:

> The cash paid to this agent is almost double the funding for all @EFL @SkyBetLeagueTwo clubs put together. WAKE UP @ premierleague.
>
> ...

The @EFL is like a starving peasant begging for scraps off your table @premierleague. Owners might ruin clubs, you're destroying the game ... Bodies involved in football are disparate ... [governing bodies] have their own interests to look out for not the health of the game.

His comments would have struck a chord with many supporters and observers of the game – don't forget more people go through the turnstiles in the English Football League than the Premier League. So the response Holt provoked was extremely surprising. According to the *Guardian*, the Premier League responded by saying it would write to Holt to ask if he wanted the organisation 'to continue the support' it provides to his and other Football League clubs. 'The Premier League supports all clubs in the EFL with solidarity payments,' said its spokesman,

and provides significant funding for their community projects and youth development schemes – all things that Accrington Stanley benefits from.

It is only because of the interest in our competition and in Premier League clubs that we can support Accrington, the wider football pyramid, and communities and schools across the country.[31]

This was an unusually blunt response, very much out of keeping with the normally diplomatic and PR-friendly style of Premier League communications. The message was very clear: the English Football League should be grateful for the support it receives from the Premier League. The 'pyramid' was described in a way that suggests it is an entity that exists outside the Premier League, not something that the top division is a part of. Andy Holt, it seemed, had struck a nerve. Welcome as the Premier League's support for the wider game was when the European Super League was proposed, we should not forget the context – the state of the game today reflects explicit choices made by those in charge of the game over the last four decades.

Similar themes dominated at the *FT*'s Business of Football Summit in London in May 2019. Andrea Radrizzani, chairman of Leeds United and founder/chairman of Eleven Sports, identified several challenges facing Championship clubs, starting with parachute payments: 'I cannot compete with clubs coming from the Premier League with a £100 million budget who can come to our place and steal our players easily.' He went on to criticise the financial regulation in the Championship by highlighting the case of the sale of Derby County's stadium to the club's owner: 'Technically the rules seemed to allow [Derby] to do that. But we should revisit the rules and the way they are written.'

With echoes of the discussions that ultimately led to the Premier League breaking away from the Football League in 1992, Radrizzani turned to the TV deal for the Championship, noting that 'We need to sit down and have a different strategy to help the clubs generate more revenue,' while also arguing that sharing the EFL TV rights income among all seventy-two clubs, 'is maybe too many in professional football to be competitive and self-financed so they are sustainable'. His message was backed up by Samantha Gordon, CFO at Nottingham Forest, who said the Championship 'has to get more media attention and TV rights income – owners are not going to just keep coming and spending. It's not going to go on forever.'[32] The similarities with the battles in the Premier League are clear: at every level of the game the battle between profit and win maximisers and between clubs of different size continues to rage.

In such a dog eat dog environment, it is inevitable that clubs will explore every avenue to improve their financial position. Derby's sale of Pride Park was the second, following Reading's, of what turned out to be a series of such transactions. Aston Villa and Sheffield Wednesday were quick to follow, selling their ground to a company controlled by the club's beneficial owners, and agreeing a leaseback deal to allow them to continue to use the stadium. The sums involved were significant, running up to £60 million, and hence of a scale that enabled all three clubs to comply with the EFL's profitability and sustainability rules. As Radrizzani identified, transactions of this nature are not prohibited by the EFL's rules, though they are arguably not in line with the spirit of the regulations. The EFL CEO at the time subsequently admitted that an unintended loophole in the regulations was what stopped them from intervening. Following eventual EFL investigations, only Sheffield Wednesday would receive a financial penalty, but this was for 'how and when' the stadium sale was handled, not the sale itself.[33]

There are three fundamental factors driving the financial stresses across the pyramid: first, the huge differences in revenues that create cliff edges between divisions; secondly, weak and inconsistent regulation across the divisions; and finally, the power of players at the higher levels of the game in the labour market.

As the comments above illustrate, parachute payments to clubs relegated out of the Premier League attract the most criticism, as they are perceived as skewing the competitive landscape in the Championship. They do, but they are a symptom of the problems in the game's financial structure – used to try and compensate for the financial dominance of the Premier League.

With analysis showing that wage levels are a weaker predictor of success in the Championship than the Premier League, the impact of parachute payments on competitive outcome is less than often claimed. It is likely, however, despite the evidence to the contrary, that the belief that parachute payments will impact results on the pitch does push up wages and transfer fees in the EFL.

Removing these payments alone will not remove football's imbalances, because in an integrated system like English football, decisions taken at one level can have direct or indirect consequences at others. This is especially true in the market for players, where the balance of power in the relationship between owners and players continues to be as important as it was when the professional game started in 1888. Much of the criticism of the financial management of Championship clubs, for example, glosses over the fact that the level of wages they pay is influenced by decisions in the Premier League. Clubs in the second tier are forced to compete in a labour market shaped by the actions of the top clubs and owners. While their high wage bills relative to their revenues of course reflect their own objectives, an average Premier

League wage double that paid in the other major European leagues clearly has an effect on Championship wages

Interdependencies between divisions are even clearer in the transfer market. Jose Mourinho is one of several managers who have identified the problem of 'English prices': the distortion caused by the combination of the requirement for clubs to have a minimum number of England qualified players and the Premier League's vast spending power.[34]

The reforms to the football labour market, together with the internationalisation of the workforce, have added to the stress on the pyramid from top to bottom. According to Deloitte, in 2018/19, of the £1.86 billion gross amount spent by Premier League clubs on transfers, 67 per cent was spent with non-English clubs, seven times the £175 million spent with clubs in the English Football League, and only £360 million (19 per cent) remained in the English game.[35] In 1991/92, the year before the launch of the Premier League, total transfer spend was £75 million, with the top division's share £46.4 million accounting for 62 per cent. Almost none of the money left the UK game, and nearly a third flowed from the clubs in the top division to the rest of British football, with the lion's share going to English clubs.[36]

It doesn't end there. As football has commercialised, agents facilitating transfers have grown in significance. In 2018/19, £261 million, was paid to agents by Premier League clubs to facilitate deals and a further £57 million by EFL members. Let's dwell on that: *more money paid to agents than the annual turnover of Leagues 1 and 2 combined.* That is money that could be spent on players, facilities or community activities. The £261 million was 50 per cent more than the value of transfer fees paid by Premier League clubs to teams in the English Football League:[37] more money spent on agents than players.

It is not only global growth that has changed the profile of the transfer market. A gradual increase in the Premier League clubs' control over talent development in the UK has significantly reduced the opportunities for revenue generation available to smaller clubs in the transfer market. With the gradual relaxation of rules over the recruitment of young players into academies, Premier League clubs have been able to hoover up a greater share of the talent. Extra scouting resources and the glamour of the top division make it hard for smaller clubs to compete. Breaking the local ties that used to shape the market for talent has reduced the likelihood that a club outside of the upper echelons will unearth a gem who can be sold at a significant profit in future. The virtuous circle of income flowing within the game has been broken.

The additional requirement for a minimum number of 'home-grown' players in Premiership and European competition squads increased the value of English players, incentivising clubs to scour the country looking for promising players from a very young age. The number of young players in top academies has grown as clubs hedge their bets. The same clubs also cast their nets wide across the globe, as young talent identified early and brought to England can, under certain circumstances, be classified as 'homegrown' under football's nation-ality rules. It is a competitive and sometimes murky world – as the 2019/20 season dawned, the new Chelsea manager Frank Lampard, their first full-time English manager since 1996, faced a two-transfer window ban on signing new players due to breaches of youth recruit-ment regulations.[38]

The desire to sweep up all the available talent also fuels the loan market, long a feature of the football business model. David Beckham's time at Preston North End and Harry Kane's stints at Orient and Mill-wall are examples of the richest clubs sending their young players to lower-division clubs to gain first-team experience and accelerate their development. Before the introduction of transfer windows, loans were used by clubs to bolster their squads during the season, such as when injuries might create gaps in squads.

The modern loan market has developed into a business of its own. The clubs with the most resources can employ large numbers of players and then loan them to other clubs. In England, Chelsea led the way, with reports suggesting that in the 2018/19 season they had forty-one players out on loan. These loans to a range of clubs, with several joining other Premiership teams, a number going out across Europe, and others moving to English clubs in the lower divisions. Other Premier League clubs also loaned significant numbers of players, with Man-chester City offering twenty-eight, Wolverhampton Wanderers twenty-seven, Brighton & Hove Albion sixteen and Everton with four-teen the most active. In what I believe is the most extreme case, in 2018/19, Atalanta in Italy had seventy-six players on loan to other clubs, a number that goes way beyond what may be perceived as reasonable under any system.[39]

If clubs are allowed to recruit significantly more players than they are ever likely to need, they are effectively removing talent from the market and, in turn, opportunities to profit. First, transfer fees and wages are inflated as clubs compete for a restricted supply of players due to the large clubs' hoarding. Secondly, loaning players can be a lucrative business. Kurt Zouma's loan from Chelsea was rumoured to have cost Stoke City around £7 million for the season, once loan fees and wages were paid.[40]

Premier League squads are allowed a maximum of twenty-five players, plus an unlimited number of young players under 21. As the numbers above are consistent with around 200 players being on loan, I estimate an additional 30 to 40 per cent of the elite player base in England is controlled by the top clubs. On its own, such a volume of players distorts the market. Loans may also disrupt the competitive balance of the Premier League. In 2017/18, Chelsea had five players on loan, each to a separate Premier League club.[41] As loan players are not allowed to play against their parent club, Chelsea that season had ten games – two against each of the five teams – when they faced weaker opponents than their rivals in the competition.

The rules governing recruitment, development and transfers have led to clubs outside the top division having a weaker talent pipeline than historically, which reduces the interest of Premier League clubs in the English market. This, together with a very flexible global market, has reduced the flow of money through the English pyramid.

Cut off from the bulk of the money flowing into the English game, the clubs in the lower three divisions of the English Football League have agreed on their own forms of financial fair play and cost management. Since 2016/17, the Championship limits the losses that clubs can make to £5 million a season or £13 million if their owners provide equity of £8 million to bridge the gap. In Leagues 1 and 2, the financial controls were, until 2020/21, based on a limit on the percentage turnover that can be spent on wages.[42]

It is a well-intentioned but very poorly designed approach that ignores the core characteristic of the pyramid: it is an integrated system. It is relatively easy for a closed league like the NFL to introduce rules to regulate its own affairs, but an open competition requires coordination. English football has a system of governance that has two major flaws: no single body with the power to provide overall, integrated leadership that considers the whole pyramid on each issue; and self-governance by the clubs in each division that always tends to mean self-interest prevails over a collective view.

If teams are to have the opportunity to move between divisions with a chance of staying up, then adjustment mechanisms are required to smooth the process, create the right incentives and help clubs manage the risks within reasonable bounds. Parachute payments on their own are too blunt an instrument for the huge task of compensating for revenue inequalities and the huge level of spending on wages and transfers in English football compared to our European peers. We require a more sophisticated approach based around a new approach to revenue sharing and more effective regulation of the football labour market including: policy on loans, young player development and possible revisions to the quotas on non-England qualified players; a relegation impact smoothing mechanism such as a pre-agreed adjustment to player contracts on relegation together with salary caps consistent across the pyramid. We have to move away from siloed, partial solutions that often cause more problems than they solve, a 'one game' approach is required.

It is a mess. But there is a positive angle too. The debate is now out in the open, and the fantasy economics of the competition are there for all to see. As I suggested earlier, football is not a typical business, indeed in many aspects it is not a business at all. If nothing else, the discussion in the last three Chapters has confirmed that football requires a different approach to regulation than has been pursued for the last three decades. Similar ideas can be found in the proposals in areas such as governance, salary caps and TV rights distribution set out in

Project Big Picture and the European Super League. I was struck that both initiatives explicitly identified the 'football pyramid' as something they sought to support. It is not immediately obvious their proposals would have achieved what they claimed, but our challenge is to build on this and turn aspiration into reality.

The consensus for change based on greater redistribution of income and a new governance structure is building. The challenge is finding an approach that doesn't just reflect the interests of a small number of clubs at the expense of other stakeholders. Clubs across the pyramid play a central role in linking football to its communities, most directly through their most loyal stakeholders: supporters. I turn now to exploring how change in the game has impacted this group.

6 WE'LL SUPPORT YOU EVER MORE

Interviewed immediately after his team had lost to Bayern Munich in the 2020 European Champions' League final, Ander Herrera of Paris Saint-Germain gave one of the most open and honest post-match assessments I can recall. Encouraged by the player's mood and eloquence, the interviewer moved on from discussing the game to ask Herrera how he felt playing in stadia without fans. The answer was unequivocal:

> It's s***, horrible. For me, fans are the key in this sport, they're the most important thing in football. Football without fans is nothing. I hope all the people realise football is for fans. The business had to continue because it's a big business. For people suffering it's been a good escape for them to watch football.[1]

It was welcome recognition for loyal supporters who, when it comes to football's power brokers, can often feel hard done by.

The Football Supporters' Association (FSA) is a very active advocate for supporter interests, describing its mission as: 'to drive positive change in football through supporter engagement at every level of the game.'[2] It is a very democratic organisation – policy is determined by the members, and the leadership is incredibly determined to understand and articulate the membership's wishes. When the European Super League proposals broke, it was the FSA and the supporters' groups at clubs around the country who led the response. These bodies really are the voice of football supporters.

In stark contrast to Herrera's endorsement, the FSA's research is clear: supporters feel they are not properly valued. Almost 96 per cent of supporters surveyed by the Football Supporters' Federation (now merged with Supporters Direct to form the FSA) in 2017[3] felt TV had too much sway over the game, and just under 68 per cent of respondents felt clubs prioritised overseas supporters to the detriment of their local fans.

Yet feeling undervalued has not stopped people flocking to football matches. Going to watch English football live has never been more popular: spectator numbers have risen significantly during the Premier League era. In the first season, the average attendance was 21,125, ranging from 37,004 at Liverpool to 8,045 at Wimbledon. By 2018/19, the average gate was significantly higher at 38,484. Manchester United were the most watched team, their average crowd of 74,879 per game being more than double the 35,084 they attracted when winning the inaugural title in 1992/93.[4] Six other clubs – Arsenal, Tottenham, West Ham, Manchester City, Newcastle and Liverpool – attracted over 50,000 people to a game on average.

Larger stadia for a number of the richest clubs have helped boost crowds, but it's not only the top division that has grown in appeal. Average attendances in the Championship almost doubled during the period, from 10,626 to 20,193, and League 1 crowds increased by around 40 per cent to an average of 8,690 per game in 2018/19. League 2 crowds were the slowest growing, but spectator numbers rose by over 1,000 spectators per game to an average crowd of 4,526 in 2018/19, a third more than in 1995/96. Across the whole of English league football, total crowds have increased from 21.8 million to 32.8 million in the Premier League era, a growth of 50 per cent.[5]

How can we explain this apparent paradox: unhappy spectators going to more games? The headline on the BBC Sport website in August 2018 provides a clue: 'Eleven out of twenty [Premier League] clubs could have made profits in 2016–17 without fans at games.'[6] According to the BBC's research, income from the crowds attending Premier

League matches in 2016/17 made up less than 20 per cent of income on average for clubs in the top division, a huge decline from the 50 per cent when the competition started in 1992/93. Match day income has become *relatively* less important not because of falling spectator numbers but because other sources of revenue, primarily TV rights and commercial sponsorship income, have grown much faster.

As we saw in Chapter 3, supporters are just one source of income for football clubs, and as there are limits to how much more money clubs can raise in their home market, their focus continues to shift elsewhere. Supporters are feeling undervalued because other stakeholders are becoming more highly valued. A quick glance at the Campaigns section of the FSA's website suggests this is what fans believe has already happened. On the day I browsed the site, the highlighted topics included:

> *Away fans matter*
> *Kick-off times*
> *No to European Super League*
> *Stand up for choice*
> *Twenty's plenty*
> *Watching football is not a crime*

Concerns over the organisation and management of the game, rather than the cost of football, dominate the list. ('Twenty's plenty', a call for lower-priced away tickets, was the only financially based campaign.) The negative sentiment of many fans towards the game is about much more than money. Supporters, the lifeblood of the game, desperately want the authorities to show respect for the traditions of the game and the people who watch it. It doesn't seem too much to ask. Indeed, as we will see, clubs and administrators have failed to appreciate how important supporters are to the financial success of the game. Affording supporters the attention they deserve would benefit all football.

As we saw in the research on Manchester United's global reach, Kantar used fans and followers to identify different levels of engagement. As it was an international survey, neither group were regular match day attendees. It is an important point: there are a range of different segments interested in football. How committed they are on a scale from attending every game through to occasional TV viewers differentiates them.

Lord Taylor's aim of improving the match day experience was a critical moment in the history of English football – stimulating an investment in stadia that would change the economics of the game. Although his focus was very much on match day supporters, his proposals changed the relationship with the game for all groups, primarily through the boost they provided for the growth in football broadcasting. Understanding how these changes have impacted the different groups following the game in England will help us develop ideas for the future. While international football lovers are stakeholders in the English game, their fate rests in the hands of their TV broadcasters.

Fever Pitch by Nick Hornby is an emotionally raw, at times uncomfortable, account of what being a football supporter – in his case an Arsenal one – meant to him at different stages in his life. His characterisation of his involvement as an 'obsession' is hard to argue with. Many supporters will recognise his reflections on finding himself watching Saffron Walden versus Tiptree in May 1983: 'I will watch any football match, any time, any place, in any weather conditions.'[7]

Hornby's loyalty and commitment, not least in time and money, to following Arsenal laid bare the depth of the relationship between a supporter and their team. The bonds run deep: in the 2019 EFL Fans Survey, 40 per cent of respondents identified proximity to where they grew up and 39 per cent family ties as the primary reason for supporting their club.[8] And supporters love going to games: 89 per cent of those surveyed said that it is the matchday atmosphere that motivates them to attend games. The overall package football offers is like a drug, creating as it does the risk that addiction could lead to supporters being exploited.

Economists describe such relationships as 'inelastic demand'. The demand of motorists for petrol or smokers for cigarettes are the textbook examples. In such situations, suppliers have significant freedom to increase the prices of the goods and services they sell, confident in the knowledge that so strong (or essential) is the demand that most customers will pay the higher prices. Even if a few buyers are lost, the increased prices mean total revenues will rise.

In football, intense supporter demand allows clubs to put up ticket prices and regularly market new products such as replica shirts, and (through broadcasters) to sell TV subscriptions to watch games. And taking ever larger amounts of money off supporters is only part of the story. Administrators and clubs feel able to impose other burdens, such as inconvenient kick-off times, to suit TV schedules, safe in the knowledge that, although fans may complain, they will continue to follow their team. Supporters are the heart of the relationship between love for the game and money.

The FSA's research tells us that supporters think the way they are treated is unbalanced. Yes, the match day experience has improved across all English football in the Premier League era, and it is reasonable that clubs have sought to recover some of the costs of providing this from supporters, but it is clear that the majority of supporters believe they have contributed more than their fair share for the benefits they have received. Do they have a case?

Lord Justice Taylor's proposals for all-seater stadia[9] transformed match days. Anyone who had visited the old Wembley Stadium, or the pre-modernised Old Trafford or St James's Park, can't fail to be impressed by the transformation in scale and quality. At Wembley alone, the difference between a trip to the men's toilets today and back in the 1990s is like moving from a youth hostel to a luxury hotel. (In truth, 'trough' was a more accurate description of the facilities at the old stadium.) Lord Taylor's objective has been achieved: stadia are much more comfortable; catering and safety are significantly better; and there is much less hooliganism than was the case in the 1980s, inside and outside grounds.

However, these improvements have come at a cost. As identified in Chapter 2, having been provided with overly optimistic assessments of the costs of his reforms and failing to secure more funding from public sources, Lord Taylor was too optimistic about the impact recovering the costs of improving stadia would have on supporters, appearing to have believed that it would involve only a marginal increase in the price of football. Despite his reservations over the competence of both owners and the game's administrators, he certainly didn't call for any safeguards to protect spectators against potential exploitation.

So did clubs exploit the opportunity offered to them?

As Lord Taylor's proposals focused on match days, ticket prices are the logical starting point. But first, an important caveat. Economists invariably find comparing the prices charged for any good or service over time challenging. There are always issues with obtaining accurate historic data and measuring like-for-like when the offer changes over time. Statisticians nowadays have to measure inflation in an era of rapid technological change: the latest top-of-the-range smartphone will cost more than its predecessor but come with new features such as a better camera and face recognition. How much of the price rise is due to higher quality and how much simply to inflation? Similarly, it seems reasonable for fans to pay more for games taking place in better stadia with better players on show, but adjusting prices to fairly reflect this improved quality is challenging.

The most comprehensive piece of research on ticket prices I have found was undertaken by Andy Kelly, an Arsenal fan, who collected data on the club's ticket prices from 1980 to 2015. It is a rigorous and fascinating piece of work. In his 'History of Arsenal ticket prices since 1980'[10] he compares the prices for a similar seat, in terms of view, at Highbury and the Emirates. Again, this seems a fair basis.

The conclusions are clear. First, as Arsenal put seats into Highbury's Clock End and rebuilt the North Stand, prices rose 250 per cent to help fund the investment – an increase of two-and-a-half times the rate of inflation in the eleven seasons between 1980/81 and the start of the Premier League. In one year alone, between 1991/2 and 1992/3, Arsenal's season prices went up an eye-watering 38 per cent. It is hard to think of many businesses which rely on loyal customers that could move prices upwards so much, so quickly, if ever.

The second major shift in Arsenal's ticket prices occurred in the decade from 1995/96 to 2005/6. This time, the higher revenues in this period were used to help pay for major increases in the club's wage bill.

As the Premier League developed and players gained more contractual freedom, wage inflation surged. The average ticket price went from £12.50 to £38 during the period, while Arsenal's wage bill increased from just over £10 million to almost £83 million. Despite the regular rises in ticket prices from the 1980s, 1995/96 was the first ever season that Arsenal's wage bill was greater than its gate receipts, at 100.9 per cent. Since then, the gap has grown larger, and wages in 2015 were nearly twice the value of gate receipts.

The declining importance of match day revenues was illustrated perfectly in his final piece of analysis. My sense is that clubs were starting to recognise supporters had little scope to pay more and that, even if they did, the impact would be marginal compared to other sources of income.

Since the move to the Emirates, [up to 2015] ticket prices have risen 17.2 per cent [2.5 per cent of which was a VAT rise that the club had no control over], RPI has risen 26.5 per cent and the average UK wage has risen 23.8 per cent. Technically, it is cheaper to watch Arsenal at the Emirates than it was at Highbury and, as a percentage of the average UK wage, it is as cheap to watch Arsenal in 2015/16 as it was in 2004/5.

The story of Arsenal's ticket prices is one of the changing economics of the Premier League. Arsenal initially used higher revenues to help fund investment in the stadium, before moving to use ticket income to contribute to paying higher wages. More recently, following the surge in television income from 2007 and the growth in other sources of income, the club has been less reliant on ticket income and has moderated the pace of price rises.

Kelly's analysis of how ticket prices have increased relative to the UK minimum wage helpfully illustrates how inelastic the demand for football is. To watch football at Arsenal in 2014/15, a supporter on the UK average wage would have to spend three times more of their income compared to the level in 1981/82. The situation has improved slightly since, but the cheapest season ticket at the Emirates in

2018/19 was £891, representing 2.9 per cent of the average wage, still more than double the share of the average wage it cost in 1980.[11] This is a huge shift in income shares, an effect of a scale we rarely see across the economy. Faced with having to spend more of their income on football at the expense of buying other things, supporters couldn't say no.

I expanded Kelly's fascinating work by looking at average prices, rather than at individual club ticket costs, across the pyramid. What I found supports his analysis. In 1992/93 the average ticket price in the Premier League was £7 to £8. The most recently published estimates of the mean and median price of tickets in the top division are around £30, suggesting that the average has increased by around 300 per cent in the Premiership era.[12]

There are more examples of the huge rises that were introduced in the earlier years of the Premier League. In 1989/90, the Football Task-force commissioned research that found the average season ticket at Old Trafford was £96 and the equivalent for Anfield was £60. By 2010/11, the equivalent figures were £532 at Manchester United and £725 at Liverpool. If ticket prices had increased in line with inflation in the UK, they would have been £170 and £106 respectively. Everywhere we look the message is the same – prices across all divisions have increased significantly over the period.[13]

This average picture masks huge differences between clubs in the Premier League. In 2019/20 Burnley offered the cheapest season ticket at £325, and Tottenham Hotspur the most expensive at £1,995.[14] Nearly two thousand pounds a season is a huge sum to pay to watch football.

With Lord Taylor having omitted to propose any financial protection for supporters, spectator loyalty was exploited and prices soared. The pace of recent rises has been much slower than in the early years of the competition, but tickets today to watch English professional football cost significantly more both in absolute money terms and compared to real wages than when the competition started. Even allowing for the significant improvement in the quality of the football on offer and in the match day experience, supporters who attend games have more than paid their way.

Lord Taylor's real blind spot was how the pay-TV market would evolve. With clubs and the football authorities willing to do whatever was required to maximise the value of rights, supporters and fans desperate to watch games found themselves at the mercy of the TV companies. Initially Sky used its monopoly of top-flight games to build up its customer base. As a result, fans typically had to incur the upfront costs of having a dish installed and buy a set-top box as well as signing a contract for a minimum subscription period. As we have seen, neither the UK Government nor the relevant public regulators acted to curb Sky's operations in any meaningful way. The initial investigations into Sky's market power ended inconclusively, and it was left to the European Commission to make the first significant intervention, requiring that the rights be divided into packages to ensure more than one company won a share. This created a fragmented market that required supporters to subscribe to multiple platforms to watch all games. It took several years for this to be resolved through regulation and the courts. The failure of either the Premier League or clubs to feel the need to intervene in this process at any time tells us a great deal about where supporters are in the pecking order.

Unsurprisingly, as the amount paid for TV rights has soared, the pricing of subscriptions has followed suit. It is difficult to compare the situation before pay television launched with the situation today. The volume of televised football is much greater than in 1992/93. In a typical week there can be ten or more live English games on the various channels, not to mention Spanish games, German matches and more – one or two free games a week was the norm before the Premier League launched. But this much greater coverage comes with a hefty price tag. Looking at published TV subscription prices, I estimate supporters in 2019 were faced with paying out a minimum of around £450 for a season of televised football, and potentially more in the range of £600 to £700[15], due to the way packages are designed. By any measure, these are significant amounts of money for the average supporter, many of whom will also be buying season tickets.

Lord Justice Taylor appears to have been too trusting of football's leaders to do the right thing by supporters. Add in the underestimation of the costs of improving stadia – a common failing with major construction projects – and the outcome was vastly increased expenditure for supporters. While Lord Taylor could have addressed the lack of protection for support due to weaknesses in the game's governance, he could not have been expected to forecast how the economics of football would change in two key respects.

First, there was the Bosman ruling. Although players had been increasing their share of football's cake since the reforms of the 1960s, Bosman provided a turbo-boost. Secondly, the emergence of new owners willing to take huge risks in the pursuit of success further stimulated spending. Lord Justice Taylor rightly identified an opportunity to generate more revenue from football; he simply failed to appreciate how *much* revenue would have to be raised because expenditure increased way more than he could have ever envisaged.

Once set on the path to commercialisation, football went beyond anything Lord Taylor had imagined. Clubs would turn out to be willing to squeeze supporters very hard. Whole new businesses would emerge as clubs became more commercial. The replica shirt is the best example.

To begin with, the replica shirt revolution passed me by. As I spent the late 1980s and 1990s travelling internationally with work and playing football on Saturday afternoons when I could, I only went to live football in the week and during holidays. Most of the football I watched was on television.

It was at the Cricket World Cup semi-final at the Sydney Cricket Ground in 1992, the game that became famous for rain interruption rules that meant to win South Africa suddenly had to score 21 runs off one ball, when I became aware of the replica shirt. 'That's it: Coventry City away!' announced one of my friends during a break. 'That completes the set!'

When I asked him what he was talking about, he explained that he'd been keeping an eye on the replica shirts in the crowd at England games we had attended. Most of these were typically worn by the children of emigrants, a badge of pride in their history. The brown Coventry City away shirt was the last one he needed for his set of all twenty-two teams in the then First Division.

Stride, Catley and Headland's study[16] of the evolution of replica kit identifies the launch by Umbro in 1959 of the Umbroset for Boys as 'the first selling of kit targeted at individuals rather than "teams"'. I remember receiving Umbro replica kits as presents when I was growing up. These typically didn't have the club badge, so the kit didn't feel particularly authentic. It was common at the time for park and Sunday League football teams to wear lookalike kits without the official badges.

'Umbro used "dress like your heroes" marketing,' explain Stride, Catley and Headland,

> with branding provided by Manchester United's manager Matt Busby, and later by striker Denis Law. The sale of a full kit with an 'Improve Your Game' soccer skills insert, indicates that, through being actively marketed as a replica, this was still assumed to be for child footballers to play in.

They point to the game-changing move by Bert Patrick in December 1973 to bring the Admiral Sportswear brand into the replica kit market by signing a deal with Leeds United to redesign and copyright their away kit, in return for a fee of £10,000. By the 1977/78 season, the study shows, eighty-four of the ninety-two English Football League clubs displayed a manufacturer's logo on their shirts, often accompanied by badges and distinctive trim to create the sense of the kit being unique to the club.

Although adults could have afforded to buy replica kits in large numbers in the mid-to-late 1970s, the actual demand remained low. There were still cultural barriers to overcome: several respondents told the authors' survey that wearing a replica would suggest they considered themselves good enough to be a professional footballer. 'It's just wrong,' said one: 'to try and look like a player when you should know better is weird ... No!'

The paper identifies 1988 as the year the replica shirt industry began to target all adult male football supporters more systematically. (There is much less data on female supporters and replica shirts, but what evidence there is suggests only around 1 per cent of females wore a replica shirt in games up until 1991, but the number increased to 15 per cent by 1996). In a watershed moment for the replica shirts market, Umbro announced in 1993 that XL was the most popular size, confirming the shift from the children's gift market to a must-have item for all fans. This trend has continued to the extent that wearing a replica shirt to games, often a retro version, is now more the norm. Many supporters will have home and away kits, and often a third-change kit in their wardrobes.

Once the replica kit market started to take off, there was no stopping clubs. The 2000 Premier League Charter contained a proposal for clubs to only change their home kit every two seasons. It had a limited impact: The 2010/11 season was the first when every club launched a new home kit. (It wasn't just clubs: in the same season the FA introduced the England Euro 2012 shirt – the forty-seventh new one in forty-four years.)[17] There is no dispute that clubs need a change of kit for matches when there is a colour clash with their opponents – but do they need *three* kits? The evidence suggests not: in 2017/18, clubs wore their home strip twenty-eight times on average compared to eight times for their away one, the eleven teams selling a third set of colours wore them on average four times, and two clubs only wore their official change strip on one occasion.[18]

It is a big and profitable business. The numbers are staggering. According to a study commissioned by talkSPORT,[19] between 2011/12 and 2015/16, Manchester United averaged 1.75 million shirt sales globally every season: nearly double the 900,000 of second-placed Chelsea. Liverpool with 852,000 and Arsenal with 825,000 per season were the next two best performers. These are huge numbers and reflect the global appeal of the Premier League's largest clubs, but even the 80,000 sold by Everton is an impressive number: double their average attendance. The shirts are not cheap items to buy. At the start of the

2020/21 campaign, Manchester United had the most expensive shirt for the 2020/21 season at £70, Burnley the cheapest at £45.[20]

The emergence of the replica shirt is another illustration of why supporters feel disillusioned: once an opportunity presents itself, football clubs appear to exploit it to the maximum. Clubs could survive with lower replica shirt prices, shirt sponsorship is lucrative in itself. The twenty clubs in the English Premier League had shirt sponsorship deals for the 2019/20 season worth £363.6 million, according to analysis by Sporting Intelligence, an increase of almost £80 million on the previous year and equivalent to about 50 per cent of match day income – fans who buy shirts end up paying for the privilege to become walking advertisements.[21]

Research in 2019 by the financial firm e-Toro demonstrated exactly how successful football clubs have been in generating income from supporters. It estimated that just the supporters who attend matches will spend £1.3 billion following their teams in the 2019/20 season – a 31 per cent increase since 2014/15. The analysis further showed that while the rise in ticket prices had slowed – they increased by 1 per cent as the 16 per cent fall in away ticket costs helped offset any increase in the charges paid by home supporters – over the same period the cost of TV subscriptions increased by 41 per cent. The sum paid for the other components also increased, but by less than the 31 per cent average, with merchandising increasing by 21 per cent, food and beverage by 11 per cent.[22]

Looking solely at match day revenues as the BBC did gives a partial view that fails to capture the real contribution of supporters to the financial performance of English football. In the 2019/20 season, supporters who attend games were spending a comparable amount again on TV subscriptions as they were on match days. Taking the example of Arsenal fans again, the average supporter was spending a four times greater share of his or her income on attending and watching football in 2020 than in the early 1980s.

Applying this analysis to the £5.2 billion total turnover of Premier League clubs in 2018/19 allows us to estimate the share contributed by domestic supporters. Despite the growth in foreign TV income and commercial revenues, I calculate that significantly more than half the revenue generated by the Premier League comes from domestic supporters, fans and followers, even before considering their indirect value as, for example, an audience for advertisers and sponsors. Compared to 1992/3, the amount spent has grown by more than ten times the rate of consumer price inflation and five times the growth in average wages.[23] We can adjust for population growth and for the higher quality of the football and match day experience as much as we like, but whatever we do, the conclusion is the same: supporters are vital to the financial viability of English football, and pay much more today than in the past.

The ability of domestic fans to spend on football, especially of Premier League teams, is close to 'maxed out'. What eToro defines as the most dedicated segment of supporters – those who travel to away games as well as having a season ticket – will in the 2019/20 season, it estimates, spend close to 8 per cent of average UK take-home pay following their team. It's a huge commitment. According to the Office for National Statistics, in the year to March 2019 a typical household spent 10.6 per cent of its income on food and non-alcoholic drinks.[24] In many households' budgets, therefore, football is, quite simply, as important as food and drink.

Despite this economic reality, supporters are convinced that clubs and the Premier League afford the interests of the television companies, sponsors and foreign fans a much higher priority than those of match-going supporters. Even before we heard traditional supporters described as "legacy fans",[25] it was clear they have a point. I have already described how the Premier League acted to make Friday evening games a regular part of its schedule, and the insensitivity in proposing a Christmas Eve game between Arsenal and Liverpool. But it was listening to a Radio 5 Live pre-match discussion ahead of Arsenal versus West Bromwich Albion on Monday, 25 September 2017 that brought home to me how little thought is given to the treatment of supporters.

Playing the game on a Monday, one of the commentary team pointed out, meant that Arsenal's last seven games had all taken place on different days of the week. Contrast this with when I started going to live football matches. Clubs would work hard to accommodate their supporters. Stoke City home games normally kicked off at 3.15 on a Saturday afternoon, rather than the more common 3 p.m., to allow workers from the pottery industry and local coal mines time to finish their Saturday morning shifts and get to the ground. In the twenty-first century the idea of football managing kick-off times to accommodate paying spectators seems very far-fetched.

Throughout the 2017/18 and 2018/19 seasons, scheduling issues dominated fan discussion boards. The FSA and others have long battled against the timing of games selected for live TV broadcast. The announcement deadline is five weeks before the original kick-off, but this often comes too late for supporters looking to book travel in advance to take advantage of cheaper tickets. Worse still, the five-week limit is often breached – the FSA reported that in 2017/18, the Premier League moved half of matches later than its deadline.[26]

Over half of all Premier League games (200 out of 380), will be broadcast each season under the three-year TV deal that started with the 2019/20 season.[27] This near-saturation coverage means the options for more innovation on timing of games in England are limited: nearly all slots are taken. Recognising the limits on looking at the clock for further changes to the schedule to generate more revenue, the Premier League turned to the map.

The strategy first showed itself in 2008 when, under Richard Scudamore's lead, the Premier League proposed a *thirty-ninth game* – an extra week of competition going beyond the thirty-eight-game season of reciprocal home and away matches. The proposal was that this thirty-ninth game would be played outside the UK, to boost foreign interest while generating incremental television and commercial income. Scudamore described it as 'an idea whose time has come'.[28]

Unusually for the normally efficient and slick Premier League, the proposal had not been pre-sold and supporters, the government and the FA all expressed their surprise. FIFA was opposed from the start: 'Football cannot be like the Harlem Globetrotters.'[29]

The abandonment of the 'the thirty-ninth game' was a rare, lone victory for supporters, but it was another Pyrrhic victory. The proposed extra game was just another step on the journey to internationalise English football that had begun in 2003 when the Premier League launched the Asia Trophy in Malaysia. This competition has been held every two years since, moving around countries with a different set of English teams competing each time. The 'thirty-ninth game' may have been shelved but, with the value of foreign TV rights and sponsorship continuing to increase, the Premier League and the clubs were not going to pass up the opportunity to maximise returns. In recent years the number of games outside the UK involving Premier League teams has increased steadily.

Clubs, especially the richer ones, have dramatically increased the share of international games in their pre-season programmes, working closely with local sponsors.[30] Launched in 2013, the International Champions' Cup operates across continents with teams drawn from a range of countries. In the summer of 2019 AC Milan, Arsenal, Atlético Madrid, Bayern Munich, Benfica, Chivas of Mexico, Real Madrid, Fiorentina, Inter Milan, Juventus and Tottenham Hotspur joined Manchester United in a tournament played in the USA, Singapore, China, Sweden and Wales.

Manchester United's pre-season tour was based around this competition and, after friendly games against Perth Glory and Leeds United in Australia, matches against Inter Milan in Singapore, Tottenham Hotspur in Shanghai and AC Milan in Wales formed the basis of their participation. Clearly designed to bolster the club's Asian fan base, the schedule offered little or no opportunity for local supporters to see the team prior to the start of the season.

When Project Big Picture (PBP) was launched during the pandemic, the interest of the clubs with the strongest global brands in the international market was poorly disguised – one of the proposals was for Premier League clubs to be allowed to sell eight of their games direct to the foreign market, keeping the receipts for themselves. Inevitably, time slots would be selected to maximise foreign audience and advertising income; domestic supporters will just have to cope. For supporters of those clubs pushing for change in European competitions, the situation is even worse – the costs and challenges of following their team are likely to increase significantly with more European fixtures every season.

Interestingly, PBP offered the prospect of capping away tickets at £20. Superficially this suggested an awareness of the financial squeeze supporters have been subjected to, but my view is that it reflects the value of the atmosphere travelling fans create in the international TV market: it is self-interest disguised as benevolence.

Nowadays the approach is there for all to see. Faced with a home market reaching saturation, overseas expansion is the logical move. It is a classic corporate strategy that we would expect from a large business. There is a difference, though. If Unilever, one of the world's largest consumer goods companies, pursues overseas expansion, it has little if any impact on its UK customers. By contrast, playing more matches in foreign countries and changing kick-off times to suit different time zones will impact home supporters.

My concern over the treatment of supporters was the starting point for this book. In the Premier League era their financial and emotional contribution has been undervalued. English football supporters have been much more accepting of their lot as the game has changed all around them than might have been expected. There have been examples of significant protests – Manchester United fans made their feelings known in a campaign against the Glazers – but, whatever their grievances, they have generally continued to turn up to watch, buy replica shirts and pay for TV subscriptions.

Have supporters been too passive? Have they failed to recognise how important they are to clubs? On some of the rare occasions when fans have flexed their muscles, they have won concessions. In the early days of the Premier League era, fans at Arsenal, West Ham and other clubs protested extensively as debenture and bond schemes were proposed to fund ground improvements.[31] Years of exploitation and lack of consultation appeared to have worn fans down. But the tide may be changing.

In February 2016, following the announcement of ticket prices for the following season, Liverpool supporters' groups organised a walkout in the seventy-seventh minute of a home game against Sunderland. The timing was chosen to highlight the proposed introduction of a £77 match ticket, an increase on the previous high of £59 – one of several proposals that the fans objected to, another being a £1,000 season ticket. The *Guardian* estimated that up to 10,000 out of the 44,179 crowd left the ground. At the time Liverpool were leading 2–0, but Sunderland fought back to earn a 2–2 draw.[32]

At first the club responded by claiming that the new pricing structure would generate better availability for local fans and offer greater accessibility and affordability. However, following the protests, the owners quickly reconsidered. 'The widespread opposition to this element of the plan has made it clear that we were mistaken,' they wrote in an open letter to supporters.

> A great many of you have objected strongly to the £77 price level of our most expensive GA [general admission] seats and expressed a clear expectation that the club should forego any increased revenue from raising prices on GA tickets in the current environment. Message received.[33]

The campaign for fairer ticket prices for away supporters is another example of supporter power being exercised successfully, this time on a collective basis across clubs. When setting prices for their own fans, clubs aim to reward loyalty and create opportunities for new and different groups of supporters to come to games. The incentive to look after away supporters is much lower, and there are few constraints – historically, clubs have been free to charge what they liked. In the BBC's Cost of Football Study in 2015, West Ham's highest priced away ticket was £85 (their lowest was £25), Arsenal's prices ranged from a high of £64 down to £26, and Chelsea had a narrow range from £59 to a 'cheap' ticket at an eye-watering £47.[34]

In January 2013, therefore, the Football Supporters' Association launched its 'Twenty's Plenty for Away Tickets' campaign, calling for 'clubs at all levels of the game to recognise and reward the amazing contribution of away fans by getting together to agree an across-the-board price cap on away match tickets of £20 (£15 for concessions).' Kevin Miles, the chief executive of the FSF, underlined the importance of away supporters to the atmosphere in grounds.

> Nobody wants to watch a game played out in front of empty stands ... Away fans in particular bring noise and colour to grounds, adding to the spectacle immeasurably. But following your side on the road can be expensive and, despite football being wealthy, we believe very little of it is used to reduce costs for match-goers.[35]

The FSA's campaign did finally have an impact, with the Premier League finally agreeing in 2016 to introduce a £30 cap for three seasons on the cost of tickets for visiting fans. With wide acknowledgement that away fans add significantly to the atmosphere at grounds, I was surprised how long it took for clubs and the Premier League to agree to something that had a minimal financial downside and a significant upside.

I had the same feeling during the Covid-19 lockdown that began in spring 2020. Faced with the prospect of lower revenues, clubs outside the elite were forced to place staff on the government's 'furlough' scheme, under which 80 per cent of their wages were henceforth paid by the state. While supporters and commentators recognised the stress many clubs were under and acknowledged these were sensible decisions, moves by Liverpool and Spurs to use the scheme were widely criticised, with the supporters' groups of both clubs leading the way. Both clubs subsequently withdrew their proposals and continued to pay their staff themselves.[36] This was fans engaging on non-football-related issues, making the owners and management of their clubs aware that they would be judged on wider grounds than purely footballing success. After years of a lack of values in the leadership of English football, might we be seeing fans stepping up to fill the gap?

It is certainly needed: however much it claims to value supporters, the Premier League's actions increasingly suggest the opposite. Throughout the Covid-19 pandemic, its leaders failed to show any empathy for the wider game. Recognising that football on television, albeit behind closed doors, was a boost to supporters everywhere, the Premier League and its broadcast partners showed every game of the resumed Premier League season of 2019/20 live, even allowing the first ever live Premier League game to be broadcast on the BBC. Yet as it became clear that the 2020/21 season would have to remain spectator-free for longer than initially expected, the Premier League announced that games not selected for broadcast would be available on pay-per-view for £14.95 per match. This despite many supporters having paid for season tickets that had not yet been refunded.

Condemnation of the move was swift and widespread. The respected Times journalist Henry Winter took to Twitter: '£14.95 to watch a game on pay per view is disgraceful … It's disgusting. The creed of greed is in @premierleague DNA but this truly stinks.' Sky Sports' pundit Gary Neville voiced a similar opinion: 'This is a really bad move by the @premierleague to charge £14.95 for single matches that have been shown free for 6 months.'

Supporters of Burnley and Newcastle announced plans to boycott games and make donations to charities that were helping people cope with the challenges of Covid-19.[37] Eventually the Premier League backed down and offered the games for free during the UK's second national lockdown.

Nothing though illustrated the power of supporters better than the response to the launch of a European Super League in April 2021.[38] Within twenty-four hours, supporters gathered at Elland Road to make their feelings known and similar protests were seen at Stamford Bridge the following evening. Recognising the mood, the Government finally delivered on its manifesto commitment to a 'fan-led review of governance', even hinting that the German '50+1' model of supporter ownership could be an option. Supporters were suddenly in the vanguard.

It is about time. I thought Gary Caffel of MoneySavingExpert.com made an interesting choice of words when reflecting on the situation of supporters, He was quoted by the *Guardian* as saying that fans were being treated as 'cash cows'.[39] In classic business school strategy, a 'cash cow' identifies a business that is mature and has little growth potential but can be milked for cash to fund investment in other areas. It is a reasonable assessment of the treatment of supporters. Even before Covid-19, there were signs that supporters were reaching the limits of their ability to continue increasing their spending on football. Even inelastic demand eventually snaps. The Premier League's support for a £30 cap on away tickets might in part have hinted at a recognition that fans were close to their limit. Certainly, the rate of increase in top-flight ticket prices has also slowed in recent years. The Premier League may have high occupancy rates on existing seating, but at today's price levels there is scant evidence of additional demand. Only Everton of the clubs outside the group with ground capacity in excess of 50,000 are planning to increase capacity to any significant extent.

There were other signs of a possible slowdown in supporter revenue growth before the Covid-19 pandemic struck. In a report entitled *Peak Football Revenues and Post-boom Scenarios*,[40] the leading media industry analyst Enders highlighted falling pay-TV subscriber numbers for Sky, Virgin Media and all other providers as an illustration of their concerns over future income streams. Even after including the growth of 72,000 in subscriptions to the cheaper Now TV service in 2018, Sky's overall fall of 114,000 subscribers meant it lost 186,000 of its higher-paying subscribers during the year. The suspension of matches during lockdown heightened the pressure on the TV companies. Many people who paused their subscriptions could choose not to renew them, or the economic shock delivered by the pandemic may make many of them simply unable to do so.

Not only could TV audiences be lower, but some supporters who have been unable to attend games during lockdown may also just get out of the habit of going to games. Others, mindful of potential health risks, may no longer be willing to attend mass events. Whatever the future after Covid-19, it seems likely that clubs will need to work harder to attract and retain supporters in the coming years, which will require a shift in attitude.

Tradition is central to the supporter journey. Football club loyalty tends to be passed down through families, with the first live game you see often defining the team you support for life. Speaking on Radio 5 Live, Mark Palios, the Chairman of Tranmere Rovers, described the process as 'Someone buys from you aged five and buys from you for the next seventy years.'[41]

There are signs that the cycle is not replenishing as it used to. With attendance levels close to sold out in the Premier League, there is a risk of crowding out younger supporters – the future of the game. Certainly, Premier League crowds do appear to be older than the equivalent old First Division supporters. Research by the *Guardian* in 2014 suggested that the average age of a Manchester United spectator had increased from seventeen in 1968 to over forty by 2008.[42] This is not that surprising – the increase in the cost of watching football in this period risks pricing younger fans out of games. There is more evidence of this trend from other clubs. In 1992, 25 per cent of the Aston Villa crowd were aged between sixteen and twenty, and this age group made up 17 per cent of the gate at Arsenal. By 2007/8, the average share of Premier League crowds coming from this age group was 11 per cent, although the Premier League claimed it had risen to 19 per cent when it introduced a new sampling method.[43] In 2014/15, the Premier League noted that 40 per cent of crowds in that season were aged between eighteen and thirty-four years, higher than the 29 per cent of the UK population this group accounts for.[44]

Detailed information on the profile of Premier League games is not readily available. What we have suggests that the primary risk to future participation arises from the relatively low share of spectators at the younger end of the eighteen-to-thirty-four-years age distribution. In 2018/19, EY's ticketing study[45] found that 70.4 per cent of tickets were for adults, 10.1 per cent for senior citizens, 12.5 per cent for juniors and 4.6 per cent for young adults. With young adults typically defined as being aged eighteen to twenty-one by Premier League clubs, it does appear that the number of young adults attending games has fallen over time. With only 12.6 per cent of tickets sold in the junior category, which covers a longer age range up to eighteen, the concern over the relatively limited numbers of younger children at matches seems valid.

The reasons for the decline in the share of younger fans at Premier League games are not hard to identify. In their 2017 'Cost of Football' study, the BBC commissioned research of 1,000 eighteen-to-twenty-four-year-olds on their football-related activities. Eighty-two per cent of the fans interviewed identified the cost of tickets as an obstacle to attending games, and 65 per cent the cost of travel. Fifty-five per cent of respondents said they had stopped going to games owing to cost. Possibly in part looking for alternative ways to engage, 61 per cent said they regularly played games on a PC or console.[46] Whatever the reasons, the Premier League appears to be at risk of pricing out young fans, creating what Justin Madders, the MP for Ellesmere Port and Neston, calls 'a demographic time bomb'.[47]

The combination of high cost and difficulty in obtaining a one-off ticket to watch live football risks weakening the bonds between supporters and clubs in future. Speaking on the twentieth anniversary of the publication of his book *Fever Pitch*, Nick Hornby, shared his concerns on this very point.

> The thing about the really cheap prices, being able to decide on the day whether you went or not, is that it creates an addiction. We made up our mind whether to go on Saturday lunchtime. You can't do that any more. Most kids see live football, like theatre, as a treat three or four times a year. Whether in twenty years' time those kids will still want to go, feels as though it will be different.[48]

A modern stadium full of older supporters, sitting in reasonably comfortable seats, also has a very different atmosphere to a ground with a young crowd packed in on the terraces. If the grounds lack an intense atmosphere, one of the key elements of the Premier League's appeal to foreign TV viewers will be diminished.

Atmosphere is important. It is one of the main reasons supporters go to a game, and players value it too. The modern player is seen as very distant from supporters, compared to the past, but this does them a disservice – players feed off the emotion of the crowd. Interviewed by the *Financial Times*, the former Manchester City captain, Vincent Kompany, shared the results of the research he undertook for his MBA at Alliance Manchester Business School into the relationship between atmosphere in stadium and team performance.[49] Premier League football clubs, Kompany concluded, should cut ticket prices to help *the* 'right communities' attend matches. He also shared his view that clubs had to draw a 'moral line' and make sure working-class fans who have supported them for generations can afford to go to games.

What was most interesting, though, was why Kompany was thinking this way. He identified a link between a better home game atmosphere, generated by more passionate fans, and team performance, arguing that in the long term this could benefit all parties.

> You wonder whether there's not more value in the Premier League as a project by making sure that every single stadium is bouncing for every single game, versus trying to squeeze everybody for the last [penny] ... There's an entire business model that at the moment stands in the way of even coming near to exploiting home advantage to the maximum.

For his research, Kompany spoke to twenty-five top current and former players, including Thierry Henry of Arsenal and Chelsea's Frank Lampard. He concluded that a full stadium with a passionate crowd drawn from the local community improved the home team's performance, partly by inhibiting the visiting team's players: 'If we go towards neutral stadiums where tickets are paid by the highest bidder ... because they are neutrals it will invariably have an impact on home advantage.' Leading him to conclude: 'Winning more football matches would be far more beneficial than actually putting up the prices ... and therefore leaving some of those people from the right communities out of the stadium. [They are the] people who care.'

Unsurprisingly given the frequency with which Germany is cited as an example of a country where fans are treated well, the clubs that ranked highest for atmosphere in Kompany's research were mainly in Germany. We shouldn't be surprised that a player rather than an owner, manager or official has identified that supporters are the lifeblood of football – it is about emotion first and foremost. Vincent Kompany's insight is to show that football is about more than money. The whole experience is what creates the magic.

Further evidence for the importance of fans and the atmosphere they create emerged when football returned after the Covid-19 lockdown. The first academic study to look at the impact of no crowds, by the IZA Institute of Labour Economics,[50] found that results were marginally impacted, but home teams still won more games than away teams. However, there was a statistically significant difference. 'Without a crowd,' noted the authors, 'fewer cards were awarded to the away teams, reducing home advantage. These results have implications for the impact of social pressure and crowds on the neutrality of refereeing decisions.'

In other words, referees were less influenced by crowds. This seems a likely explanation, although it could be that the absence of crowds led to changes in how teams played and this, rather than refereeing decisions, was what caused the change.

More support for the impact of crowds on games emerged during the 2020/21 season played out in empty arenas. Away teams achieved their highest ever success rate in the Premier League.[51] The inference is clear: atmosphere matters and hence so do supporters.

There is no doubt that supporters contribute much more than the money they pay and the noise they make inside grounds. Most importantly, fans embody and own the traditions of football and are a living link to communities. Above all, they are the conscience of the game.

The gap between the people who run football and manage clubs on one hand and their supporters on the other was really brought home to me in the summer of 2019. Bury Football Club was placed into administration, the first club since 1992 to be forced to drop out of the English Football League. I listened to Radio 5 Live's *Football Daily* podcast, with reporter Steve Crossman describing the mood among Bury fans in the run-up to the deadline for the decision on the club's membership of the Football League.[52] I found a story describing how one supporter came to the ground almost unbearable. He approached slowly, tied his blue and white scarf to the padlocked gates, kissed it one last time and walked away. He was too emotional to talk to the media.

Other fans did manage to articulate their feelings. 'I might not have a football club to support next week,' reflected the BBC reporter and Bury fan Mark Crossley. Jean Hall described her 'pain and anger', and when asked how she planned to spend her Saturday afternoon said she would 'sit there and cry'. Another supporter revealed that no fewer than forty members of his family held season tickets. 'I just want to watch a game of football,' he lamented.

Any football supporter listening would have empathised. This was not a defeat in a local derby, a promotion opportunity missed or the pain of relegation, all of which feel like the end of the world at the time. It was the end of the line. 'How would I feel if Stoke City went out of business?' I asked myself.

Subsequent investigations, most notably by the Select Committee of the Department for Culture, Media and Sport,[53] unearthed a litany of bad practice and failures of regulation by the football authorities. What leaps out is how the warnings from supporters that things were not right at Bury were ignored. Given how much supporters contribute to the game, financially and emotionally, it was striking, Malcolm Clarke, Chairman of the Football Supporters' Association, told the committee, how little they are consulted or involved, either by people running the national game overall or in the administration of their own clubs. The FSA is staffed and resourced by committed people who have typically made the transition from supporter to administrator and even director when crises have hit their clubs. Yet even beyond the FSA, Clarke pointed out, there is so much professional expertise and experience of football among supporters that could be made available to clubs to draw on – potentially a huge benefit, especially to smaller clubs with limited resources.

The FSA suggested the FA, Premier League and EFL create a Supporters' Ombudsman to hear supporters' concerns about how clubs are being run. (There already exists an Independent Football Ombudsman, but this role is to deal with commercial disputes from supporters as customers). The new position would address issues such as those raised by the collapse of Bury, but football should consider being more ambitious with supporter involvement. There is a strong case for involving supporters more formally on questions like ticketing and kick-off times that directly impact them.

And there is an opportunity to widen the role and participation of supporters in football clubs that goes further than consultation. FC United of Manchester, founded by Manchester United supporters who opposed the takeover by Malcolm Glazer, is now the largest fan-owned football club in the UK, and is democratically run by its members, who all have equal voting rights. Fan ownership is often dismissed as unworkable in relation to the Premier League because of the scale and complexity of the operations, but FC Manchester is evidence of successful fan intervention.[54]

Admittedly, as Chris Porter's *Supporter Ownership in English Football*[55] points out, the English experience of fan ownership leaves questions about the long-term benefits of the model. Most incidences of fan ownership were in response to either a financial crisis, such as at Northampton Town, AFC Bournemouth and Exeter City, or a conflict with the existing owner, often in conjunction with financial problems, such as at Brentford and Notts County.

While the track record of supporters in intervening to saving clubs from financial collapse is strong, maintaining the momentum over the long-term has proven more challenging. There are notable examples, like Brentford, though this may in part reflect the fact that the Supporters' Trust ultimately sold their shares to an owner, Matthew Benham, who was also a supporter. But as Porter shows, there are challenges in finding the right structure to allow supporters to feel represented while at the same time enabling them to play an effective role in the governance of the club when working alongside other interests. Most of the supporter interventions to date have been via a wholly owned trust that owns the supporter shares, separate to the main football club structure.

The Bundesliga is the most commonly cited example of best-practice operation of a major football league. With top-quality games, high attendances, low ticket prices and a vibrant fan culture, the German equivalent of the Premier League attracts admiration from football fans worldwide, and according to Vincent Kompany's research is loved by players. This success is largely accredited to the 50+1 rule. This requires that a majority of the voting rights are controlled by the club's members or supporters' trust. The remaining share is available to all parties, including investors.

The approach of Germany's most successful club, Bayern Munich, to season ticket pricing, exemplifies the difference between German and English clubs. Uli Hoeness, Bayern Munich's president, explained the philosophy that guides his club, European Champions in 2020, very clearly when it came to ticket pricing: 'We could charge more than €104. Let's say we charged €300. We'd get €2 million more in income, but what is €2 million to us? In a transfer discussion you argue that sum for five minutes.', going on to reject the profit maximising, 'cash cow' strategy: 'We don't think fans are like cows that you milk.'[56]

It is not complicated; it just requires the adoption of a different model and mindset from the one so deep-rooted in the Premier League. At the core are values and identity, the precise things that fans bring to a club. That German clubs were not among the initial list signing up to the proposed European Super League is an illustration of the potential benefits of involving supporters in governance.[57]

Comparison with Germany provides clues as to why establishing supporter ownership in the UK has been challenging. In part it reflects differing approaches to corporate governance across the economy. Worker and other stakeholder representation on boards is much less common in the UK than in Germany, while the presence of supervisory board structures in Germany also provides a framework for incorporating other interests into decision-making roles. There is also a different history. By the time the law requiring German clubs to be members' associations was changed to allow the 50+1 approach in 1998, Premier League clubs had already listed their shares on stock markets, sold stakes to cable television companies and welcomed the first foreign owners.[58]

Changing a well-established, economy wide, ownership model would not be a simple task in any circumstances. The presence of a large number of foreign investors in England, especially in the most valuable clubs, makes it even harder. A forced shift of governance would risk running into international disputes on investor protection. Having sat on the Government's Trade Advisory Group, I find it hard to imagine the UK Government being willing to risk jeopardising foreign investment flows into the wider economy post-Brexit. Starting from where we do, it is unlikely that the wholesale adoption of the German model could be successfully achieved in the English game.

Equally, as many large European clubs like Barcelona, Real Madrid and Bayern Munich all operate governance systems with some form of fan involvement, we should not accept the status quo. We need to identify a new approach reflective of the unique nature of the English game and the surrounding legal and commercial environment. It is not necessary for shares to change hands. What is required is a process that ensures decisions on those aspects of a football club's operations that potentially affect supporters and communities reflect the interests of all stakeholders.

Change is required: in English football the relationship between clubs and supporters is out of balance. With fans seen more as consumers than stakeholders, clubs are happy to take their money, but don't recognise what they are missing in supporter engagement. The emotional commitment of supporters to their team allows clubs a huge amount of leeway in how they treat their fan base. Without any effective regulatory intervention by either Government or the football authorities, Premier League clubs have been able to maximise the commercial opportunities available to them. With stadium utilisation at 97 per cent the chances of securing a ticket are relatively slim for many fans;[59]TV coverage is the only way they can see their team. For Premier League clubs this is a win-win: they capture supporters one way or the other.

Secondly, while some progress has been made on improving the gender and race balance of supporters inside grounds and, albeit belatedly, better disabled fan provision, over time there is a risk that demand for tickets among younger people may drop further. With the aftermath of Covid-19 likely to reduce growth in overall revenue flowing into football for some time, clubs need to re-engage with their supporters beyond the financial relationship. Fans embody the tradition of the game and bring knowledge of the culture of the club and its community, often to a greater extent than the owners and management themselves. It would make football a better game.

Coming with supporter influence at its highest in living memory in the aftermath of Project Big Picture and the European Super League saga, the government's 'fan-led review of governance'[60] is a potentially game-changing development.

Speaking as the review was launched, the Chair, Tracey Crouch MP, promised: "It will look closely at the issues of governance, ownership and finance and take the necessary steps to retain the game's integrity, competitiveness and, most importantly, the bond that clubs have with its supporters and the local community." There is no doubt that the action (and inaction) of the elite clubs during lockdown has caused the pendulum to swing in favour of supporters – they have scored a huge political own goal.

As clubs look to build a global brand, there is a growing requirement for business to act in a socially responsible manner, and we could see fan discontent and protests impacting the profile and image of clubs and competitions on a regular basis. After arranging the funding for the European Super League, investment bank JP Morgan had their sustainability rating downgraded by Standard Ethics, a specialist ratings agency[61]. Such events are something both the brand- and marketing-focused football club executives and their commercial sponsors would be very keen to avoid. Any hint that the bond between supporters and club is broken hits at the core of the football story being sold around the world. Fans should not be shy of flexing their muscles.

So what should they ask for?

Supporters should demand to be front and centre in the game's governance, empowered to ensure the game's values feature in decision-making and capable of protecting supporter and community interests. In Chapters 9 and 11, I will consider in more detail how this might work both at the national level and within clubs, such as the '50+1' model and seats on boards. For now, there are at least two areas where change offers the opportunity to rebalance football towards supporters.

The first area is broadening matchday attendance. In addition to pushing harder on existing efforts around gender, race and disability, clubs should be encouraged to think more about how to make a number of tickets to games available to a wider group of people on an occasional basis.

Alongside ticketing, TV offers the scope to make more games available. We know from audiences attracted to England's men's team games that football is extremely popular, and the viewing figures on pay-TV channels are constrained by the number of subscriptions that are sold. Covid has shown us how audience figures will surge for free broadcasts. It should be possible to insist a small number of games per club are broadcast free-to-air every season.

Supporters and clubs are the visible face of football's wider impact, but the game reaches much further into society. Let's move on to explore football's best-kept secret; its work in the community.

7 YOU'LL NEVER WALK ALONE

'YOU ARE ON THE BIG SCREEN AT THE LONDON STADIUM,'
shouted the text from my West Ham-supporting friend on a wintry
Saturday afternoon.

'I don't understand,' I replied.

'They have just played a video before the kick-off against Spurs,
and you were there alongside Baroness Brady and the first-team squad.'

Several more exchanges of messages later, I understood what he
was talking about. A week earlier, at an event held at the former Olym-
pic Stadium, I had shared the findings of a Premier League-funded
assessment of the impact of the Players' Project – West Ham United's
hugely impressive community programme.[1] The club had played a
summary video of the day to the crowd before the start of the home
game against Spurs. Choosing to give the event such a high profile
shows how important this activity is to the club.

It was an inspiring day, hosted by the club's vice-chairman Karen
Brady, the passionate chair of the club's Community Foundation.
West Ham organised a set of stalls and demonstrations to give
everyone a feel for what the club does, ranging from encouraging
learning in schools to help with mental health. The highlight for me
was meeting the members of Any Old Irons, a group for and run by
older supporters, using a shared interest in football (mainly but not
exclusively in the Hammers) to tackle loneliness and support people
with age-related disabilities, especially dementia. They meet regularly
for a meal and a chat, interspersed with visits by current and retired
players. Their impressive line in memorabilia is another tool to

reach out to people – it is a fantastic programme, really well thought-through and implemented.

This was a whole club effort. No-one was left in any doubt how important the local community was to the club's men's skipper, Mark Noble, who spoke passionately about growing up in the area, and how he felt that if anyone nearby went hungry or didn't have a bed for the night then it was the club's duty to act. Gilly Flaherty, the captain of West Ham United Ladies, explained how much the players enjoyed working in the community, admitting Any Old Irons was a favourite. The manager at the time, Manuel Pellegrini, had a simpler take. The high rewards for people working in football, he argued, in a way a Latin American socialist politician would applaud, created a moral responsibility to give something back.

Because money shapes the English game, I have devoted a significant amount of this book to analysing the financial flows into, out of, and within English football. Only in the vast North American market do we find domestic competitions that generate higher revenues in a season, and even the second tier, the Championship, is one of the top ten football competitions in Europe in revenue terms. Yet in the UK corporate arena, never mind on the world stage, the Premier League is a minnow. In 2018/19, the combined turnover of Premier League clubs was around £5 billion. This was roughly half the revenue achieved by Marks & Spencer, a retailer that at the time employed just over 75,000 people – about seven times the number directly employed by the Premier League and its twenty clubs.[2]

But as West Ham's efforts demonstrate, football can be – is – about much more than money. The game's evolution from village green through the mill and factory towns of the North and Midlands to the global reach it enjoys today has shaped its position in society. On one hand, English football is an iconic global brand; on the other it is entwined in the fabric of families and friendships and communities. Goldblatt, Tempany, Hornby and others[3] have described just how central the game is to daily life within England. Football is not just an idea: it has a real and visible physical presence. Across the nation, football grounds are to be found nestled in the hearts of cities and towns, hubs in the urban landscape. And it is locally where the game has its real impact.

Competitive games are the face of English football. Yet most clubs only play one or two games a fortnight at their home stadium, and none in the summer months. It was only when I started working with the Premier League to understand the economic and social impact of the competition that I realised how matches are just the tip of the iceberg.

When working for EY, to understand the scale of a club's contribution to its local community, I went to meet Lee Charnley, Managing Director of Newcastle United, and his team. I turned up at St James's Park on a typical midweek day to find the place buzzing. Corporate and private social events were taking place in the ground's dining and conference rooms; club officials were meeting suppliers and partners; huge light frames that simulate sunlight were being moved across the pitch to boost grass growth. If I had visited on a summer day, I might have stumbled on preparations for a concert: the Ed Sheeran shows St James's Park hosted in May 2018 generated an average daily increase in trade for businesses in the city centre of 57 per cent.[4]

The stadium was not the only place where people were busy. At the Benton training ground, players were preparing for the next match with coaches, nutritionists, fitness specialists and medical staff. Spread across the city, staff from the club's Community Foundation were working in schools, colleges and other institutions.

If we concentrate solely on the Premier League and its finances we miss so much of football's economic impact. Clubs reach into the local economy to source temporary match-day employees like stewards and catering staff, transport and advertising services and goods such as food and programmes. On a typical match day Manchester United employ up to 1,300 temporary staff, I was told, to deliver hospitality and catering, while Manchester City estimated that the £200 million spent on their training complex led to 883 contracts being awarded to local companies.[5] The numbers of people travelling across the country and visitors coming to the UK to watch games are significant: in 2016/17, around 686,000 tourists travelled to the UK on a trip that included a Premier League game, spending an estimated £555 million.[6]

Taking account of all this activity, we estimated that the management and the twenty clubs in the Premier League were responsible for supporting around 100,000 jobs in the UK during the 2017/18 season: 52,000 in the supply chain, and the other 35,000 through the expenditure of players, club employees and those workers in the supply chains.[7]

This is only the first-round effect of football in the UK economy. A significant amount of additional activity is generated in a range of related industries such as sports clothing, footwear, gambling and news subscriptions. Without doubt, the Premier League has played an important part in strengthening the UK's position in key industries. E-gaming is a growing sector worldwide, and the UK has an emerging industry helped in part by the profile of the Premier League and its players in some of the most famous games, like the FIFA series by EA Sports. The Premier League has also enhanced the UK's reputation in the worldwide media industry: its international broadcast value is greater than the sales of all other UK television shows combined.[8]

Though the Premier League's economic impact is impressive, like its corporate status, against a total UK economic income of £2 trillion and more than 34 million people in work it is still relatively small. It is locally where it is more significant. In 2016/17 Stoke City's operations supported around 1,800 jobs in a city with total employment just below 135,000 (in other words, about 1.3 per cent of the total jobs).[9] Deloitte estimated that in 2017/18 the 4,564 jobs Liverpool FC created in the Liverpool city region represented around 4 per cent of local employment.[10] Clubs act as economic anchors: a very important role, especially when the national economy weakens. But there is much more.

Back to Newcastle. It was a cold February evening when I alighted from the train at Newcastle Central and made my way up the hill to Murray House, in the centre of the city just around the corner from St James's Park in the midst of dense housing and small industrial premises. The building is hard to describe, a cross between a hangar and a gymnasium, with a wooden, varnished floor reminiscent of my old school basketball court. Newcastle United's Community Foundation has an ambitious plan to turn Murray House into a new, state-of-the-art hub for its activities. The club had taken over the building from a local charity, and that Thursday evening was holding an event to explain its plans and launch a fund-raising drive. My job was to explain how valuable club's community work was and suggest how large the impact could be once the new building was up and running.

That dark Thursday night, Murray House lit up the city. Guests were greeted by a projection on the front of the building of an artist's impression of the development when it is finished – it was truly awe-inspiring. Around 200 people turned up to hear the ambitious plans for a £12 million redevelopment: public space on the ground floor, learning and technology facilities in the middle and a 4G pitch on the roof: something for everyone. Radio 5 Live's John Murray hosted the evening, and kicked things off by introducing Lee Charnley, who made it clear how committed the club were. A series of interviews and panels featured the local MP and police chief, members of the council and youth workers, all of whom shared their vision of how the centre would help young people. This was a football club embedded in its city and community.

The centrepiece of the evening was a discussion between John Murray and the ex-Newcastle player Shola Ameobi, now patron of the Community Foundation. John set the scene by explaining that the player he had commentated on scoring for Newcastle at the Nou Camp in a Champions' League game against Barcelona had started his career playing at Murray House. Ameobi went on to explain his vision for the venue, and why it was so important for kids like him growing up in the city to have a place to call their own.

The Murray House project is an extremely ambitious attempt by Newcastle to make a difference to people's lives and a positive social impact in the local community. The club's unique emotional bond to its supporters creates the opportunity to corral resources to make a difference. Despite the building having only a few small electric heaters on a freezing night, no-one left until the event was over.

Murray House demonstrated that, even though Newcastle United's activities support around 2,000 jobs in a city with around 200,000 people in employment,[11] football's real value is its potential to change lives through its community activities. As a senior Department of Education official said to me, football helps reach children that other public and private sector initiatives are unable to. At Westminster 'levelling up' the UK economy is currently the hot topic. Football has been quietly doing so for decades.

Typically, football clubs in England deliver a range of community programmes through a charitable foundation. Each defines its strategy to reflect the specific challenges of its local area. When I worked with the Liverpool FC Foundation, they were supporting veterans in the city, Alder Hey Children's Hospital and numerous other good causes. And clubs do take on tough challenges – Crystal Palace's Palace for Life foundation runs a programme calling Breaking the Cycle that seeks to tackle youth crime in South London.[12]

The typical programme combines physical activity (not just football), improving educational outcomes, especially for young people, enhancing employment prospects and promoting healthy living. As clubs have become more deeply engaged in their local communities, so their ambitions and capabilities have increased, leading to more complex attempts to encourage social cohesion and community building like facilities such as Murray House and food banks, all with an emphasis on inclusion and diversity.[13]

Most clubs mix Premier League-funded, centrally developed activities with their own initiatives, usually funded by donors, the club's supporters' organisations and direct fundraising, along with charging for programmes like football coaching. In 2017/18, Premier League clubs worked with national organisations such as the Prince's Trust, Save the Children, Children in Need and the National Citizens' Service as well as local councils and organisations.

In my experience, anyone dropping in to watch will be impressed by the professionalism of the staff and the energy and commitment of participants – these are well designed, constantly evaluated activities.

In 2016/17 over 500,000 young people participated in Premier League-funded programmes, of which 38 per cent were female, 26 per cent BAME and 27,000 with a disability.

Premier League Kicks is one of the most long-established programmes, dating back to 2006, and designed to appeal to young people defined as hard-to-reach. In 2017/18 sixty-nine football clubs were supported in this programme by the Premier League across 800 venues, two-thirds of which were in the 30 per cent of the most deprived communities in the UK. Every season 70,000 young people participate in Kicks, including an ever-increasing number of girls –12,500 in 2017/18.[14]

Running football courses is something I suspect most people would expect from football's community activities. Useful in getting kids exercising, but maybe not life-changing. Kicks works as an entry point: Premier League Primary Stars goes further. This programme sees clubs working with schools to improve the educational achievement and skills of children and young people. Schools receive curriculum-related materials for PE, PSHE, maths and English, and community staff from clubs will go into schools to run activities. Schools also receive football kit and equipment.

Stoke City offer a range of Premier League-funded programmes like Kicks and Primary Stars as well as others like the Stoke Challenge: two days a week of targeted group work and one-to-one support to help young people aged sixteen to eighteen develop the skills and abilities needed to return to education or employment or training. My favourite was a twelve-week course developed for football fans in England by European Fans in Training (EuroFIT). Stoke City's version targets men between thirty and sixty-five. The programme offers a toolbox of skills and techniques for living a healthy life and the chance to get fitter and feel better.[15] Each session includes physical activity led by Stoke City's community coaches at the bet365 Stadium, and the attraction of training at the ground in the same facilities as the players means attendance and completion rates are very high. It is a very clever way of leveraging the appeal of football.

Newcastle's own tailored programmes include NE1 Works, for young people outside the job market, in which the club and Foundation work with ninety-four local employers to identify work experience opportunities and match young people to them. In 2017/18, the programme led to thirty-one work starts. The Foundation also supports volunteering, an activity shown to improve community cohesion and mental health outcomes, which generated 8,800 volunteering hours in 2017/18. Since its inception in 2007/8 the Newcastle United Foundation has increased its spend over each decade from £400,000 to £3.6 million.[16]

When football invests in community activities, it is understandably keen to understand the value created. It is not just football. A couple of years ago, I presented the Premier League's analysis of its impact at an event hosted by Pro-Bono Economics, a charity that provides economists to assess the impact of social programmes. It can be a relatively small effect such as improving people's health, where we can use published studies to estimate the probable reduction in their use of NHS services, or measured in the wages of someone helped to find a job they would not otherwise have secured.

Analysing each element of the programmes offered, we estimated that in 2016/17 the Stoke City Community Trust spent £1.3 million and generated a social return of £14.4 million, comprising £8.9 million from improved physical well-being, £2.9 million from improved mental well-being and £2.8 million through education and skills enhancement. In total, a return of £11 for every £1 invested.[17]

The evidence from Newcastle's Community Foundation paints a similar picture. In 2017/18, £22.5 million of social value was generated on an investment of £3.2 million, a return of £7 for every £1 invested, the lower multiple primarily reflecting a different mix of activities.[18]

These are impressive social returns, and significantly above average – a study by Sheffield Hallam University found a return of 1.9 times on every pound invested in sports participation.[19] We shouldn't be surprised: both clubs operate in cities challenged by economic changes over the last three or four decades, each seeing their major industries – pottery, shipbuilding, steel and coal mining – shrink dramatically. Community efforts have been impressive, but there are fewer resources than in the UK's two or three largest cities. The football clubs therefore become not only a source of economic activity but also ever more important providers of social support. In many ways, the Murray House project is the next stage on the journey.

All of football has the potential to contribute beyond the confines of the game itself, and some of the best work is done by smaller clubs embedded in their communities. Burslem is often described as the 'mother town' of the Potteries. The headquarters of Synetics Solutions doesn't stand out as you walk past the town's Victorian mansions and commercial buildings and head up the hill towards Vale Park. The building lies in the shadow of Port Vale FC's ground, convenient as company and football club now have common owners in Carol and Kevin Shanahan.

Synetics is a family-owned, leading-edge IT services company. I first met Carol when she spoke at an event in Hanley, another of the Potteries towns, hosted by the *Guardian*, one of a series reflecting on Britain after Brexit. The next time we met was at the Synetics Solutions offices. In the boardroom she introduced me to her latest project, the Hubb Foundation, which Synetics had helped to establish. The charity provides meals out of term-time to children and their families who would otherwise struggle to replace the free meals they receive at school. Since then the Foundation has grown at breakneck speed and during the lockdown was able to provide 1,000 meals a day. To date it has served around 300,000 free meals, a huge contribution to helping some of society's most vulnerable people.[20]

Food is only part of the story. Local and national businesses have been drawn in, and a typical day for the families helped involves events, games, art and craft and much more than just a meal. No detail is left to chance: even the name Hubb was selected for its significance in Arabic, so as to make the Potteries' Muslim community feel included.

In the summer of 2018, Kevin and Carol were finally able to achieve their ambition and acquire control of Port Vale football club. Carol was already on the board of the Port Vale Community Foundation which supported the Hubb effort, but this was the chance to go further and create a true community club.

From day one, the couple have thrown themselves into the job, accompanying the team to Largs in Scotland for pre-season training, running a series of discussion sessions for supporters and being hands-on across the operations – including the design of the new kit. The pair have implored wavering supporters to buy season tickets, offered contracts to local businesses wherever possible, strengthened links with the local university, especially for work experience, and asked for volunteers and donations. After a very difficult period under the previous ownership, within a few months the pair had re-established the bond between Port Vale and its supporters and local community.

Just before Covid struck, the club announced a concert by Port Vale supporter and global recording star Robbie Williams, to be held in summer 2020, the proceeds to be shared between the Hubb Foundation and Williams's own charitable activities. As would be expected, the return of the local boy-done-good sold out in minutes.

In just over twelve months, new owners have turned Port Vale from a club that had lost touch with its supporters into a true community club. Supporters now know they will be listened to – Carol regularly answers questions on social media – and almost every move seems designed to maximise the benefit to the local area. It is an example of how much football can do with the right intentions, high-quality management and adequate funding.

Anecdote and analysis lead us to the same conclusion: football has the potential to improve communities and change lives. But participation in football, as player, coach, administrator or supporter, has huge potential benefits too. Of course, this requires facilities, and funding to support the running of new grounds once they have been built. Wander onto a football pitch in England and there is a good chance that the Football Foundation will either have helped with the funding or provided support to one of the teams based there.

The Football Foundation is a partnership between the FA, the Premier League and the government, via Sport England. Clubs and organisations can apply for funding for pitches, changing rooms and other facilities. Other schemes offer support to start up female and disability teams and to keep men's teams playing. Founded in 2000, the Football Foundation had by 2018 helped to create 747 new artificial grass pitches, over 3,000 real grass pitches and 1,024 new changing rooms. Over £1.5 billion's worth of projects have been supported, and 2,050 grants made for stadia improvement funding.[21]

By building or improving facilities, communities can come together and create lasting legacies. A study by the economic consultancy CEBR quantified the Football Foundation's contribution, finding that in 2011 for every £1 invested in facility development an additional £1.53 of economic benefit was generated.[22] Typically, the Football Foundation provided one-third of the funding, stimulating additional investment from other partners and so multiplying the impact of its resources. By the end of 2018, according to an investigation by the *Evening Standard*, the Premier League had invested £302 million, the FA £299 million and the government £273 million – a total of £874 million.[23]

Yet all is not well. When the Football Association announced it was planning to sell Wembley Stadium, Martin Glenn, its chief executive, said the primary reason was to generate funds to invest in 'the grass roots', providing new pitches and facilities up and down the country. How could the country with the richest league in the world – a competition ostensibly set up to boost the fortunes of its national team – be having to sell off one of the most iconic football stadiums in the world to raise money to provide football pitches?

At the time the Premier League clearly believed it was doing enough. 'The amount we invest in good causes, communities and the wider development of the sport outside the Premier League is unprecedented in global sport,' said its spokesman. But a *Daily Telegraph* investigation in December 2018 used the FA's own research to paint a less rosy picture.[24] It found that:

- Only one in three grass roots pitches are of adequate quality
- In the 2016/17 season 150,000 matches were called off due to poor facilities
- One in six matches are called off due to poor pitch quality
- Thirty-three out of fifty county FAs are without their own 3G pitch

Even more striking is that the number of 3G pitches in England is half that in Germany. Artificial surfaces can be used much more intensively and are more resistant to bad weather, allowing games throughout the year. For the country to be lagging so far behind one of our European peers, despite having the richest football league in the world, is inexcusable. It is not just Germany that appears to have found a more effective approach.

The Gothia Cup is one of the most impressive football events in the world, and yet is probably unknown to most English football supporters. Every summer, the Swedish city of Gothenburg plays host to a tournament often referred to as the 'unofficial youth world cup'. Teams from Under-11 to Under-18 travel from all over the world to compete for a week, first in group stages and then a knockout competition. The opening ceremony in the Ullevi Stadium can attract a crowd of up to 50,000, with excited schoolchildren very much in the majority. Schools and other organisations convert classrooms and offices into dormitories where squads of up to sixteen players bed down. Public transport is reconfigured to provide service between grounds, enabling thousands of players to move around the city. Apps allow real-time tracking of matches – I followed the team one of my sons was playing for in a penalty shoot-out while watching his brother play live. Young referees, Sweden's future elite officials, take charge of the games.[25]

In what was a fabulous week, the lasting memory I took away was the pitches. No fewer than 1,700 teams from eighty countries play close to 4,500 matches during the week on 110 pitches. The quality of the pitches is unimaginable in England, with a predominance of 4G surfaces – the local clubs typically have several artificial pitches to offer. During the Swedish football season, with matches able to be played one after the other, the constant use of the facilities, especially on Friday evenings and over the weekend, allows the clubs to reach into their communities, with boys and girls playing matches around adult and veterans' games. It is a model England should aspire to: large-scale participation on high-quality surfaces, available for the wider community.

Sadly, the outlook is not promising. 'When you look at where local government finance is', Andy Burnham, the Mayor of Greater Manchester, told the *Daily Telegraph*,

> the grass roots are looking at a pretty bleak decade if there is not change. It can't be difficult for football to create a permanent revenue stream for the grass roots; from agents and transfer fees, as well as betting and the TV deal – that could create a really solid sustainable fund. The elite game depends directly on the grass roots – that's where the future revenue comes from.[26]

Lord Faulkner, like Andy Burnham a member of the Task Force that first proposed the 5 per cent levy, offers a solution.

> The game has become fabulously wealthy, and I support the principle of there being an independent football commission which receives income from various sources and spends it in the interests of the game, rather than be dependent just on the goodwill of the Premier League.
>
> A proportion would come from the television income. What would be quite good is if, in each transfer deal, a proportion of these proceeds would go to this new commission. It would not need to be a large proportion, but would certainly mount up if it applied to everybody.[27]

As the UK entered its second Covid-19 lockdown, I found myself talking to David Bernstein, the former FA chairman, about the proposals for reforming the governance of the game he had worked on with Andy Burnham, Gary Neville and others.[28] This was just his latest effort; he has campaigned long and hard for more money for grass roots football, previously calling for a levy to be introduced on Premier League income to solve what he calls the 'disgrace' of dilapidated grass-roots facilities. What struck me was how the same senior figures crop up time and time again. Their efforts to reform and improve the game may have been rebuffed, but they keep coming back for more. When busy people who have lots of demands on their time continue to work for the greater good because they love the game it should give us hope.

There is much to admire in the administration of grass roots football: for all its weaknesses in dealing with the senior game, this is where the FA's organisation comes into its own. Anyone who has been involved will be aware of the scale of the effort. It is a very different model to that found in FA headquarters dealing with the professional game, the England team, running the FA Cup and managing Wembley Stadium. A devolved model led by county Football Associations combines a small paid staff and large numbers of volunteers to see leagues run, referees trained, coaching courses held and regular visits from FA staff to run workshops in areas from coaching to child protection and training part-time assistant referees.

It is only when you are on the inside that you appreciate the scale of the commitment. For just over a decade, I managed teams that my two sons played in, including one incredibly stressful, not to be recommended season when I managed both their teams – especially challenging on the Sundays, when they had kick-offs at the same time in different places! By chance, the administrator of both age groups was Graham Ekins, whom many people became aware of when he published a powerful and insightful letter[29] highlighting the challenges facing youth football in England.

Running two teams, I got to observe his efforts at close quarters. Not only did he referee games on a Sunday morning, once ruining my weekend with (what I believed to be) a controversial decision to deny our team a last-minute equaliser in a top-of-the-table clash, but he also scheduled all the fixtures, collected results, tracked player registrations and managed all disputes, often while travelling internationally in his day job. Notwithstanding the disallowed goal (made worse as we had to drive all the way back to London from Sussex soaking wet), it was impossible not to admire his efforts and knowledge. He was scrupulously fair, in no small part from having seen every trick in the book many times before – I tried a few, believe me.

The FA has a much wider set of objectives, though, across all forms of football. On its website it defines itself as a body that 'grows participation, promotes diversity and regulates the sport for all to enjoy'. 'The FA', it says simply, 'keeps the grass roots game going'. The reality is that the FA is extremely good at *running* junior football, but lacks the resources to lead the way on protecting and growing the grass roots game because it is reliant on others to fund investment in facilities. Although the FA invested £22.5 million into the Football Foundation in 2018[30] this is a small share of the total required. However hard the FA works, it will always find its lack of influence over the Premier League's finances a major constraint on its ability to deliver for grass roots football – nearly all of football's resources are in the professional game, primarily with Premier League clubs. The FA has made positive steps in recent years in boosting interest and participation in women's football, but the number of men's teams continues to fall, and the quality of facilities remains a real issue. The challenge is to do more and to a level that fairly reflects the financial resources available in the game.

While the failed attempt to sell Wembley Stadium didn't cast the FA in the best light, it did highlight the need for more resources for the grass roots. Boris Johnson, leader of the victorious Conservative Party in the 2019 General Election, stated during the campaign that he would allocate £550 million extra for grass roots football to support a bid to bring the 2030 World Cup to Britain. The money would be used to provide 2,000 new Astroturf pitches and repair 20,000 grass surfaces to ensure that within ten years 'every family in England will be, on average, fifteen minutes from a great football pitch.'[31] Forty per cent of the spending would be allocated to the most deprived parts of the country, with an additional requirement to ensure female football would benefit. But the new administration had barely settled into Westminster when the pandemic hit the country. The launch of Project Big Picture restarted the process. Its proposals recognised the need to allocate more to grass roots football, reportedly offering £180 million.[32]

As we saw in Chapter 2, in 1999, after discussions with the government to head off a challenge to the collective-selling model for TV rights, the Premier League was said to have made a voluntary commitment to allocate 5 per cent of its revenues to 'good causes', primarily for investment in 'grass roots' – a principle that originated from the government's Football Task Force. Andy Burnham, then a young Labour MP, was an administrator on the Task Force and remains adamant that the eventual 5 per cent was agreed as part of their backing for the league's lucrative collective-selling policy, but has always acknowledged that the Premier League's and the Task Force's conceptions of this were subtly different. 'I think the Premier League has always seen the five per cent as a slightly movable, renegotiable commitment,' he says, 'and we never saw it that way – we saw it as a clear commitment.'

'Good causes' and 'grass roots' are open to interpretation too, which makes establishing what the Premier League and its clubs spend on them slightly challenging. In 2018/19, the accounts of the FA Premier League, the official name of the company set up to manage the competition, show a turnover of £3.3 billion. Five per cent of £3.3 billion would be £165 million, but according to the accounts,[33]

- £130 million goes to 'wider football support/good causes', of which there is reported expenditure of £6.5 million on football stadia improvements. £13.4 million goes to supporting wider football development and £109.9 million to solidarity, youth development and community activities.
- £77 million goes to 'charitable activities', comprising £17.3 million to the Football Foundation, £25 million to the PFA's charitable activities and £34.5 million to 'other community activities'.

The Premier League is always keen to stress its support for the wider professional game in England, and the 'solidarity payments' of almost £110 million cover support to teams outside the Premiership, to help with their ongoing operations. Over 90 per cent goes to clubs in the English Football League, but there is an allocation to the two tiers below the professional game. This is an important source of revenue for football in England but, like the football stadia fund, is expenditure going primarily to the professional game and not to 'grass roots' football. It seems that around £10 million of this total spend might be classified as actually going to 'good causes' rather than the football business.

All the items funded in the 'charitable activities' category are worthy causes. The investment in facilities by the Football Foundation is very important, especially as local authorities are under significant funding pressure. The PFA's charitable activities help both former players and communities, but only a portion of the expenditure can reasonably be classified as going to the 'grass roots'.

Overall, it appears that around £100 million went to good causes/grass roots, as loosely defined in 2018/19. On revenues of £3.3 billion, it is 3 per cent. If we include the solidarity payments, which I would argue are a payment for the benefit the pyramid provides in keeping the Premier League dynamic, the figure is just over 6 per cent. Using the lower, current TV deal, the figures are 3.3 per cent and 6.6 per cent.[34]

By comparison, in the 2018/19 season, the Premier League spent £273 million on parachute payments to clubs relegated. A payment designed to address a structural competitive imbalance is worth more than eight times what the Premier League donates to its charitable fund. Even more strikingly, in 2018/19 Premier League clubs spent just under £1.9 billion gross on transfers, of which £261 million was payments to agents – over £50 million more than the total of payments to good causes and for solidarity. Juan Mata launched an initiative to donate 1 per cent of his salary to good causes: with a wage bill of £2.9 billion, if all players joined, this alone would generate £29 million, very close to the effective charitable donation of the whole Premier League in 2018/19.[35]

It is not a generous approach by any reckoning. The good news is that Project Big Picture confirms even the elite appear to have realised that the current settlement is indefensible. Project Big Picture proposes both a significant increase in solidarity payments, which we will explore in the next chapter, and increased funding for grass roots and good causes to £180 million.

We now seem to have a unique opportunity to transform English football's relationship with its communities. With government willing to engage and provide resources, and two of the country's largest clubs recognising the need to allocate more to wider societal improvement, football must come to the table. A hundred and eighty million is a good starting point – approximately 6 per cent of Premier League TV revenues – but it represents less than 4 per cent of the total turnover of the Premier League and its clubs. There is scope to push a bit harder.

The next steps are an agreed vision with clear objectives, defined activities for the charitable, community side of English football, and an effective governance model. Football should provide the resources, but be only one of the voices deciding how the money is spent. Governance of any programme needs to be much more transparent and robust. An independent body is required. This fits naturally with the government's promised 'fan-led review'.

However, before moving on to solutions, there is one more aspect of football's transformation that we need to consider – the priority afforded to the men's national team. Improving the fortunes of the England team the FA's decision to support the creation of the Premier League. Let's see how it turned out and what the implications are for the future of the game.

8 IT'S COMING HOME

According to Alex Fynn,[1] who was there at the time, improving the performance of the England men's team at major tournaments was a major reason for the FA agreeing to support the creation of the Premier League in 1992. The record was dismal: Italia '90 had been the first time since the 1966 World Cup win that England had reached the last four of the competition, and the national team's first semi-final in any tournament since the 1968 European Championships. Once the generation of players who delivered the success in 1966 began to fade from the scene, England hit a particularly bad patch, failing to qualify for the 1974 and 1978 World Cup finals.

English football in the 1980s was a marathon, not a sprint. With no restrictions on the number of replays in cup competitions, clubs like Liverpool that were successful on the domestic and European fronts would face a daunting schedule of games, many on heavy, muddy, injury-inducing pitches. In winning 3 trophies in 1983/84, the club played 64 matches including 3 to beat Fulham in the third round of the League Cup and a replay to overcome Everton in the final.

Reducing the burden on the elite players was believed to be the way to improve the nation's footballing fortunes, offering more rest and time to work on technique. Hence, in the move towards creating the Premier League, the opportunity to reduce the top division to eighteen teams was the star prize for the Football Association.

While we have already identified how the operation of English football is not consistent with normal business practice, the most striking illustration of its unique nature is the way international football operates in parallel to the club game – it is highly unusual. Several times during the season and then again after the club campaigns end, players go off to play for another team with different management playing in competitions that offer no benefit to their employers, often returning with injuries – Stoke City goalkeeper, Jack Butland, missed over a season due to an injury sustained playing for England.

No other industry shuts down its operations for a few weeks every so often to allow its talent to go off for a few weeks to work for another business. So unique is the potential conflict between club and country, we shouldn't be surprised that it is so difficult to find the right balance. It is another example of why football, and other sports, can't be treated simply as normal businesses.

The Premier League couldn't come soon enough for the FA – the goodwill from England's successful campaign at Italia '90 had already faded after the disastrous campaign at the 1992 European Championships. But the new era didn't start well.

In 1993 I was in a packed Ullevaal Stadium in Oslo when Graham Taylor selected what must be one of the least organised England sides ever to take the field in a World Cup qualifier. English football is very popular in Norway. During the 1980s, games were broadcast live to Norway on Saturday afternoons, providing an opportunity for people to meet and have a few drinks before heading out on Saturday night. With alcohol very expensive due to high taxes, football provided a perfect excuse for 'pre-loading', as my children now call it.

Familiar, therefore, with the English game, once the starting XI was announced my Norwegian hosts started asking me what the England formation was, as the players didn't appear to fit into a recognised shape. They were correct: Gary Pallister as the left-sided centre back was completely dominated by Jostein Flo, and Lee Sharpe was all at sea as the wing back outside him. The loss was England's second in five days, and a subsequent defeat against Holland meant England failed to make the 1994 World Cup in the USA.

Journalist Joe Lovejoy summed it up: 'It was a bold imaginative game plan, but after only one training session in the new shape, England were always going to need time to sort themselves out, and, while they were doing so, Norway won the game.'[2]

The tactical acumen of Terry Venables then created a team able to interchange positions fluidly, more like the great Dutch teams than an English one, but the successful run to the semi-finals of Euro 1996 in England was a one off: it was not until Russia 2018 that the national team would again progress to the last four of a major tournament. In World Cups, England flattered to deceive. It sometimes felt like losing heroically was becoming the norm, such as in 1998 and 2006, when they lost on penalties against Argentina and Portugal respectively, having played with ten men for large parts of both games. But there were low points: being humiliated 4–1 by Germany in a last-sixteen knockout tie in South Africa, when the contrast between England and a young Germany was painfully evident; and limping out of Brazil with one point from three group games against Italy, Uruguay and Costa Rica.

Performance in the European Championships was no better. England were unable to better hosts Portugal in 2004 and lost on penalties to Italy in 2012 – the team had no grounds to complain, having been embarrassingly outplayed by their opponents. But a 2–1 defeat to Iceland in 2016 was the nadir.

As the England team returned home flushed with the success of their best World Cup run for nearly three decades, fans were trying to understand whether or not it represented a step change in performance. Would Russia be the start of an era of success? Had it just taken longer than we hoped for the Premier League to improve England's fortunes? The evidence was mixed. While it is true that England played well to beat Sweden in the quarter-final in 2018, the other two wins were in group games against Panama and Tunisia, arguably two of the weaker teams in the tournament, the latter only after a last-minute winner. More tellingly, in their three games against teams ranked in FIFA's top 20 in the world,[3] the Three Lions edged to a win on penalties against sixteenth-ranked Colombia, lost 2–1 to twentieth-placed Croatia, and were beaten twice by third-rated Belgium. By contrast, on an unbeaten run to the final, winners France defeated Peru (eleventh), Uruguay (fourteenth), Argentina (fifth) and Croatia and Belgium. England came up short against the strongest teams in the world – not that surprising for a country ranked twelfth going into the tournament.

Taking place 26 years after the launch of the Premier League in 1992, which was itself 26 years on from England's triumph in 1966, Russia 2018 provides an ideal basis to compare performance in the two eras. Assessing the performance of international teams over time is difficult because England's win ratio has increased in recent years as a result of an increased number of competitive fixtures against lower-ranking and smaller countries. To take this out of the equation, I analysed England's performance in the final stages of the World Cup and European Championship against countries that were in the top three of the world rankings going into the tournament – a total of 12 countries over the period from 1966 to 2018.[4]

Comparing results in the final stages of tournaments over the period 1966 to 1992 with those between 1993 and 2018, England's performance against the top twelve ranked teams declined from a 58 per cent of available points won before the Premier League was established to 39 per cent in the last twenty-six years. The win ratio since 1992 is also lower than the long-term average of 44 per cent against these twelve teams. If we take success in qualification for major tournaments as the basis of comparison, rather than the results in the final stages of the tournaments themselves, the findings tell the same story: no sign of significant progress up to and including 2018.

England's run to the final at the delayed Euro 2020, was a huge boost for the country still battling Covid-19. Reaching a semi-final and a final in successive tournaments was the team's best performance since 1966 and 1968.

While there are hints of an upturn, even after Euro 2020, there has been no upturn in results in the Premier League era. As in Russia, the team benefited from the draw in Euro 2020. Although victories over 13th-ranked Germany and 12th-ranked Denmark were welcome, England were unable to overcome the one team they faced from the world's top ten.

There is a perception that the England team underperforms. What level of performance is reasonable to expect from the national team? Actually, 'perception' is not strong enough – it is a widely held belief. Certainly, as anyone who has witnessed the build-up of excitement and anticipation before England depart for a major tournament and the intense post-mortem afterwards can testify, English football supporters expect the team to do well. But is it valid? The results above suggest England struggle against the world's best teams, but does this mean the team underperforms?

In *Soccernomics*, Simon Kuper and Stefan Szymanski argue that when we take experience (how many international matches a country has played), population size and national wealth into account, the England men's team has historically performed largely as would be expected.[5] In their view, it is the public's unrealistic expectations of the team that create the sense of disappointment that accompanies each failure to win a trophy. If we were more realistic, we might end up praising the team for what we often view as heroic failures.

It is the classic worry of suburban Britain – not keeping up with our neighbours. Since the creation of the Premier League, Euro 2020 is the only time England have reached a major final. By contrast, in the same period, Spain won the World Cup and two European Championships, Germany succeeded in both a World Cup and a European Championship as well as losing a final in each competition, and Italy won a World Cup and lost a final, and won one European Championship and lost in two finals. The French national team has been the most successful, winning two World Cups in 1998 and 2016, one European Championship in 2000, losing a final in each competition and winning the FIFA Confederations Cup twice, in 2001 and 2003. All but Germany have improved their success rate since 1992, and even Germany has won both the World and European competition in the last twenty-eight years. England did not have to open their trophy cabinet, never mind order a larger one.

Even if we accept the view that, over time, England has performed largely as might be expected, our results have declined relative to Italy, France and Spain by some margin during the Premier League era. If we want to ensure the improved results at Russia 2018 and Euro 2020 are the start of a new era, we need to start by understanding why the national team of the country with the richest league in the world lags behind its European peers on the international stage.

So intense is the sense of disappointment when England do leave a major tournament – recall the vitriol directed towards David Beckham after his sending-off against Argentina in France 1998[6], or the constant agonising over England's failure to win a penalty shoot-out – there is never a shortage of post-mortems to explain the outcome. In recent times, once the immediate anger has faded, the two most common reasons advanced to explain England's performance are: the long-standing concern over tiredness due to the demanding schedule; and the low number of English players in the Premier League.

Although modern Premier League players don't play the same number of games as the stars of the 1980s, does the competitive intensity of the Premiership and the fixture schedule help explain the performance of the national team? What could be significant is that the England team tends to be drawn almost exclusively from the Premier League: in Russia 2018 it was the only top nation to have a purely domestic-based squad.[7] If the competition is more demanding than others it could well leave players too drained to perform at their best in end-of-season international tournaments. Having noted that England didn't score in the second half of games in World Cup Finals in Japan and South Africa, Kuper and Syzmanski asserted: 'If there is a single culprit for England's summer failures, we suspect it's more likely to be fatigue than the foreign influx.'[8] For them, the high number of non-England qualified players in the Premier league was not to blame.

Modern top-flight football is a very physically demanding sport. When the 2020/21 campaign got underway, later than normal and with a shorter break from the previous season, injuries started to mount quickly. By early February, Liverpool had lost three central defenders for the season, and the absence of nine first-team players due to injury was clearly a factor in Southampton's 9–0 loss to Manchester United. Managers were quick to blame the schedule, arguing adequate rest periods are vital for player welfare.

Euro 2020 provides further evidence for the role fatigue can play. The suspension of football during the early stages of the pandemic led to a more compressed schedule for the 2020/21 season across Europe. As a result, the England team didn't arrive at the end-of-season tournament with its normal disadvantage.

It seems therefore reasonable to conclude that the Premier League's reluctance to accept a mid-season break, a feature common across Europe, has contributed to some extent to hampering the England team's chances. Even when one was finally introduced in 2019/20, it was a half-hearted scheme that appears unlikely to have a significant impact on player fitness for a summer tournament. With the 2022 Qatar World Cup to be played in the winter, we will have another opportunity to test the hypothesis on fatigue. All players from the European leagues will have had very similar schedules. Following on from success at Euro 2020, if England win the tournament, the case for more rest will be significantly strengthened.

Nothing is ever easy in English football. The research undertaken at Liverpool University I drew on previously found that games over the Christmas period attracted 10 per cent more viewers on average than might be expected. Here we have a reason for the reluctance of Premier League clubs to embrace the calls for a mid-season break: it is the most lucrative period of the calendar.[9] And supporters are not in favour of a mid-season break. In the 2017 Football Supporters' Association Survey, 50 per cent of respondents were opposed to any pause in the season even if it did not affect the Christmas schedule.[10]

Let's assume the game's owners and supporters can be persuaded to change to help the national team. Even if we can reshape the fixture schedule, will it be enough on its own to improve performance? What about the lack of England-qualified players? Has the internationalisation of the English game adversely affected the performance of the national team?

Cross-border trade, migration and capital flows are seen as beneficial by the overwhelming majority of economists, offering as they do opportunities for specialisation, knowledge-sharing and the generation of new ideas and working practices. Indeed, there is a view that the English game has been too insular, failing to take advantage of the knowledge available in the other countries that have outperformed England on the international stage. As Kuper and Syzmanski put it: 'England can have an excellent league, or it can have an English league, but it can't have both.'[11]

As we have seen during Brexit, and through the increasing number of trade disputes between major powers such as the USA and China, openness is not without its challenges: trade can increase overall wealth, but at the same time have distributional impacts, affecting groups in society in different ways, creating winners and losers. The UK government's focus on 'levelling up' the economy, an attempt to share the benefits of economic growth more equally across the country, is in part an admission that policy has failed to address some of the adverse impacts of an open economy.

Do we need specific policies for English football to mitigate the adverse impact of the internationalisation of the national game on the England team? In the pre-Bosman world, players from outside of the British Isles were a novelty. In the early 1980s, Argentinian World Cup winners Ossie Ardiles and Ricky Villa were a high-profile, pioneering duo at Tottenham Hotspur who memorably helped Spurs to win the FA Cup in 1981 – before they were forced to return home temporarily as a result of the Falklands War. But they were the exception: on the opening weekend of the Premier League in August 1992, only eleven non-British or Irish players featured in starting line-ups.[12]

The Bosman judgement came at a time when the funds flowing into the Premier League were just starting to grow. The impact was immediate. A much greater range of players was now available and, with English clubs having more resources than their foreign peers, the inflow of foreign talent accelerated rapidly. On Boxing Day 1999, four years after the Bosman case ended, Chelsea started their game with a fully non-English team, the first time this had happened. On Valentine's Day 2005, Arsenal were the first team to have no English players in their match day squad of sixteen.[13]

In pursuit of success, clubs have deployed their vast resources to attract the best talent in the world. On one weekend in December 2018, only fifty-three England-qualified players started Premier League games (fewer than three per team), going below the previous low of fifty-eight set during the 2015/16 campaign.[14] Chelsea and Newcastle United both started their matches that month without an English player in their eleven.

English football is an extreme case of globalisation. For the 2020/21 season, according to Transfermarkt, only one in every three of players in the twenty-five-man squads nominated by Premier League teams was England-qualified at the start of the campaign. In the Championship, League 1 and League 2, the percentage of foreign players, at 47 per cent, 34 per cent and 24 per cent respectively, was smaller but still significant. Over 40 per cent of all footballers in England were not qualified to play for the national team.[15]

This is an extremely high level of internationalisation. To put it in context, the highest level of non-UK workers in any of the major sectors of the UK economy at the time of the referendum on EU membership was food processing at 39.7 per cent.[16] As is so often the case, football has gone further than any other industry.

Just as in the wider economy, migration has benefitted the English club game. Firstly, the quality of football is higher, with the impact of new players going beyond match day – David Beckham, Gary Neville and their fellow Manchester United members of the 'Class of '92' have spoken of how Eric Cantona's approach to training inspired them to work harder.[17] Secondly, I believe the spectacle is more interesting than when English football was dominated by British players. Supporters have the chance to watch some of the world's best in the flesh. Thirdly, signings such as those of Japan's Kagawa and China's Sun Jihai by Manchester United and Manchester City respectively raise the profile of the game in their homelands, opening up new markets.

It is not clear that the Premier League is quite as elite a competition as it would have us believe. As I showed in Chapter 5, across a range of metrics, such as players featuring in World Cup-winning squads, winners of the Ballon d'Or and the success of domestic teams in Europe, the Premier League never comes out on top. Having looked at the issue in several ways, my view is that La Liga in Spain has the strongest claim to be seen as the league with the highest level of elite players. While there are more foreign players in England, quantity does not necessarily equate to quality, we should continue to work to ensure the quality in the English game is as high as possible.

Whatever the benefits, the current England manager is certainly concerned about the impact of the changing mix of players on the national team. Interviewed by the *Guardian* in 2019, Gareth Southgate said,

> We've got to arrest the slide ... Because it isn't correct to say we're not developing good players. There's tremendous work going on at our academies. The big concern for me is this graph continues to fall away and that we end up in ten years' time with an England manager who has got 15 per cent of the league to choose from. Why would that not happen? It is a big danger for us.[18]

Is there any evidence that the decline in the share of domestic players in the Premier League has hampered the England team? Looking at the successful international teams, Kuper and Syzmanski demonstrated that experience matters[19], but as international football only consists of a small number of games each season, I believe we need to consider club football as well as international caps to form a comprehensive view. As club competitions have expanded in size, today's top players now find themselves playing significantly more games in European competitions. With the richest clubs spending ever more to assemble talented squads, a match in the later stages of the Champions' League is of at least equivalent and potentially higher quality than an international contest between two of the leading football countries. The same is true of the Premier League: Manchester City versus Liverpool is a clash of footballing powerhouses.

To analyse the potential role of club-level experience in the success of international teams, I compared the number of senior club games in total played by the starting XIs in the tournament final of the five European countries that won the World Cup during the Premier League era. On average, the successful teams fielded line-ups boasting over 2,500 top-flight and 400 lower-league games under their belts. (European Champions' League winners throughout the 21st Century have had a similar average with only 3 of the 20 successful teams having a significantly lower total of senior games). Throughout most of the period England teams, during the game in which they were eliminated from the competition (I used this as a comparison as England didn't reach any finals), tended to have similar profiles. (2010 was an exception, when England's team had over 3,500 appearances, reflecting the last hurrah of the 'Golden Generation', with players possibly going to one tournament too many – the defeat to a young Germany in that tournament certainly seemed consistent with this view). Up to 2014, there is little evidence that English players were not obtaining the top-flight experience they needed to be competitive. To illustrate the point – the squad at the 2006 World Cup contained a set of household names, Beckham, Ferdinand, Gerrard, Lampard, Owen, Rooney sufficient for to name a starting XI of outfield players who had won the Champions' League. It seems other factors such as fatigue, poor tactics or selection are more likely to have determined the team's fate in this period.

In England's last three tournaments, however, in 2016, 2018 and 2020, the signs were that the higher share of foreign players in the Premier League is becoming a more significant influence on the experience levels of the England team. In the 2016 competition, England's last starting team had under 2,000 top-flight appearances and less than 400 lower-level games. The numbers fell to around 1,600 and 800 respectively in 2018, before edging closer to the 2016 levels at Euro 2020. A Premier League dominated by international players appears to have begun to restrict the opportunity for young English players to gain top-flight experience, leading many to spend time in the lower divisions to secure first-team professional football appearances. (This does provide further evidence of the important contribution the pyramid makes to the English game, of course.)

Just as we drew a distinction between the quality and quantity of elite players between leagues, so we should consider the type of experience the young players who do break into the Premier League acquire. In the semi-finals of Europe's two major club competitions, the Champions' League and the Europa League, in 2020/21, sixteen England qualified players featured in the first leg games, and eleven started in the two finals.

Although there is a reasonable case for believing fatigue may have hampered England's performance over the Premier League era, it is less clear that the number of non-England qualified players in the Premier League has hampered England's performance consistently during the period. The evidence suggests that only in the last few years have young English players struggled to gain the volume of experience historically needed to compete on the international stage and even then, the individuals who do break into the elite teams acquire valuable game-time at the highest levels of club football.

However, in England's two recent semi-finals, the absence of a midfielder able to control the game, as Modric and Jorginho did, highlights the detrimental impact of clubs relying on the international market in certain areas of the pitch. Our focus should be on the quality of players we develop not the quantity.

Turning to other possible explanations, has the national team suffered because the English game has been too insular rather than too open? Should the FA have been faster to appoint a non-English manager to lead the national team? While open to international players, has the English game been too inward-looking and failed to seek out the best leadership talent capable of bringing new techniques and ideas to bear?

It was probably inevitable that, as the number of foreign owners and players in top-level English football increased, so knowledge of the English game became less and less of a requirement for managers. Certainly, after Bosman, in the never-ending search for competitive advantage, owners turned to the international market for leadership talent, but have the English game and the England team benefitted from this inflow?

Who was the first foreign manager in English top-flight football? It's a great quiz question. I suspect many people would wrongly answer Arsène Wenger but he was actually fourth. Dr Jozef Venglos, who arrived at Aston Villa in the summer of 1990, was the first. Ossie Ardiles became the first foreign Premier League manager in 1993, and Ruud Gullit took over as player-manager at Chelsea in the summer of 1996.

Although not the first to arrive, Wenger was, it is widely acknowledged, the foreign manager who had the most significant impact on the Premier League, completely changing the approach to training, diet and management at Arsenal as well as introducing a European style of play. Other clubs began to copy his approach, but the transition to foreign managers was still relatively sedate. By the time Sven-Göran Eriksson became the first non-English manager of the England team in 2001, only ten foreigners had managed in the top division of English football. Of these, three had been at Chelsea and two at Tottenham Hotspur. By the time Avram Grant replaced Jose Mourinho in 2007 and Juande Ramos took over from Jacques Santini, both Chelsea and Tottenham Hotspur had hired five non-English managers, then Liverpool and Portsmouth with two each were the only other clubs that had recruited more than one.

The successes of Wenger and Mourinho, the first two managers to break Alex Ferguson's near-monopoly of the Premier League, increased the appeal of international talent. At the start of the 2018/19 season, only six Premier League teams were led by English managers. By 2020/21, the total was up to 8 as well as two other British managers in Brendan Rogers and David Moyes. Even so, this was a far cry from the inaugural campaign, when all twenty-two managers had spent the bulk of their playing careers in England, with fifteen Englishmen, five Scots, Welshman Mike Walker at Norwich City and Wimbledon's Irish international, Joe Kinnear (although he grew up in England from the age of seven). Even more strikingly, no English manager has ever won the competition. Reflect on that for a second: in the 'home' of football, the most prestigious competition has never been won by a manager from within the country. The Premier League truly is a competition without geographic boundaries.

Attitudes to hiring foreign managers in boardrooms vary widely. At the end of the 2019/20 season, forty-nine teams had played at least one season in the Premier League, and of these, twenty-four had had a foreign manager for at least a full season. Of the clubs never to have a non-British manager, many had not spent long in the top division, but clubs that had clocked up lengthy stays in the top flight, such as Stoke, Queens Park Rangers, Burnley and Bolton, had remained with British managers. Crystal Palace dipped their toe in the water with a combination of a brief caretaker arrangement and then the ill-fated seventy-seven days of Frank de Boer, but the total time under foreign leadership does not add up to a calendar year. Similarly, the half-year of Roberto di Matteo and the 123 days of Pepe Mel didn't quite get West Bromwich Albion to a full twelve months and Slaven Bilic's tenure only lasted 4 months of the 2020/21 campaign.

Even within the clubs willing to look outside of the United Kingdom, the propensity to hire an international boss varied significantly. By the summer of 2020, only seven clubs had been led by a non-British manager for more than half their time in the Premier League. No surprise that Arsenal led the list, with twenty-five of their twenty-eight seasons in the hands of Arsène Wenger, Unai Emery and Mikel Arteta. Next were Chelsea, with only five of their twenty-eight seasons entrusted to a British manager. Then came Liverpool and Tottenham Hotspur, both heading towards two-thirds of their Premier League tenure under foreign leadership. Finally, Manchester City, with just over half of their twenty-two seasons piloted by non-British bosses. (Watford and Huddersfield Town make up the list, but their top flight stays have been too brief to draw any firm conclusions). Alex Ferguson's long tenure at Manchester United explains why the Red Devils are the only one of the Big Six not to have had majority non-British leadership, but after the brief tenure of David Moyes all the club's recent hires have been from outside the UK.[20]

It is hard to compare the performance of foreign and British managers, as circumstances at different times make direct analysis difficult. I decided to use performance by club in the Premier League as the basis to try and identify trends. From my research, among the Big Six clubs non-British managers have done better than their club's average over time in every team except, for obvious reasons, Manchester United. Elsewhere, though, the picture is more mixed. Imported managers have performed better than the club average position at Leicester City, Everton and Southampton, but below the average at Newcastle, Aston Villa, West Ham, Fulham and Sunderland and others. In perhaps the most direct comparison, Wigan finished two places lower than their average position over eight years in the Premier League in the four seasons that Roberto Martinez led them – but he did lead them to FA Cup success.

Overall, when we account for differences in wages and transfer spending, the evidence is far from conclusive that appointing an international manager will lead to better results, and certainly doesn't support the dominance of non-English bosses in the top-flight.

Just as with players, the internationalisation of managers has benefits and costs. At times it has felt as though hiring a manager from abroad is the default option for certain clubs. Barney Ronay of the *Guardian* highlighted one of the strangest episodes – the career of Marco Silva: 'The sacked Everton manager has been in English football for three years, but has not grown roots at any of his three clubs, built no notable team and won only thirty-two league matches.'[21] It was a remarkable story: Silva was very much in demand for a time, despite little supporting evidence.

Fashions change, however, and the tide may be turning. There were eight English, one Scottish and one Welsh managers among the twenty that started the 2020/21 season, the highest share for some time, and Chelsea's Frank Lampard became only the second English manager to lead a team in two Champions' League campaigns, following in the footsteps of Sir Bobby Robson. 'Sometimes I think we have managers at home who can do the jobs as well,' pondered Lampard of his achievement.[22] Unfortunately, his tenure was a short one, replaced by German Thomas Tuchel, fresh from being fired by Paris Saint-Germain.

Turning to the national team, Fabio Capello's record as England's most successful manager, with a win rate of 76 per cent, appears to support the claim for the superiority of foreign managers. However, once more the case is not clear-cut. As previously identified, care is required with comparisons over time, because the higher number of fixtures against smaller countries in the modern era boosts success percentages – six of the eight England managers to have success rates above the average level between 1872 and 2020 have held the position since the launch of the Premier League. That Capello's successors, Roy Hodgson and Gareth Southgate, have success rates of 72 per cent and 74 per cent respectively (almost 76 per cent for Southgate if we exclude performances in the highly competitive UEFA Nations League that he is the only manager to have led England in)[23] suggests Capello's relatively strong performance may reflect the quality of the opposition he faced as well as his own ability. The championing of foreign managers also ignores the fact that the six times England have reached the semi-finals of major tournaments have all been with an English manager at the helm.

Even though the evidence suggests we should be careful in assuming that managers drawn from the global market are necessarily superior to domestic talent, it is undeniable that the likes of Arsène Wenger, Jürgen Klopp and Jose Mourinho have brought new ideas and practices to the English game, improving the quality on offer. It is a similar story elsewhere. The Spain-based football journalist Graham Hunter identifies the arrival of Johan Cruyff as manager of Barcelona as the catalyst for a change in Spanish football, from an aggressive, physical game to one of high technical quality.

> The influence which Cruyff had on all of Spanish football [is huge], not simply the fact that he worked several times at Barcelona ... There was an awareness, a jealousy and a will to adapt to intelligence, technique and ball retention, that stemmed with the Dream Team from 1989 onwards. Teams, coaches, youngsters all around the country said, 'That's how I want to play, that's what I admire.'[24]

Results since Cruyff arrived in Spain support the thesis. Spain successfully enhanced its own capabilities with ideas from elsewhere, and the results were spectacular for a country that had never previously won a major trophy. We should, though, be careful about drawing too much from one case: football does go in cycles, based on either a few talented players or an approach that others eventually find a way to counter. Germany's previous domination of the international stage is a good example, and Spain's recent pre-eminence has now ended. The next wave of success in Europe might well be based around the 'gegenpress'. As Jonathan Wilson has written in the *Guardian*, the Barcelona-inspired, possession-dominated model has come under

threat from a German model that focuses more on regaining possession than retaining it.[25] It is a more aggressive, physical school of
thought than the highly technical skills-based Spanish version.

Germany and Spain offer a contrast to England. Although English
football is known for its speed and power it hasn't been associated
with any specific innovation in playing style in recent seasons. In truth,
it is a long time since England provided the world with a tactical tem-
plate: it is telling that 'English Pragmatism' features twice as chapter
headings in Jonathan Wilson's masterful study of tactics over time,
Inverting the Pyramid.[26].

Identifying a national style is clearly a subjective exercise. Even
when England won the World Cup in 1966, Alf Ramsey's 4–4-2 (more
4–1-3–2 in big games), 'the wingless wonders', was a system he devised
rather than took from the domestic game – it was only adopted by
English clubs after the tournament.

Since then, while there has been an English way of playing the
game, it has typically been based on the physicality of the approach
often combined with the long ball game rather than any attempt to
dominate possession. Liverpool's success in the 1980s and 1990s was an
exception, centred as it was around passing and movement. Even the
most passionate believer in the superiority of the national game has to
accept that English football has never given rise to a widely accepted
tactical style such as *catenaccio* or Total Football in the modern game.

'Pragmatic' doesn't in any way do justice to the sophisticated management that Gareth Southgate has brought to the England team on and
off the pitch. However, his ability to extract the maximum from a squad
loaded with attacking and defensive wide players of the highest quality
but lacking a true elite central midfielder able to control the game, reflects
a pragmatic and realistic approach grounded in logic and deep analysis.

With no clear national style, why have England's best tournament
performances come under an English manager? That no country has
won the World Cup or the European Championship with a foreign
manager hints at the answer. Maybe the unique nature of international
football, a small number of games with little time to prepare and then
intense end of season tournaments places a greater premium on

knowledge of the players and motivation? Hence, managers who have developed in the same system as the players may be better placed to produce successful teams under the unusual circumstances international football operates under. Certainly the FA appear to have stumbled onto a manager with a unique appreciation of the pressure players face when representing the England men's team.

If this logic is correct, the consistent preference clubs have for foreign managers works against the national team by reducing the talent pool of English managers with top flight experience. Going into the 2020/21 season, of the Big Six teams that most England national players are chosen from, two had Spanish managers, while the other four were led by English, Norwegian, German and Portuguese coaches (and Frank Lampard, the English manager, would be fired in mid-season). Developing a larger group of experienced, elite English managers could be one factor in improving the national team. It is another example of the challenges the FA faces in trying to build a competitive national team while not having the control over the key decisions necessary to effect change.

What about players? We know from the analysis of the drivers of success in club football that the quality of players, measured by wages and transfers, is a key driver of success. Players from the Premier League certainly should have the quality to compete on the international stage. Since Marseille won the Champions League in 1992/93, the season the English Premier League started, Monaco and Paris Saint-Germain (aided by huge financial backing from its Qatari owners) are the only other clubs from France to have reached a final. By contrast, the Premier League has provided four winners and six beaten finalists. Yet, over the same period, while England have played in just two major semi-finals and one final, the French national team has won two World Cups, in 1998 and 2016; one European Championship in 2000; lost a final in each competition, and won the FIFA Confederations Cup in 2001 and 2003. Rather than simply celebrating the welcome upturn in England's performances, fans should now be asking, 'what is required now to ensure France, the country with the weakest major domestic competition in Europe does not outperform England, home of the richest domestic competition in the world, in future?'

The answer in part lies in the different balance in priorities in the two countries between the elite league and youth development. The French football authorities have invested in their national team over a long period of time. After years of under-performance, culminating in a disappointing campaign in the 1978 World Cup in Argentina, the French Football Federation completely revamped its approach to youth development. In 1988 a national academy was established at Clairefontaine outside Paris, the hub of a network of eleven regional academies.[27] Investment in youth has helped France produce world-class players and teams on a regular basis – fourteen of the twenty-three-strong 2018 World Cup-winning squad played abroad at the time of the competition.

The FA can claim success in its efforts to boost the England Women's team, the Lionesses, with two third-place finishes in the last two World Cups suggesting sustained progress, but it has yet to deliver on its promise to improve the England men's team to any measurable degree. It is not for want of trying. The FA recognised the need to improve the talent available to it, launching a number of efforts to improve the development of young players. The last was led by former England international, Trevor Brooking, a well-liked figure in the game. It came to an abrupt end. On 30 September 2010 the *Guardian* reported that the FA had retreated to concentrating on training coaches, developing grass roots players and offering support for international players, ceding control of player development to the professional game. 'Alex Horne [Brooking's boss as FA general secretary] has pulled Trevor round by telling him he was in danger of losing his legacy,' said an insider.[28]

The Elite Player Performance Programme (EPPP)[29] scheme emerged from that decision. Under EPPP, the FA undertakes the early-stage development of young players in schools or local clubs and the education of coaches, but then hands over responsibility for player development primarily to Premier League clubs. The FA is hoping that its investment in young players and coach education will create the platform from which Premier League clubs can develop future England players. The reality is that the coaches working with players under the EPPP will inevitably be influenced primarily by the management and objectives of the Premier League club they work for, and not by the future performance of the

England team. It is a difficult situation: the FA is relying on coaches it doesn't even employ to deliver success on its number-one objective.

In a sign that the FA recognised the benefits of the approaches to youth development adopted by Germany in 2000 and Spain in 1995, on 4 December 2014 the English FA unveiled an ambitious performance plan called the 'England DNA Philosophy' at the national football centre, St George's Park. Its aim was to create a unified philosophy to produce more quality players for the England team.

There are five main elements of the programme: who we are, how we play, the future England player, how we coach and how we support. From under-15 to senior level, every age group is meant to play the 'England way'. This means that, when in possession, England sides will 'intelligently dominate by selecting the right moments to progress the play and penetrate the opposition'. Out of possession, they will win the ball back 'intelligently and as early and efficiently as possible'.[30]

An inherent conflict between developing players for a Premier League club and for the England team is nothing new. From the first Football League proposal to shape the future governance of the game in 1990, the conflict between club and country was an issue. Clubs have every interest in shielding their players from international duty to ensure they are rested when the club needs them. By backing EPPP to deliver future England players, the FA is beholden to the clubs in the Premier League. Will clubs embrace the England DNA Philosophy? Given the profile of Premier League owners and managers, it seems unlikely.

EPPP is extremely favourable for Premier League clubs relative to other teams in the League pyramid. An academy requires significant funding, which will make it unaffordable for many clubs outside the top flight. Add to this that EPPP removed the ninety minutes travelling rule between a player's home and their club, reducing the ability of smaller clubs to capture some of the talent pool. Faced by competition from the richest, more glamorous clubs, the economics of investing in player development have become less favourable for smaller clubs. Under the current regime, clubs in the EFL help young players develop on loan but don't share in the future transfer proceeds.

Money matters in player development – Spain provides an example of how much effort and resource is required to develop young talent. In the Spanish version of *These Football Times* magazine, Nathan Bliss quoted Jon Townsend's identification of the role of the Spanish football federation in driving player development.[31]

> The commitment of the Real Federación Española de Fútbol (RFEF) to prioritise high-level, accessible and comprehensive coaching education through a national program ensured that talent from all over the country had access to the necessary resources, most notably the qualified coaching methodologies, from a young age.

Bliss compared Spain and England in 2013. At that time, the average cost of taking a UEFA A Licence course in England was £2,965, with a prospective English coach having to spend over £4,000 to go from UEFA Level 1 to UEFA A, and approximately 250 hours of teaching needed in order to qualify. In Spain, the cost of the UEFA A Licence was just €1,200, but 750 hours of teaching were required. Football coaching in Spain is much cheaper, but by the time they qualify coaches have more hours of teaching and experience under their belts.

This has had a profound impact on the number of coaches England and Spain produce. As of 2013, according to the UEFA Coaching Convention Statistics, there were just 1,395 English coaches with either UEFA A or Pro qualifications. Spain had 15,423, an incredible 1,000 per cent more. Just 203 coaches in England held a UEFA Pro Licence, the highest possible coaching level, while Spain had 2,140 – again, almost a thousand per cent more. There are no short cuts to success: time and resources are required.

The FA has identified the success of the England national teams as its number-one priority. While aiming high is to be applauded, the reality is that it is far from clear the FA has either the power or the resources to deliver on its ambition. Under the current governance structure, the FA has a limited influence over the development of young male players, reliant on its brief contact with them during international breaks and tournaments. It can choose the manager and coaching team, but players are owned and managed by clubs on a day-to-day basis. This has not always been successful. Between 2002 and 2012, the FA hired two foreign managers, but their tournament win records against the world's best teams were under 40 per cent.

On no measures has the England team's performance improved during the Premier League era. Despite the FA's optimism when it supported the creation of the new competition, the conclusion is unsurprising when we look at the structure of elite English football today. Majority foreign-owned and managed, with the highest number of non-national team-qualified players of any major league and with a governance structure biased towards clubs, no incentives exist in the Premier League to favour the England team. In a stark contrast to the situation in France, the FA gave away much of its control over English football at the top level when it agreed to the creation of the Premier League.

Alongside improved tournament form, there are other signs of progress. The creation of a national centre at St George's Park has been a success and, despite the limited control the FA now has over the development of young players, within just two-and-a-half years of the launch of the England DNA programme, England's youth teams started to achieve success at international tournaments. Successes so far have included: Under-17 European Championship runners-up, Toulon Tournament winners, Under-20 World Cup winners, Under-21 European Championship semi-finalists, Under-19 European Championship winners and Under-17 World Cup winners.

We also need to draw on the depth of the English game to maximise our chances of developing talent. Beyond its inexperience – the least number of caps in a squad since Terry Venables' group in 1996 – the most striking feature of the line-up selected by Gareth Southgate for Euro 2020 was how many players had gained experience outside of the Premier League. The whole of the pyramid contributes to player development and we must continue to support and sustain it.

There are as many theories for England's performance as there have been failures. I don't believe there is a simple answer. In my view we need to focus on several areas: continuing to work on improving the approach to talent development; considering if the changes to the rules over domestic players in squads can be tweaked to increase the top-flight club experience of promising English players; recognising that although the internationalisation of playing squads and managers has brought benefits to the game, it does appear to have made it harder to create a clear playing identity for the national team; investment in the development of managers and coaches, offering the additional benefit of making the game more diverse given the low number of BAME coaches in top level English football; and ensuring England teams are as rested as possible before major tournaments.

However, there is a conflict between the interests of the national team and those of the national game. Internationalisation has improved the offer and commercial reach of the Premier League, but at some cost to the England team. While either a mid-season break or fewer fixtures would offer more opportunities for players to rest, both could potentially have a negative impact on the commercial performance of clubs, especially if European club competition is expanded.

The first step therefore is to decide if we want to bring football home and have a more successful England team. Supporters appear to be in favour: 66 per cent of respondents to the EFL's 2019 survey of supporters identified the England team as important or very important compared to 12 per cent who had the opposite view. In addition, respondents to both the EFL's 2019 survey and the FSA's 2017 Supporter Survey viewed the inclusion of local players in teams as important, 83 per cent and 78 per cent respectively – investment and promotion of domestic talent is something supporters want.[32]

There is no mention of national teams in the brief of the fan-led review of governance. Without an agreed way forward, the game will be locked in a continual battle between competing camps – we should include it in our conversation.

We have come full circle. The men's national team was central to the moves to create the Premier League but is currently not on the radar of the current debate about the future of English football. Now is a good time to turn to the governance. What do we need to do to ensure we get the game we want?

9 YOU DON'T KNOW WHAT YOU'RE DOING

Montenegro would not have been most people's choice as the opposition for the 1,000th competitive game played by the England men's football team. While it is always good to win landmark games, the team's 7–0 victory was achieved too easily to fire the imagination of the Wembley crowd on a cold November evening.

Doing what it does so well, however, the Football Association pulled out all the stops to commemorate the occasion. Although no members of the Royal Family graced the match on 14 November 2019, football 'royalty' was out in force: World Cup winners Geoff Hurst and George Cohen; Paul 'Gazza' Gascoigne; Fabio Capello and many other leading lights. They provided the cabaret for the assembled representatives of the constituent parts of the Football Association: an overwhelmingly white, middle-aged, male audience in their blazers and suits. I remember thinking how much it illustrated the scale of the challenge facing my host for the evening, Sanjay Bhandari, the newly appointed chair of Kick It Out, the organisation dedicated to tackling discrimination in football. My personal highlight of the pre-match festivities was Matt Lorenzo's interview with Paul Gascoigne, during which, in the space of barely a minute, the Geordie maestro made a joke that would have failed most PC tests, spoke passionately about football and ended up overcome by emotion.

By contrast, the Football Association Chairman Greg Clarke's speech was low-key. At such a feelgood event, I was surprised he chose to reiterate what he had said earlier in the year at a Digital, Media and Sport Committee of the House of Commons, on the FA's role:

> Historically, the Football Association is a stakeholder organi-
> sation run by its stakeholders. We have the National League, the
> Premier League and the Football League ... For as long as I am
> aware ... the competitions have written their competition rules
> and enforced them. They have never been enforced by the FA.[1]

Where to start? It is an interpretation of football's history that ignores much of the past. When professional football emerged out of Northern and Midlands towns in the nineteenth century (there were no clubs from the south of England among the twelve founder members of the Football League), the amateur-led, southern-based Football Association embarked on a struggle to protect its leadership role. 'The rivalry between the Football Association and the Football League', as Alex Fynn says, 'goes back to the origins of organised football itself'.[2]

It was not an easy task. In order to maintain a balance between finance and competition while ensuring financial stability, the two bodies were forced to collaborate to restrict the commercial freedom enjoyed by both owners and players. Despite a loosening of the constraints on player wages and contracts in the 1960s, these efforts were reasonably successful in balancing interests until the richest clubs began a concerted push for more commercial freedom in the late 1970s/ early 1980s.[3]

Faced with mounting pressure from both owners and the Football League, the FA tried to take control of the game, but was unable to stem the tide of reform. To reduce the demands on top players, it agreed to support the formation of the Premier League, which was to be 'governed by a committee of the FA'. Charles Hughes, the FA's Director of Coaching and Education at the time took this to mean 'The FA would run the new league.'[4] When the breakaway clubs went back on their commitment to move to a league of eighteen clubs, the FA nevertheless acquiesced. The 'Big Five' richest clubs had got what they wanted – probably more than they expected, and certainly more easily than they could ever have imagined.

Speaking to David Conn of the *Guardian* in 2004, Graham Kelly, Chief Executive of the FA at the time of the breakaway, had seen things very differently to Greg Clarke:

> We at the FA missed a golden opportunity. The clubs were desperate for their freedom, and they would have given virtually anything to be granted that. We could have done so much more to get it right, by saying the FA is here for the good of the whole game, and developed a structure which worked. So many things have come back to haunt us, which could have been dealt with by establishing principles then: on the financial integrity of the game, on agents, good management of clubs, putting country before club. I still do not believe that big clubs should subsidise small clubs which are badly run, but we should have ensured a more equal distribution of the money, not allowed them to keep it all. We were guilty of a tremendous, collective lack of vision.[5]

It was a brutally honest assessment of the FA's failure to take the opportunity to entrench itself as the guardian of the game's legacy and its guide for the future. Kelly identified the components of an effective framework for the regulation of the game that is as valid today as it was then: have one body responsible for the whole pyramid; shape the game's finances to reflect the interests of the whole of English football; clearly define the relationship between club and country; and introduce a structure for regulating finances and conduct.

Kelly was right. The creation of the Premier League was a watershed moment, creating a third force, alongside the FA and Football League, in an already ineffective structure for managing the game. The abject failure of leadership by the FA left the elite of English football free to pursue their commercial agenda largely unconstrained by financial regulation. Almost a century of work to balance the commercial and sporting dimensions of the game was undone. Ever since, the FA has struggled to define its role in the English game. Even when things appear to be improving, a crisis is never far away. The summer of 2018 was no exception.

When the England men's team touched down at Birmingham Airport after their widely acclaimed campaign in the 2018 World Cup in Russia, sentiment towards the national team was at its most positive since Euro 96. 'Three Lions' was back at number one in the charts, the team was being feted for its diversity and humility, and the sports pages were full of calls for manager Gareth Southgate to be knighted. Twenty-six years after the Premier League was launched, the England team had matched its performance at Italia '90 and the Football Association had delivered national men's team success of a sort – one of its original justifications for supporting the creation of the Premier League. It seemed too good to be true.

It was. Within weeks the FA had embroiled itself in more controversy.

All summer, the FA's proposal to sell Wembley Stadium to raise funds for grass roots football had been bubbling along in the background. Barely had the England players boarded their flights for Ibiza, Mykonos and Florida when things started to come to a head. Yet rather than devoting all its energies to completing the transaction, the FA, presumably to capitalise on the favourable mood after Russia, went off on a tangent, floating the idea of bidding to stage the 2030 World Cup. For observers of the FA's actions, it was Groundhog Day. Rather than enjoy its moment in the sun, the FA chose to bring the two issues that had caused it huge problems in the recent past back into the headlines.

When it supported the creation of the Premier League, the FA effectively gave up its position as head of the professional game, leaving itself with three major assets: Wembley Stadium; the FA Cup; and the England men's team (in the early 1990s the FA paid little attention to the women's game) plus its position in the global game. Over the next three decades the management of all of them would turn out to be extremely problematic, eroding the FA's reputation and credibility. (As we have seen in Chapter 8, it was not until success in 2018 and 2020 that the FA could claim it was making progress with the men's national team.)

Built for the Empire Exhibition in 1924, and hence often called the 'Empire Stadium', Wembley Stadium was opened by King George V on 28 April 1923 for the FA Cup Final between Bolton and West Ham. Exactly how many people attended the game is unknown, but most estimates suggest it was around double the stadium's capacity of 127,000, with thousands more locked outside. Bolton won 2–0 in a game that became known as the 'White Horse Final' because of the role a white police horse named Billy played in pushing the crowd that had spilled onto the pitch back behind the touchlines to ensure the game could take place.

After such a challenging opening, Wembley recovered and acquired legendary status amongst sports fans the world over. It staged famous events such as the 1948 Olympics and Henry Cooper's World Heavyweight Title fight with Cassius Clay (later Muhammad Ali). The 'Matthews Cup Final' in 1953, England's 6–3 defeat to the Hungary of Ferenc Puskás and Nándor Hidegkuti, and England's only World Cup win in 1966, are three of the many historic football games staged there. Wembley was a flexible venue too, hosting world-class speedway and Rugby League Challenge Cup finals and in 1985 hosting the UK leg of Live Aid, as well as regular greyhound meetings.[6] Hard though it is to imagine today, the owners of Wembley Stadium refused to cancel the scheduled greyhound racing during the 1966 World Cup, forcing Uruguay–France to be played at the White City Stadium.[7]

Legendary as the venue was, the torrential rain that poured down on 7 October 2001 for the whole of the last game at the old stadium left everyone inside the ground in no doubt that it was time to move on: old-fashioned seating, awful toilets and outdated catering facilities. It was substandard for a modern stadium in every respect – even the executive box I was in was a relic from another age. A 1–0 defeat to Germany that provoked Kevin Keegan's resignation as England manager was a suitably downbeat ending for a venue long past its peak.

In *Broken Dreams*, Tom Bower forensically dissects the process through which the new stadium eventually emerged.[8] Although the FA acknowledged that a new stadium was required, it dragged its feet, leaving Sport England, backed by National Lottery funding, to take the initiative, launching a competition to design a new national stadium in

YOU DON'T KNOW WHAT YOU'RE DOING   201

1994. Once again, the FA was on the back foot, but in 1999 it eventually bought the old stadium and set up Wembley National Stadium Limited (WNSL), chaired by Ken Bates, the controversial chairman of Chelsea. In the press at the time there seems to have been little concern with the appointment of a man who had once suggested that an electric cattle fence might be an effective means of crowd control.

Growing interest in a bid by London to host the Olympics led to calls for a stadium capable of hosting football and athletics, along the lines of the Stade de France. Dual-purpose arenas, especially for football and athletics, usually fail both sports: the design suffers, and the costs go up. Crucially, the French government recognised the problem and allocated the Stade de France project £500 million of funding, significantly more than the £120 million allocated to Wembley by Sport England. After a very acrimonious process, Wembley was left to be redeveloped as a football stadium, and the Government decided to build a new London Stadium as the centrepiece of the 2012 Olympics.

The UK, or more accurately London, thus ended up with two world-class venues, both with significant financial challenges. In 2013, in a move to ease the burden, the Mayor of London reached an agreement to allow West Ham United to use the London Stadium in winter, with the stadium converting back to an athletics facility when needed in summer. Anyone who has watched football there, particularly as an away fan seated at a very strange angle to the pitch, would agree that football and athletics don't mix. Correct as the FA was to push for a football-only venue, the way it handled its campaign meant it lost significant amounts of political capital along the way.

If the battle over the design of the stadium was painful for the FA, the problems in the delivery of the project did even more damage to its reputation. Tom Bower reports that the original estimate for the project was £136 million. It eventually cost £798 million[9] before financing costs, suggesting a total expenditure of around £1 billion – probably 50 per cent more than the Stade de France, and at the time comfortably the most expensive association football stadium in the world.

The venue finally opened in early 2007, four years late. Even after completion, the stadium continued to attract criticism. Even though the pitch was re-laid ten times between the stadium opening and 2010, a plethora of managers and players, including Sir Alex Ferguson, David Moyes, John Terry and Slaven Bilic, criticised the surface. 'It's a disgrace,' said Spurs manager Harry Redknapp after losing to Portsmouth in the 2010 FA Cup semi-final. 'You have to spend the whole time making sure you don't fall over. That can't be right, can it? How can you play on a pitch you can't stand up on?'[10]

Insufficient sunlight making it onto the grass was identified as a reason, but other factors undoubtedly played a part. Needing to generate additional revenues to cover the stadium's cost, Wembley agreed to host the NFL International Series of American football matches. There is a reason why most NFL teams have Astroturf pitches. Gridiron games, based as they are around intense scrimmages in the middle of the pitch, can cause significant damage to a grass surface on wet autumn days. The nadir came when the FA allowed Tottenham Hotspur to use the stadium while their new ground was being built. When Spurs played Manchester City the day following an NFL game, the American football markings and NFL logos were still visible on the turf, and there was worn grass in the centre and on the touchlines.

The rebuilding of Wembley Stadium exposed the weaknesses of the FA's structure and its lack of the managerial, financial and political skills required to run an effective major delivery programme. This failure to execute plans successfully is a theme that recurs across the organisation's activities at home and abroad, and nowhere more so than in its bids to host future World Cup tournaments.

The first bid was for the 2006 World Cup. The Labour Party were enthusiastic backers, setting out their support in their 1997 election manifesto. The bid was in trouble almost before it started, states Tom Bower, with the major European nations making it clear that they were supporting Germany because they believed the FA had agreed to support the German 2006 bid in return for being awarded Euro 96. Bert Millichip, the FA Chairman, continued to deny he had made this verbal agreement, and the FA pressed on regardless of the opposition.[11]

England then alienated many of their allies when they backed Sepp Blatter for FIFA president rather than the President of UEFA Lennart Johansson, believing Blatter would back an England bid. Ham-fisted attempts to win the support of Thailand and the Caribbean Federation vote (via Trinidad and Tobago) were unimpressive but not terminal. By contrast, the revelation that FA Secretary Graham Kelly and Chairman Keith Wiseman had authorised secret payments to the Welsh FA to gain support for Wiseman in the election to be a FIFA vice-president was the final nail in the coffin.[12] Both men were forced to resign, and England went out in the second round of voting with two votes.

With lessons apparently learnt, especially the need to resource the bid properly and be more effective in building relationships within FIFA, a bid for the 2018 World Cup, backed by both main parties in their 2010 election manifestos, was launched. Unfortunately, as David Conn reported in detail,[13] international football politics had moved on and were now even murkier. The *Sunday Times* acquired recordings of conversations that made it very clear votes were for sale,[14] a BBC *Panorama* investigation[15] linked FIFA officials to secret payments for the selling of broadcast rights, and Lord Triesmann, FA Chairman between 2008 and 2010, claimed the same in evidence to a select committee.[16] Unsurprisingly, the revelations didn't endear the FA to FIFA delegates. It was no surprise when the English bid, despite backing from the Prime Minister, the Duke of Cambridge and David Beckham, secured only two votes and the competition was awarded to Russia. With hindsight, the bid was probably unwinnable from the start given the way the process unfolded, nevertheless having raised expectations, the FA's image did take a hit with the footballing community.

Seemingly oblivious to the painful experiences of two such chastening campaigns, that if nothing else had demonstrated how unpredictable the bid process is, the FA appeared keen in the summer of 2018 to embark on a third. This was a surprise to say the least. Two years earlier, the organisation had launched the FA Strategic Plan for 2016 to 2020, a very wide-ranging programme which defined the FA's role as to 'support and grow the grass roots game while continuing to strive for success at the elite level ... Our number-one goal', it went on, 'is to improve the tournament record of the England senior men's team.' Seven priority objectives were identified:

- **England teams**: England men's and women's senior teams ready to win in 2022 and 2023.
- **Education**: A world-leading education programme for a diverse football workforce.
- **Female football**: A doubling of the player base and fan following of female football.
- **Participation**: Flexible, inclusive and accessible playing opportunities for everyone.
- **Digital engagement**: Direct engagement with every fan, player and participant.
- **Regulation and administration**: Trusted regulation, efficient administration and world class competitions.
- **Venues**: Management of Wembley and St George's Park.[17]

There was no mention of a World Cup bid. Yet in the summer of 2018, the FA chose to take on a major new commitment, despite being involved in a series of protracted investigations into historic governance issues. Such was the seriousness of these issues, stretching managerial resources to pursue an aim not identified in the existing Strategic Plan was a major gamble.

In mid-November 2016, disturbing allegations started to emerge of widespread historic sexual abuse at football clubs dating back to the 1970s.[18] The FA, supported by the NSPCC, set up a helpline, which within a week received 860 referrals from around 350 individuals alleging abuse. In the same month the FA announced it was to set up an internal review, led by independent counsel Kate Gallafent QC,[19] to identify exactly how much Crewe Alexandra and Manchester City knew of the activities of the convicted paedophile Barry Bennell, who had worked at both clubs. An ex-minister for sport, Gerry Sutcliffe, proposed that an independent body should look at the issue rather than the FA investigating itself: 'What I've seen in football over the years is that they're very narrow, very insular, and may not do a proper job even though with the right intentions.'[20]

After several iterations, Clive Sheldon QC assumed responsibility for the inquiry. In March 2018, it was reported that the scale of evidence provided, plus the 'chaotic nature of the archiving', had delayed the inquiry team's sift through the FA's legal files.[21] The level of activity was immense: around 500,000 pages of material from 6,000 files were uploaded to a digital platform. The scope of Sheldon's review went beyond Crewe and Manchester City, including incidents at Aston Villa and Leicester, because of the crimes of the late Ted Langford, and Newcastle, owing to the club's involvement with George Ormond, who is serving twenty years for sexually abusing boys over three decades.

In July 2018, it was reported that the FA's independent inquiry had found no evidence of an institutional cover-up or of a paedophile ring operating within football.[22] When Sheldon finally reported in March 2021, his findings were stark. He concluded: 'This was an institutional failing by the FA, for which there is no excuse,' going on to say: 'The FA did not do enough to keep children safe,' adding: 'Child protection was not regarded as an urgent priority for the FA.'[23]

Further questions about the FA's leadership arose after England women's international, Eniola Aluko, convinced she had been unfairly dropped from the national team, wrote to the FA to make a grievance report in January 2016. Although an initial internal FA inquiry and a subsequent investigation led by barrister Katharine Newton found no evidence of wrongdoing, Aluko was paid £80,000 by the FA.[24] After more evidence emerged, a third investigation led by Newton was commissioned. The barrister concluded that Mark Sampson, manager of the England Women's football team, had racially abused Aluko and her teammate Drew Spence.[25] Although the FA apologised to Aluko, when interviewed by the *Guardian*, the player clearly remained unhappy about her treatment, describing the process:

'It was about Eni Aluko versus the FA – David versus Goliath. The PR machine of the FA was "Make Eni look as bad as possible". It was a smear campaign.'[26]

The FA's handling of the Aluko case highlighted the broader lack of significant progress in addressing racial inequalities in the English game. Since 1990, one in four – just under 25 per cent – of retired England internationals have been black or from an ethnic minority background (BAME). This does not translate into management roles, as the ratio falls to around one in seven.[27] A report in 2015 by the Sports People's Think Tank found just twenty three of 532 coaches in senior coaching positions in the English game came from a BAME background.[28] In 2018, the sports journalist Jonathan Liew wrote that just 7 per cent of the Premier League and Football League managers at that time, and 2.6 per cent of all the permanent managers in Premier League history, were BAME. According to the League Managers' Association, almost two-thirds of all the BAME managers in Football League history never obtained a second job.[29]

When the FA published its 2018 annual report on progress,[30] it became clear that the organisation was struggling to deliver on its objectives. While women's football was moving forward both in terms of the national team and participation, progress on the other priorities had been weaker. Participation in men's football had continued to decline; digital engagement had been slow moving; and the education plan was behind target.

Against this backdrop, the announcements in the summer of 2018 of the proposed sale of Wembley Stadium and of a possible bid for the 2030 World Cup, neither of which had been mentioned in the strategic plan, seemed brave at best, foolhardy at worst. All organisations need to be flexible, but these new proposals raised questions about the FA's decision-making and strategic discipline, coming as they did at a time when the FA knew it was struggling to deliver on its existing priorities. If you have limited resources, don't take on more things, is a sensible rule. With an already full agenda, and after investing so much time and effort and public funding to back the creation of a new national stadium and finally getting it up and running, why would the FA consider selling it? And why embark on a World Cup bid at the same time?

As is usually the case in football, money provides the answer. In the summer of 2018, the FA still owed £112 million to public bodies such as Sport England, the Department of Culture, Media and Sport and the London Development Agency, that had helped to fund the stadium's construction. Although the FA had been successful in growing broadcasting and sponsorship revenues, the 2018 accounts showed a worrying drop in income from Club Wembley, the 10,000 premium memberships seats in the middle tier of the stadium. As the original ten-year debentures expired, under the new contracts revenues initially fell by almost £20 million.[31]

The financial burden of Wembley was exacerbated by the declining commercial value of the FA Cup. As with other areas of the English game, the rise in importance and power of the Premier League has diminished the attractiveness of a trophy that was still undeniably the most famous domestic cup competition in the world. Games like the White Horse and Matthews finals had given it legendary status, but these days it just doesn't make enough money.

In the days when football on TV was strictly limited, FA Cup Final Saturday was the highlight of the football calendar, kicking off an intense period of live football that would usually include both the European Cup and the European Cup Winners' Cup finals, the annual England–Scotland game and possibly an England tour game or tournament qualifier. Both the BBC and ITV would cover the FA Cup with a whole day of programming devoted to the build-up, with specially adapted shows such as family favourite *It's a Knockout*, and cameras in the team hotels and on the way to the ground.

With the rewards from the Premier League now so great, however, the elite clubs have chosen to deprioritise the FA Cup, fielding weaker teams – often closer to a second eleven – to rest their star names and avoid injuries. Such is the gap that has emerged between the elite and the rest that the approach of fielding weakened teams has not significantly affected the success rate of the top teams. In 2019, Manchester City were able to beat Watford 6–0 despite leaving several of their best players out of the starting eleven.

In fairness to the FA, the arrival of the Premier League and the packaging that went with it probably meant that the decline of the FA Cup was inevitable. The FA has had to work very hard to maintain interest in the competition, forced to limit and then eliminate replays from later rounds and to accept penalty shoot-outs. Unsurprisingly, average TV audiences have fallen as the competition has lost some of its appeal. Interest in the competition peaked for the 1970 final between Chelsea and Leeds, with over 20 million people watching the 2–2 draw at Wembley, followed by a record 28.49 million tuning in for the replay at Old Trafford, only 100,000 or so viewers less than watched the Apollo XI moon landing in 1969. In the last decade, viewer numbers for the final have been around 7.7 million, with the high spot being the nine million people who tuned in to Arsenal versus Aston Villa in 2015.[32] With football returning to TV after lockdown in 2020, the FA Cup Final in August attracted 8.2 million viewers.[33]

Money worries make the FA's interest in selling Wembley and launching a World Cup bid easier to understand. Divesting itself of the stadium would reduce the financial burden and generate resources for grass roots football, while a World Cup offered the prospect of a significant financial boost to the wider game, not just the England team. As the World Cup bid quickly stalled, however, owing to uncertainty over FIFA's process, it was the proposed sale of Wembley that captured the unwanted headlines.

Owning and running a stadium with a heavy financial burden is not essential to achieving the organisation's strategic objectives; quite the opposite as it eats up resources. Unfortunately, the FA completely failed to get this message across, leaving the public unconvinced about the need to give up ownership and control of the national stadium. Giving evidence to the DCMS Select Committee on the sale, Gary Neville spoke for the public:

> There is a little bit of gut instinct in this. If a multi-billionaire knocks on your door and says he wants to buy something off you, straight away you curl up into a ball and think, 'He must

know something I don't.' There is just something instinctive about that. You know what I mean. I don't know the science behind the sale, but there is something that is quite instinctive that says, 'I feel a bit uncomfortable with this.'[34]

When the preferred bidder, Shahid Khan, owner of Fulham and the Jacksonville Jaguars NFL team, pulled out of the sale citing lack of support from the FA Council, he exposed the FA's governance challenges. Although the FA board approved the sale, the discussion at the 127-member FA Council was described as 'healthy', suggesting a far from resounding level of support. Shahid Khan issued a statement:

> The intent of my efforts was, and is, to do right by everyone in a manner that strengthens the English game and brings people together, not divides them ...
>
> Following last week's FA Council hearing, it appears there is no definitive mandate to sell Wembley.
>
> My current proposal, subsequently, would earn the backing of only a slim majority of the FA Council, well short of the conclusive margin that the FA Chairman has required.[35]

As well as damaging the organisation's credibility, both the sale process and proposed World Cup bid served to divert resources away from the major challenges the FA was facing elsewhere in the regulation and administration of the English game.

Adding to the catalogue of poor performance, the 2019 annual report from the equality and inclusion charity Kick It Out noted that reports of discrimination in professional and grass roots football were up by 32 per cent from 319 the previous season to 422. 'For me, at the moment, it's like the Wild, Wild West,' Kick It Out's Development Officer Troy Townsend told the *Guardian*.

> It's a free-for-all out there. I have genuine concerns that something may happen. We see some pretty horrendous stuff. We've seen actual bodily harm. Blood pouring out of a player's face,

his shirt on the ground with blood all over it. Targeted Islamo-phobia at its worst degree.[36]

And the situation is getting worse not better. In the 2018/19 season racist incidents resurfaced in the professional game. When Manchester City travelled to Chelsea in the Premier League, footage posted on social media showed a home fan allegedly subjecting Raheem Sterling to racist abuse. This was a week after a Tottenham supporter had thrown a banana skin at Arsenal's Pierre-Emerick Aubameyang during the north London derby. West Ham, Millwall and Burnley supporters were also accused of racist behaviour during the season, as English football appeared to be heading backwards rather than forwards.[37] Even after the emergence of the Black Lives Matter movement and widespread support from all of football's stakeholders, racist incidents continue to plague the game. Kick It Out's 2020 Report found racist incidents in the professional game had increased by 42 per cent in the 2019/20 season despite a significant number of games being played in empty stadia. There are no signs of any let up: During the 2020/21 season online abuse has become a very public concern, with numerous players in both the men's and women's game targeted.

Off the pitch there are few signs of progress with only 2 BAME managers in the top two divisions in the English game in the 2020/21 season, both appointed part way through the campaign. It is time for innovative thinking. Having described football on social media as 'a battleground of hate', drawing on his extensive professional experience, new Chairman Sanjay Bhandari is driving a new data-intensive approach. 'I am angry that racism and discrimination still exists. But analytics is our strategy. We need to get better insights to have a better strategy.'[38]

The constant stream of incidents serves to highlight the FA's inability to shape and control events. As the failed Wembley Stadium sale demonstrated, the FA lacks the power, credibility and resources to lead the wider game in its current form. It defines its scope as ranging from grass roots to the elite, acting as the regulator and administrator of the game. This sounds like the scope a football association should have, but it glosses over the FA's lack of influence across the four professional divisions. Greg Clarke put the FA's case on several occasions: that it prefers to describe itself as having delegated power to the Premier League and English Football League to regulate themselves. The reality is, as Graham Kelly so honestly admitted, that the FA missed its opportunity and gave away its power.

Without real influence over the professional game, the FA cannot provide the English game with the integrated, top-to-bottom leader-ship it requires. The efforts to sell Wembley Stadium and attract a World Cup tournament demonstrate just how severe the organisation's financial constraints are. Yet, ask a typical supporter to outline what the FA does, and the chances are the answer will suggest a remit that significantly overstates its role and influence. When the financial crises in Bury and Bolton hit the headlines in the summer of 2019, the FA's inaction would have surprised many people, but in fact the FA controls the very top of the English game – the national teams – and the game *below* the four professional leagues, but it is largely absent from the huge space in the middle, the place where all the power and money sits. There is no power vacuum: the largest share of the gap in the FA's remit is filled by the Premier League.

This structure goes a long way to explaining the governance chal-lenges the whole of English football faces. Ever since it was created, in reality even before it began operating, the Premier League has been extremely successful in: protecting its own interests; maximising the commercial opportunities available to it; and heading off attempts to establish any meaningful regulatory oversight of its activities by either the Government or other football bodies. Although in theory the Premier League sits at the top of the pyramid of leagues that make up English football, it actually operates outside the pyramid altogether, free to pursue its own agenda.

As the efforts by the elite clubs to restructure the game in 2020 and 2021 demonstrated, the pursuit of self-interest alongside the emer-gence of a cadre of international owners has distanced the elite from the traditions of the game. That the attempts to reshape the game in-volving members of the so-called "Big Six" failed twice in six months shows just how out of touch they were. Reform is required to make sure the balance between the pursuit of money and the interests of the game is restored.

It is not only the Premier League that operates outside of the FA's influence: the other three professional leagues in the EFL follow their own paths. With both competitions self-governing, but each division having control over its own affairs, it is a recipe for confusion.

Fragmented governance of the English game is the inevitable consequence. In the 2018/19 season, the Premier League was using short-run cost control to regulate financial behaviour, alongside UEFA's Financial Fair Play rules. The Championship, League 1 and League 2 all had different profit and sustainability frameworks, with the bottom two divisions operating under a form of salary cap.[39]

The structure is not only fragmented; it is also ineffective. Once Covid-19 hit, all three divisions sought to adjust their financial controls to allow them to manage the financial shock. It proved very challenging. Leagues 1 and 2 introduced much tougher salary caps, but these were successfully challenged by the PFA on grounds of lack of consultation. Despite numerous attempts at reform, the Championship clubs were unable to agree on the introduction of a salary cap.

If the leagues operated independently of one another in a stable environment the structure might work. But English football is a dynamic and volatile financial arena. Promotion and relegation impact each division every season, and the battle in the Premier League for places in European competition adds a further pressure. With significant differences in income between divisions, the lack of integrated financial regulation severely complicates the leadership challenge especially, as we have seen, between the Championship and the Premier League.

Without an independent regulatory authority in a competition that includes clubs with very different financial resources, it is unsurprising that governance of the EFL is challenging. Tensions are never far beneath the surface, with some of the larger clubs expressing their disappointment at the 2019 to 2024 TV deal, believing it undervalued the competition.[40] There are echoes of the developments that led to the creation of the Premier League, as the larger clubs feel, with some justification, that, as they typically generate larger audiences, they could attract higher revenues. Based on the research from Liverpool University on the importance of games to the outcomes of a competition and the 'brand effect' in driving TV audiences and given the history and fan bases, the gap between the Premier League and EFL deals does seem wider than it should be.

Dealing with clubs struggling to balance the pursuit of success and fan expectations with the financial realities of the English game is the major challenge for the EFL. During the Premier League era, the EFL has faced difficult situations at clubs such as Oxford United, Luton Town, Sheffield Wednesday, Nottingham Forest, Portsmouth, Bradford City and Leicester City. Despite financial problems being a regular feature of the last two decades, no professional club had dropped out of the EFL since 1992/93. It seemed that whatever the problems, found Kuper and Syzmanski,[41] clubs would always find a way to keep going. The events of summer 2019 were a rude awakening.

As we've seen, Bury and Bolton ended up in financial difficulties via very different routes. Bury had worked their way up to League 1 via promotion while Bolton were on a downward path, having been relegated from the Premier League in 2012 after eleven years in the top division. Whereas Bolton survived at the eleventh hour, Bury were forced to drop out of the EFL.

The Digital, Culture, Media and Sport Committee of the House of Commons's *Inquiry into the Administration of Football Clubs*[42] subsequently heard submissions by the EFL, Premier League, FA, Football Supporters' Association and a range of other interested parties including supporters of both clubs. The process put the financial regulation and administration of English football under the spotlight, and it was not a pleasant sight.

There is so much that is worthy of comment. The most shocking revelations included: 'In the summer of 2014, one of the companies of Stewart Day, the owner of Bury at the time, took out a loan of £1.5 million at 138 per cent annual interest, secured by charges on Gigg Lane,

(Bury's ground)' and: 'In February 2015, a different Stewart Day company signed a lease with Bury for 200 parking spaces and in turn each parking space was offered at a debenture of around £10,000 with a promise of a 9 per cent return to investors.'[43]

These revelations and others formed the basis for the questioning of Debbie Jevans, Executive Chair of the English Football League, in the course of which it became clear that the 'owners and directors' test used by the EFL to evaluate a future owner is extremely limited. A prospective owner has only to prove they do not have interests in another club, and that they have not previously been banned from being a company director. As such, the fact that the new owner, Steve Dale, had liquidated his property company, Dale Acquisitions Ltd, two days before he took over Bury, did not form part of the test.

Even more surprisingly, the questioning revealed that the EFL never received information on the sources and sustainability of funding to support the operation of the club after takeover. Debbie Jevans claimed that the EFL had worked hard to obtain the information, but admitted it had allowed the club to compete in the competition even though one of the two key tests for a new owner had not been met. 'He was asked to provide the financial information,' she said in evidence. 'He did not do that.'[44] To which Committee Member, Ian Lucas replied, 'But what he needed from the club was the right to participate in the league ... You didn't have any information and yet you let him through the door.'[45]

Much of the questioning was on similar lines, with the EFL coming across as naïve and appearing to rely on processes and tests that are at best partial. The discussion on the profitability and sustainability tests identified that the focus is very much on operating results – primarily revenues and wage costs – rather than the overall financial position of a club. The question from the committee chair captured the issue perfectly: 'How could a club such as Bury be practically trading insolvent but still be compliant?' And in response to Ms Jevans' suggestion that this issue would be considered as part of the QC-led review of the EFL's processes, 'You do not need a QC to tell you that if someone cannot demonstrate that they have the funds to buy a football club and you let them buy it, you are storing up prob-lems for the future.'[46]

Despite these exchanges, Debbie Jevans stated that she did not see any need for government legislation to give the football authorities more power. 'Government have said – they believe that football author-ities should govern themselves, and I support that.'[47]

The status quo is not supported by the Football Supporters' Associ-ation. 'We personally would like to see much more located in the FA than is the situation currently,' said the FSA's Chairman, Malcolm Clarke, in his evidence. 'We feel that, historically, the FA has delegated too much to the leagues … we would ideally like to see some kind of independent unit within the FA.'[48]

The FA doesn't appear keen to step up. Having expressed the view that the FA has delegated responsibility for management to the PL and EFL, FA Chairman Greg Clarke responded to Ian Lucas's suggestion that the number of organisations in football works to the disadvantage of the game, 'I think it is a fair observation.' But, he went on, 'I believe that the way to get this lined up is for us to co-operate to address these problems, rather than draconian powers being given to the FA to tell people what to do.'

The Conservative MP Damian Collins, the Chair of the DCMS Committee on the Administration of Football Clubs, went as far as to call for an independent regulator for football:

> The Football League's handling of the Bury situation was to-tally inadequate, and really their only interest when they intervened was protecting the interests of the other clubs in the league, not trying to save Bury. It would be much better for football if there was an independent body, and the FA would be the logical one, which could intervene and act as a sort of regu-lator of clubs, that could audit them.

It is a lose-lose situation. Organisations with power in the game are reluctant to give it up, while other people in power in the game ac-knowledge there are issues, but are happy to stay within their silos.

English football lacks an effective administrative structure. While the three main organisations, the Premier League, the EFL and the FA, theoretically work together, the reality is no single body able to speak for the English game. There are two other major stakeholder groups in football: supporters and players. Fans were at least given a voice in the DCMS hearings, while the latter exist somewhat on the periphery of the game's governance though, unlike supporters, this appears more out of choice. The Professional Footballers' Association (PFA) restricts itself to intervening when the interests of its members are felt to be threatened.

Formed on 2 December 1907, the PFA is the trade union for footballers. Its aims are to protect, improve and negotiate the conditions, rights and status of all professional players by collective bargaining agreements. As we have seen, historically, the PFA has been successful in representing the interests of players through, for example, the campaign to abolish the maximum wage. In 2001, members were balloted on strike action. Ninety-two per cent voted, and 99 per cent of those votes supported the union and industrial action if necessary. This show of support and strength for the Association enabled a satisfactory agreement on the PFA's share of TV rights to be reached, and strike action was averted.[49]

The leadership of the PFA found itself in the spotlight in the summer of 2018. In the *Guardian* David Conn highlighted the size of Gordon Taylor's salary.[50] As Chief Executive, Taylor was paid £2.29 million in 2016/17, more than four times the £530,000 the PFA provided during the same period in grants to former players who were either ill, infirm, in poverty or with mental conditions – a truly staggering statistic.

Taylor clearly believed he was in the right, and when in November 2018 it became public that Ben Purkiss's eligibility to be chairman was in dispute, more than 200 players wrote an open letter calling on Taylor to stand down. Taylor responded in an open letter that promised a full and open review of the union's structure and operation. At its 2018 AGM, held in Manchester in March 2019, it was agreed that Taylor, Purkiss and the entire management committee would stand down following the completion of a 'full and open review' into the PFA's finances and its presentation at the 2019 AGM.[51]

As events unfolded at Bury and Bolton Wanderers in 2019, the PFA was, as is normally the case in such situations, heavily involved, helping players understand their rights but also providing financing to the clubs to pay wages. Players clearly understood that there were issues with the large amounts Bury FC were willing to spend on wages even when the EFL seemed oblivious to them. Speaking on Radio 5 Live's football podcast, the ex-footballer and Port Vale manager Michael Brown could not have been clearer when he spelt out his concerns over Bury's overspending: 'Everybody in football was talking about the signings that Bury was making and what they were spending on wages. There was a particular player that we went in for – we were blown out of the water.'[52]

Any reform of football should ensure that players have a more prominent role in governance. The interventions by individual players such as Marcus Rashford and team captains added to the opposition to the European Super League, while, in an unprecedented step, Manchester City star, Ilkay Gundogan moved on to the proposed Champions' league reforms, criticising them: 'More and more and more games, is no one thinking about us players?'[53] We have entered uncharted territory.

Unhelpful as the governance problems at the PFA were, the response to them has created an opportunity for change. With a new Chairman, Maketa Molango, a Swiss lawyer who played for several English clubs in his career and also had a period as CEO of Real Mallorca in Spain, empowered to implement the findings of the strategic review and move the organisation forward, it is important football doesn't waste it.

Just as players have more to offer the game's governance than has been recognised to date, so do supporters. On the same podcast, Mark Chapman cited a Bury supporter who pointed up the signing of Leon Clarke from Wolves, when Bury, in League 2, had beaten off competition from clubs in the Championship.

The FA rarely mentions the protection of supporters' interests. Historically, the balance that existed between owners and players achieved this, but Alex Fynn's work suggests it was more by accident than design on the FA's part: the FA was 'never constituted in a way that recognised football as a spectator sport. It was made up entirely of participants and officials.'[54]

It is beyond belief that, despite the development of the game, no body with an official role in the game has ever acknowledged an explicit responsibility for protecting the interests of this very important stakeholder group. Far from it: the FA has consistently either missed or refused opportunities to champion the cause of the game's followers. The consistently impressive Football Supporters' Association and others have stepped into the gap, but they are typically 'consulted' rather than entrusted with decision-making power. The knowledge and desire to identify solutions demonstrated by the FSA in its regular public statements and commentary clearly point to the potential for supporters to make a significant contribution to the game both at a national level and within individual clubs.

That English football needs structural reform is neither a secret nor new. 'Football is running out of time to organise itself,' said Charlie Whelan, Gordon Brown's confidant, in 1999. 'This Government [is] not about to sit back and watch the shambles at the top of our national game much longer.'[55]

Twenty years on, the shambles has got worse and government is still watching.

In October 2020, frustrated at the lack of football's progress in tackling the game's Covid-19-created financial crisis, a coalition of the great and good including ex-FA chair David Bernstein, Gary Neville, Andy Burnham, former Governor of the Bank of England, Lord King and others launched *Saving the Beautiful Game: A manifesto for change*.[56] This moved the dial up a notch by calling for the government to appoint an independent regulator, arguing that the FA was in no position to take on the leadership role the game so urgently needed. Powerfully, the report identified calls in 2011, 2013, 2016 and 2017 by various parliamentary bodies for the FA or football authorities to reform themselves. Frustrated by inaction, the group – comprising a number of people who have held senior roles in the FA, politics and football – felt the only option was to take responsibility away from the FA to give the organisation the time and space to reform itself.

These proposals echoed calls made in December 2016 by five former FA executives, David Bernstein, David Davies (who was also part of the 2020 group), Greg Dyke, Alex Horne and David Triesman, for the House of Commons' Culture, Media and Sport Committee to propose legislation to reform the FA. They called it outdated, saying it was held back by 'elderly white men', and unable to counter the power of the Premier League or 'to reform and modernise in a fast-changing world'.[57]

It would be wrong to accuse the FA of not trying to change. It has tried to launch reform several times. In May 2017, following the 2016 challenge, proposals were approved at the FA AGM to restructure the organisation. The key features were: establishing three positions on the FA board for female members by 2018; reducing the size of the board to ten members; adding eleven new members to the FA Council to 'better reflect the inclusive and diverse nature of English football'; limiting board membership to three terms of three years; and introducing term limits for FA Council members.[58]

However, only six months later, in October 2017, in an admission of the challenge of implementing real change, FA chairman Greg Clarke, who had already been publicly criticised by PFA Chief Executive Gordon Taylor and abuse victim Andy Woodward for comments he had made at a DCMS Committee hearing, changed tack and announced a 'fundamental' review of the FA after admitting it had 'lost the trust of the public' following the Aluko controversy.[59]

As the very public criticism of people familiar with the organisation confirms, the FA has failed time and again to reform itself. Just how out of touch Clarke was became painfully apparent in November 2020 when, having already stumbled when his attempts to underplay his role in Project Big Picture were highlighted, his comments on race and gender issues at a DCMS Select Committee led to him resigning before the end of the day.[60] It was a shocking episode, completely undermining the FA's efforts to lay claim to a leadership role in the game.

Following Clarke's departure, the FA will be under new leadership. Alongside recent leadership changes at the Premier League, PFA and the EFL, there is a real opportunity to make a fresh start.[61]

While the situation in English football is as challenging as it has ever been, public and political support for change is now very strong and visible. Football's failure to respond effectively to Covid-19 has strengthened the hand of the reformers.

Reform is not easy: responsibility is divided, and the four main organisations have all shown themselves lacking. The Premier League has clear commercial capability, but consistently fails to demonstrate a willingness to represent the needs of the wider game. Structure and personnel handicap the FA, while the EFL has nowhere near the level of resource to manage a seventy-two-team competition effectively. The PFA has historically had limited impact across the wider game.

It is the worst of all worlds. Facing a challenging financial outlook, the game is at a critical juncture with its leadership weaker and more divided than ever. When Liverpool and Manchester United launched Project Big Picture, it became very clear that the influence the Premier League had been able to wield over the game since its formation had declined. In *Off the Pitch* magazine Tom Corbett quoted an unnamed 'Premier League source' admitting that Project Big Picture 'shows a chronic level of cultural misunderstanding from those who come US-centred "closed competitions" of what makes football thrive: that is risk and unpredictability.'[62] The subsequent proposals to launch a European Super League made the situation even clearer.

The Covid-19 crisis and the actions of the Big Six have changed the landscape: players and managers found their voices and used them to great effect. We must build on this new mood. Players in particular have a key role to play. If English football is to return to profit, costs will need to be brought under control, that means wages to a large extent which in turn will require players in the higer echelons of the game to bear some of the pain.

This is a once in a generation opportunity – we need a debate on the type of game we want in England, and in particular, the balance between money, competitiveness and the game's wider community role. Is an international game dominated by a small number of clubs a price worth paying for the survival of the pyramid? Or do we want a more balanced competition enabled by stricter financial regulation and more revenue sharing? Or something in between?

We now have the platform, the 'fan-led review.'[63] In the aftermath of Project Big Picture and the European Super League incident, the terms of reference are more wide-ranging than we could ever have hoped for twelve months ago, including: "Examine the flow of money through the football pyramid,"; "Assess calls for the creation of a single, independent football regulator"; "Explore governance structures in other countries,"; and "Look at interventions to protect club identities." There really is everything to play for.

Any new model of governance must be future proofed. We want to avoid finding ourselves back in crisis in a few years. In the next chapter, as the final step before I share my thoughts on what we need to achieve, I consider what the future might hold for football.

10 WORLD IN MOTION

From late March through to the end of May 2020, I worked harder than I can ever remember. It felt as if everyone wanted a briefing on the economic outlook – client webcasts that might have 300 or 400 attendees were attracting between 1,000 and 2,000 people. I'm not looking for sympathy or praise, and certainly not suggesting what I did was in any way comparable with the unbelievable efforts and sacrifices many incredible people made during this period. But it was a busy time – every morning brought a new tsunami of analysis, commentary and forecasts. I quickly realised it was impossible to read more than a fraction.

Despite all this effort, it will be a long time before we know definitively how the pandemic has affected the economy and our way of life. Nevertheless, we can be confident that we will not go back to the way we were. Nor should we – we have the chance to reshape how we organise our economic and social activity. By forcing us to do things differently, Covid-19, or more accurately the lockdown of activity, set up an economic and social experiment that deserves the description 'unprecedented' – a word I suddenly found myself using every few minutes. We saw existing trends such as the shift against globalisation accelerate at the same time as we found out we could change the very way we work. Exactly how transformative these effects are remains to be seen, but the future will be different.

The crisis amplified football's problems too. It was hit hard. Live matches were suspended because of the risks of transmission in large crowds. (In truth, the decision was almost certainly taken too late – Champions' League matches including Atalanta versus Valencia and Liverpool at home to Atlético Madrid are widely believed to have contributed to the spread of the virus).[1] With no matches, the revenues from gate money and television fell dramatically, highlighting the fragile and unbalanced nature of football's finances. The failure of the game's leaders to agree on a rescue strategy laid bare the ineffectiveness of the game's governance. Self-interest dominated: smaller Premier League clubs reluctant to bail out Championship teams they saw as rivals; tensions in the EFL between clubs with wealthy owners willing to inject money and those without; the FA sitting on the sidelines struggling with its own financial challenges; the PFA defending its members interests; and the government, despite its promises of a 'fan led review of governance', remaining on the outside, telling the game it had the resources to resolve its own problems. As usual, supporters were not consulted.

Something had to give. Anyone with a knowledge of the history of the Premier League would not have been surprised that it was the richest clubs that took the initiative. On 11 October 2020 the *Daily Telegraph* broke the story of Project Big Picture (PBP),[2] a proposal led by Liverpool and Manchester United, subsequently backed by EFL Chairman Rick Parry, to reshape the whole game. Suddenly the divisions and problems were out in the open. Envisaging as it did further internationalisation and greater commercialisation alongside a transfer of governance to the richest clubs, Project Big Picture was an attempt to define the future of the game. That reform was needed was undeniable. That PBP was the answer was much more doubtful. Six months later a European Super League was launched and cancelled within 3 days. No-one with even a passing interest in football could be in any doubt that the game had arrived at a critical juncture: change is now inevitable.

It's easy to forget how much football has changed. At the same time as it pointed towards a different future, Covid-19 opened a window to the past. When lockdown started it was not just football viewers that were forced to adjust; broadcasters had to fill the gaps in their schedules. In one of the more innovative moves, BT Sport dipped into the archives to find programmes from *The Big Match*, London Weekend Television's flagship highlights programme of the 1970s and 1980s. It was more a history show than a football programme. I found myself transfixed by shots of poor-quality pitches, players with shirts numbered 1 to 11 and goalkeepers playing without gloves even on freezing days, only covering their hands to deal with slippery balls when it rained. The game was slower, there was little pressing, tackling was often more akin to a physical assault although yellow and red cards were only issued reluctantly[3], and it was obvious that teams were not as well-drilled tactically as in the modern game.

The re-runs of *The Big Match* illustrated just how much has changed over the last forty years: on the pitch, for supporters, and in the media. It is fitting that television provided this insight, as it is the growth of football on our screens over the last three decades that is both the highest-profile visible illustration of the change in the game and the largest single source of revenue growth. According to Deloitte, Premier League broadcasting revenues were £3,049 million in 2018/19, almost 60 per cent of the total. Income from broadcasters has increased more than sixty-fold in the Premier League era, far more quickly than overall football income. And it is not just the Premier League that benefits: TV deals and the solidarity payments out of the Premier League's TV income make up a third or more of the income of clubs across the English football pyramid.[4]

I started to write this book because I believed that English football was out of balance: commercial considerations were afforded too much weight. The contrast between *The Big Match* and Sky's current flagship *Monday Night Football* illustrates the truly staggering scale of change. A transformation of this magnitude has consequences, many of which have been unarguably positive: higher-quality stadia; reduced hooliganism; opportunities to see the world's top players up close; and a reduction in violent play. However, the downside is also clear: neglect or exploitation of loyal supporters; a growing distance between fans on one side and players, managers and owners on the other; ineffective, out-of-touch leadership; and underinvestment in community activities.

Throughout the period, clubs operated confident that, however much they asked of supporters – to pay higher ticket prices, to buy replica kit and TV subscriptions, to attend games at all times on any day – they would do so. Indeed, so loyal were they that no organisation involved in administering the game felt it necessary to consult them properly, never mind involve them in decision-making.

Before anyone had heard of Covid-19, it was clear that English football's long winning streak was coming to an end, and the game needed to change. What is most striking, four decades on, is that many of the issues likely to shape the evolution of the game were live when *The Big Match* was in its heyday: in many cases, difficult choices have been parked rather than resolved. The pandemic has heightened the stress but plans by the richest clubs to change the game had been in development for some time. Football needs to take the opportunity Covid-19 offers to take stock and think about what type of future the game should aspire to. This is not a static situation, not only is football changing – the whole environment it operates in is in a state of flux. We must look forward not back.

Football went from playing a weekly, bit-part role on terrestrial television to occupying its own dedicated channels across multiple broadcast platforms. In the Premier League's inaugural season only sixty games were broadcast live. In 2019, the committed football watcher could easily have tuned in to sixty live games a *month* on English television. Just as television was a major agent of change in football in the last three to four decades, so it is very possible that the most significant changes in future will still derive from this key part of football's commercial empire: the communications sector.

To my knowledge, no-one, not even the so-called 'visionaries' predicted how valuable or extensive TV coverage would become. Alex Fynn, described by the *Sunday Times* as 'the spiritual godfather of the Premier League' for his role in advising the FA on its creation, forecast in 1992 that broadcasting thirty games a season could generate £22.5 million in revenues, equivalent to £750,000 per broadcast game.[5] In the 2018/19 season, 168 games were broadcast live, and at an average price per game of £10.2 million from domestic TV rights alone.[6]

Sky recognised the opportunity the new Premier League offered: that so strong is the appeal of top-level football, such as the Premier

League, the European Champions' League and England internationals, that if pay television is the only place to watch it then football followers will buy a satellite dish and sign up to a subscription. It is a broadcaster's dream: must-watch content and captive customers.

From the nail-biting, last-minute decision to bet the company in the first Premier League TV rights auction, Sky moved on to revolutionise the way football was covered and broadcast, innovating across the whole range of industry activities. Yes, Sky has been a highly effective operator, bidding whatever was needed to retain TV rights, challenging regulatory decisions and always looking to disrupt competitors with new channels, new packages and innovative marketing campaigns, but it is a company with smart, professional and commercially savvy people all working to a clear strategy based on a detailed understanding of what will work and what won't. While many fans may have issues with some of the changes Sky has introduced into the English game, it would be churlish not to recognise the innovation and dynamism the company has brought to the table.

Looking back over the story of Sky, there is one key lesson for the future: the primary driver of the value of TV rights is the intensity of competition for them. The evidence from auctions from 2000 to 2018 is unequivocal: the brief emergence of NTL, Setanta's moment in the sun after 2007 and then the arrival of powerhouse BT all coincided with rises in the amount paid.

As we have seen, the auction for the rights for 2013 to 2016 was when the Thatcher government's reforms from three decades earlier crystallised. The benefits of a truly competitive bidding process to a seller of highly desired content were clear for all to see.[7]

My sense was that, on the back of two huge rises in the value of rights, the mood was very buoyant as the Premier League moved into the auction cycle for the 2019 to 2022 rights. Just to make sure, the television deal starting in 2019/20 would not only be available on more platforms but offer an increased number of games and more late-evening Saturday matches. The assumption was that supporters who had become accustomed to paying more each season to watch football on television would pay more to access games on new platforms while travelling at increasingly more inconvenient times to attend.

The other reason for the confident mood was that the Premier League was expecting new bidders for TV rights, with global technology giants such as Amazon, Google and Twitter rumoured to be considering throwing their hats in, despite the growing political worries about their dominance of markets and their approaches to taxation. Money clearly talks to the Premier League without, it appears, too much concern for who is speaking.

It would have been fascinating to have been a fly on the wall at Premier League HQ in spring 2018 when the results of the auction saw the first fall in the value of UK rights in consecutive auctions since 2004. While the new television deal was still hugely lucrative – £4.65 billion – it was around £400 million down on the previous deal, and for a higher number of games.[8]

The much-heralded arrival of the Internet giants into the UK rights auction didn't materialise. Amazon won one package of games, the smallest on offer, but for an estimated value of only £90 million annually.[9] That the deal was announced after the other bids closed suggested a significant effort had to be made to entice Amazon to sign up.

Further confirmation of the easing in competitive pressures came with the results of the auction of Champions' League rights for 2021 to 2024 in late 2019. BT retained the UK rights for £400 million a season, according to Enders Analysis,[10] a slight increase on the £394 million of the previous deal, although including seventy-seven additional games from the new European Conference. Indeed, Enders believed BT could have secured the rights for a much lower price: 'From the viewpoint of BT's shareholders, this is a disappointing result. This auction presented a golden opportunity for BT to cut its costs.'

The Premier League had been over-optimistic and probably complacent, failing to recognise that the value of TV rights is to a significant extent determined by competition in the communications market rather by football itself. Whatever the intrinsic appeal and value of TV rights, by 2018 it was clear that growth in the broadband market was slowing and hence the price of TV rights would begin to decline. BT was still coming to terms with the fall-out from an accounting scandal in Italy; together with ongoing concerns over its pension deficit and political pressure on it to accelerate its roll-out of high-speed fibre in the UK, this limited its resources for bidding. Like any well-run corporation, Sky was always looking for an opportunity to reduce its payments.[11]

Looking to the future, the market is changing in ways that may not be beneficial for UK football TV rights. Younger viewers consume more of their media on laptops and mobiles and, with home ownership ever more unattainable thanks to high UK house prices and employment increasingly precarious, consumer spending patterns are changing. The offer of a combined broadband service and subscription to a television package doesn't fit with either the lifestyles or the finances of consumers aged under thirty.

The battle for content has also moved on, as asset-light companies like Netflix, Apple, Facebook, YouTube and Amazon Prime compete with traditional content producers and broadcasters in the home and in the cinema. Despite the huge resources these new players are bringing to bear, the cost of acquiring the rights to elite English football is daunting even for them. The £1.6 billion annual value of the 2019-to-2022 domestic Premier League deal is narrowly behind the total spend on content of £1.7 billion by the BBC, way ahead of the £1,050 million spent by ITV, significantly more than Channel 4's close to £700 million typical annual outlay and very similar to its estimates of the combined UK video revenue of Amazon, Facebook, Netflix and YouTube in 2017 according to Enders.[12]

It is far from certain new media companies like Amazon, Twitter and Netflix will seek to play in a major way as an exclusive provider of a large share of the televised games. As Enders highlights, there is a real question over how Premier League TV rights for the UK fit with the strategies of scalable global model of these companies. Unlike high-quality drama, sports programming is all about immediacy rather than catch-up or replay services. Amazon has made investments in the NFL and in tennis content, and Facebook bought the digital rights to Indian Premier League cricket, but these are very different offerings. It seems possible that these companies might be interested in a share of the foreign rights in future, but whether this would generate values in excess of those achieved by the country-by-country sales model historically used to good effect is uncertain.

Sport is in any case now just one of the potential sources of new subscriber growth and may be past its peak. Certainly, the numbers of new subscribers taking channels for football has been slowing dramatically for some time, while the rate of loss of existing customers has been increasing. Enders reported that in 2018, Virgin Media lost 350,000 pay-TV subscribers, Sky's base fell by 114,000, but this was after allowing for a gain of 72,000 to its cheaper Now TV offer, and the rest of the market fell by 275,000 – a total decline of 739,000. Enders estimates that the price paid for UK TV rights for Champions' League and Premier League coverage increased by 222 per cent between 2009 and 2019, compared to an 18 per cent increase in pay-TV revenues. This does suggest that, just as we found with match going supporters, TV consumers are at risk of being maxed out. Having been acquired by the North American media giant Comcast, Sky too may act differently in future, possibly attaching a lower priority to the UK market.[13]

In the first sign of just how different the future might be, BT Sport confirmed in spring 2021 that it was in discussions; 'with a number of select strategic partners', exploring 'ways to generate investment, strengthen our sports business' to 'help take it to the next stage in its growth', hinting at a sale of some or all of the operation.[14] With the report also citing the Premier League hoping to roll over its domestic TV deal without an auction due to the pandemic, the market appears more likely to consolidate rather than expand. These developments together will the fall in the value of rights in the auctions in Germany and Italy during 2020/21[15], add further support to my view that the 2019/22 deal, slightly disappointing as it was, marks the end of the model that has underpinned the growth of the Premier League's domestic revenues since 1993, and especially the rapid growth since 2012.

But though football undoubtedly became more attractive and popular to UK broadcasters over the last three decades, this alone does not explain the rapid rise in the game's income. Top-flight football's revenue growth has consistently outperformed that of the wider economy. The changes to the UK economy and to football itself in the 1980s shifted the game from the periphery into the economic mainstream.

In the new market-led UK economy, businesses became much keener to be involved with football – taking clients to a match became a key part of relationship building activities and brands wanted to be associated with the glamorous image of the game. As we saw earlier, clubs responded to the opportunity and sponsorship and commercial revenues took off. While the home market drove the initial growth, it was income from overseas that has fuelled the recent surge in commercial income.

Following China's accession to the World Trade Organisation around the turn of the twentieth century, global trade and investment flows increased dramatically. I remember businesses and investors all excited by the possibilities offered by the emergence of the BRICs.[16] Recognising the opportunity, the Premier League led a successful campaign to grow the spread and value of foreign TV coverage, attracting broadcasting partners from around the world keen to be associated with the competition for its global reach. Despite the decline in the value of domestic TV rights in the 2018 auction, international rights sold for around £1.4 billion a season, an increase of £300 million a year.[17]

The unexpected boost from the emergence of online gambling around the world is another example of the charmed life of English football during the last three decades. Having aggressively sold foreign TV rights, the large number of viewers around the world made English football, hugely appealing to the start-up businesses seeking to attract customers. Well positioned because of the openness of the UK economy and the strength of the domestic gambling industry, clubs and their broadcast partners both gained significantly.

Advertising and sponsorship by tobacco and drinks companies, for which football had been an obvious partner (I am old enough to remember the Park Drive and then Rothmans' football yearbooks), had been banned on television – but football filled the gap with gambling companies. At the start of the 2019/20 season, nine out of twenty Premier League teams and seventeen of the twenty-four clubs in the Championship had gambling sponsors, with a significant number based outside the UK.[18]

There are three major motivations for gambling companies to sponsor English football teams. First, in the case of companies outside the UK, to boost their brand globally, exploiting the global coverage the Premier League achieves. Without a doubt, the willingness of a foreign gambling company to pay £5 million to sponsor Newcastle United reflects a desire to build a global brand rather than an interest in the UK market alone. But with the value of deals having increased dramatically over the last three or four years such sponsors may be overpaying. 'These companies – and other Chinese and Asian gambling companies – are perhaps naive of the effects of the sponsorship and misjudge the value of the shirts,' Simon Chadwick, Professor of Sports Enterprise at the University of Salford, told offthepitch.com. 'The gambling companies have certainly bumped up the price of lower-tier shirt sponsorship deals over the last two or three seasons considerably.'[19]

Secondly, gambling companies with large UK operations use sponsorship, together with advertising, to drive bets and revenues. A large amount of football betting nowadays is 'in-play', meaning it takes place after the game has started – it has been reported that bet365 generates up to 80 per cent of its football bets this way.[20] During the 2018 World Cup, gambling advertising was very prominent both before kick-off and during the half-time interval. Research by the *Guardian*[21] estimated that a viewer could have seen up to ninety minutes of gambling adverts throughout the tournament, with one in every six minutes of advertising being taken by a gambling company. Such volume and prominence led to calls for greater regulation and, sensing the public mood, several companies announced voluntary restrictions.

Understandably, given the evidence of the risk of addiction, gambling attracts a significant amount of attention from politicians, and the horrifying scale of problem gambling has seen an increasing willingness to intervene. While the restrictions the betting companies have announced on their TV advertising may buy some time, there will be increasing pressure on football to reduce its association with them.

The greatest risks to the gambling related income of Premier League clubs may well be in the international market from the third reason companies in the sector are attracted to the Premier League. In an article in the Athletic magazine entitled, 'How Premier League shirt sponsors facilitate "illegal" gambling', Joey d'Urso outlined some of the key features driving the sponsorship income from overseas gambling companies:

"What a lot of football fans won't understand is how little interest most of these firms have in the UK market and in UK bettors," says Alun Bowden, head of European markets at US research firm Eilers & Krejcik Gaming. "It's just about trying to get brand exposure in Asian markets where gambling advertising is banned or heavily restricted. It's a game within a game, and you're not playing."

D'Urso went on to quote Carolyn Harris MP, chair of the Gambling Related Harm All-Party Parliamentary Group, who characterised clubs as "actively promoting Asian firms which have no paper trail, which seek to entice gambling in China, where gambling on football is illegal". "We need immediate action on this," she added.[22]

Online gambling perfectly illustrates how circumstances that favoured the commercialisation of the English game may now be turning against it. Football embraced gambling with apparently little concern over the potential societal costs, choosing to focus on the commercial rewards, and the free hand given by politicians made that possible. Just as investors I have worked with have found investing in seemingly attractive opportunities in new markets, such as those offered by the BRICs, is not risk-free, football is finding that all that glitters is not gold.

Gambling companies have not been the only foreign investors in the English game. At the start of the 2020/21 season, fourteen of the twenty Premier League clubs were majority foreign-owned. Beneficial as this has been, there are increasing signs that it could become a vulnerability. In fact, it is already happening. 'Most Chinese-controlled foreign clubs are expected to be sold in the next couple of years,' Paul

Conway, an investment banker heavily involved in the moves of Chinese investors into European football in the last decade, told *Off the Pitch* magazine.

> It is just too politically sensitive. If you love football, the pressure from the government is to focus locally 'to improve the quality of local football to compete to win the World Cup in 20 years' ... The government views investments in Southampton, West Brom, Aston Villa, Sochaux and Slavia Prague as financially wasteful, so now it is essentially calling these investors back home.[23]

We are moving into a very different international environment. The global economy has failed in recent years to achieve the growth rates that were common before the financial crisis. Even before Covid, the emergence of trade wars and increased geopolitical tension exposed the rise of economic nationalism. Developed economies that had previously embraced open markets have started to reconsider. Although the USA under President Biden has adopted a more internationalist stance than under his predecessor Donald Trump, there is little sign of a relaxation in the emphasis on economic nationalism. Even historically strong pro-trade blocs like the European Union have begun to adjust their position.

Worryingly given its importance, there are already signs that the tension could spread from the wider economy into football's core broadcast activities. When football shut down due to the pandemic, broadcasters entered into negotiations to reduce their payments for TV rights. In China the situation became very politicised and wrapped up in other issues around the wider relationship between the UK and China. Not only did the Premier League have to terminate its TV deal with its Chinese partner[24] but there were reports that broadcasts of the competition were downgraded on Chinese TV. 'China is prepared to use football as a means through which to hurt Britain,' was how Professor Simon Chadwick characterised the action.[25]

Political risk is not just growing in the international arena. The belief in the power of markets and individual decision-making that shaped the agenda of Margaret Thatcher's governments endured long after her departure from power, beyond the financial crisis, even though the overwhelming opinion among economists was that austerity policies were inappropriate. However, with the UK, like many other economies, grappling with such challenges as an ageing population, rapid technological change and the climate emergency, there is a growing sense that more state intervention is required to shape outcomes. It is no surprise that the 2019 General Election manifestos of the Conservative, Labour and Liberal Democrat parties all promised a more interventionist approach with higher levels of public spending.

That interventionist mood has spread to football: all three manifestos specifically referred to new regulation for the game. The victorious Conservative Party's promised fan-led review 'will include consideration of the Owners and Directors Test and will work with fans and clubs towards introducing safe standing.' These commitments signalled a desire to go much deeper into the operations of football than for some time. The signs are that every move is liable to be scrutinised.

Football is not alone in facing a more complex political environment. All industries are being challenged by their stakeholders (investors, employees and customers) to be 'purposeful' and work to try and balance the interests of all groups, rather than merely maximising profit for their shareholders. For example, as the climate emergency has moved to centre stage, concerns over the impact of fossil fuel producers on the environment have led to protests about the sponsorship of the arts by oil companies and the investment by funds and foundations in these sectors.

FIFA has already faced controversy over the award of the 2018 World Cup to Russia and the following tournament to Qatar owing to concerns over human rights in both countries.[26] Other sports face similar challenges. The decision to stage the British heavyweight boxer Anthony Joshua's world title fight with Andy Ruiz Junior in Saudi

Arabia was described as 'sportswashing': enabling a country to distract attention from human rights abuses by staging a major event.[27]

English football needs to change. The potential takeover of Newcastle United by a Saudi Arabian-led consortium was one of the sagas that distracted us during lockdown. However, it is unclear how much consideration human rights were given by the Premier League compared to concerns over the failure of the Saudi government to clamp down on the illegal piracy of broadcast football in the region, with complaints led by BeIn Sports.[28]

The corporate impact of the failed launch of a European Super League was a salutary lesson. As identified earlier, JP Morgan found itself downgraded by an ethics rating agency[29] and broadcasters close to the game made clear they were not interested in broadcasting the new competition. Like every industry, football will have to pay much more attention to its social responsibility in the broadest sense going forward.

Covid has caused countries to become more introspective and consider how to boost their resilience. It appears we could enter a period of lower global trade growth and a slowing of international capital flows, with an all-too-obvious risk to international TV rights, sponsorship and commercial flows and foreign ownership. Domestically, the UK economy has been weakened, with unemployment rising and many businesses either failing or forced to restructure. This is likely to reduce spending on football in the short term. It seems likely that it will be some time, if ever, before travel, either leisure or business, returns to pre-crisis levels, that corporate entertaining expenditure will be depressed for some time and lower margins will put pressure on corporate sponsorship and commercial spending. Reflecting on the potential impact of the pandemic on sponsorship by sporting goods companies, Adidas' sales reportedly fell 90 per cent in the first quarter of 2020, Phil Knight, founder of Nike said: (it) 'will change the whole face of the business.'[30]

An effective response to a crisis starts with good governance, something we have seen football lacks. This is the environment from where Project Big Picture emerged. Absent any co-ordinated response, and with no organisation able to provide leadership to the game, Liverpool and Manchester United reportedly led an effort to develop their own proposals. It was in many ways the logical end to the journey that began forty years earlier: effectively an American takeover of the English national sport. When the European Super League followed, the scope had grown – control of a major element of the European game was effectively the aim.

The economics of PBP and the European Super League are logically sound if you are an elite club with a global brand. First, with domestic rights declining, it is sensible to focus on increasing the value of foreign TV rights and the potential growth in European fees if more games can be squeezed into the schedule. (As we have seen, discussions between Europe's richest clubs on a 'Super League' or extended Champions' League had been ongoing for some time.) PBP's proposals reflected these themes: an eighteen-team Premier League with thirty-four Saturday games to maximise global exposure while creating more midweek European slots (by ending the League Cup); selling eight games a season direct to foreign supporters (primarily benefitting the teams with the largest global fanbase by taking this revenue out of the shared pot); and taking over selling EFL games, allowing the Premier League to benefit from any potential undervaluing of EFL rights.

Secondly, it is important to ensure your club can rely on European revenues; there can be no possibility of missing out. The proposals in PBP designed to ensure this include: ring-fencing European and pay-per-view foreign income streams; replacing parachute payments with a withholding tax on promoted clubs, likely to reduce their chances of staying in the top division; reducing the share of money going to smaller clubs, effectively creating weaker teams and hence easier games for the top clubs; a wider and more flexible loan system to allow the richest clubs to control more of the available talent in the game; and giving the Premier League the power to set salary caps and other governance to allow it to control the competitiveness of EFL clubs. The European Super league proposals went even further, guaranteeing participation for twenty-three years for the founding clubs, completely eliminating any risk from under-performance on the pitch.

Thirdly, seek to head off political interference by appearing to in-crease significantly the distribution of money, with a focus on the pyramid, grass roots and especially the women's game. It is a more nu-anced proposal than it may appear on the surface. While Leagues 1 and 2 would receive more income than previously, the outlook for the Championship was relatively less generous, after taking account of the proposals for sharing Premier League revenues after promotion.

And finally, the price to be paid: under PBP a reverse takeover of English football by the Premier League, with governance vested in nine clubs, seven of which were foreign-owned at the time the pro-posals were launched, with four in London, one more based in the south of England and two from each of Manchester and Liverpool; and a new Europe-wide governance structure for elite club football as a result of the European Super League proposals.

Unsurprisingly, given the business talent available to the elite clubs, Project Big Picture was a very clever set of proposals, maxi-mising the opportunity created by lockdown by appearing to address all the major issues of the game. It carefully avoided raising potentially contentious issues like support for the England men's national team (one of the original justifications for the Premier League), and the po-tential impact on competitive balance.

It was this last issue that drove the extraordinary public and polit-ical response to the European Super League. We shouldn't have been surprised at the proposals – they were the logical end to the journey of opening the UK game up to market forces that started under Margaret Thatcher's premiership. As leading economist Chris Dillow pointed out; 'Capitalists hate competition.', illustrating his point with reference to Warren Buffet's advice to shareholders to search for; '"economic moats' – things that protect them from competition."[31]

However, as we have seen, football is not a typical business. On the field competition encapsulates football's raison d'être; the dream of success. When Leicester surprised everyone to win the Premier League title in 2016, it seemed possible we were on the verge of a new era of competitiveness. In fact, exactly the opposite happened. The response of the six clubs with the largest revenue (Arsenal, Chelsea, Liverpool,

Manchester City, Manchester United and Tottenham Hotspur) was to spend even more money on new players and salaries, leaving the rest trailing in their wake. With wage constraints further strengthening their relative competitiveness, the Top 6 seemed unassailable.

In 2019/20, the Premier League clubs decided not to renew their voluntary restraints on wages for the new TV deal period. With no constraints on wages, results in the 2019/20 and 2020/21 seasons suggest clubs outside the top six willing to invest heavily can mount effective challenges for the European places even if they are unlikely to be able to challenge consistently for the title itself. Project Big Picture and the European Super League are the elite's response: an attempt to ensure the richest clubs can distance themselves from the rest of the competition.

The UK's lockdown in response to Covid-19 showed us that alternative ways of organising our economic and social activities exist. We remembered the importance of community and our local societies, rediscovered how much we need each other. The absence of supporters at grounds not only demonstrated how important a crowd is to the game, but also made us realise just how big a part of our lives football is.

One of the most positive developments after PBP emerged was the number of people and groups willing to speak out about the future of the game. With the government also vocal in its criticism, the opportunity for a national debate is greater than at any time in the last four decades. The 'fan-led' review is perfectly timed, coming at a point in time when the power of supporters and the footballing community is stronger relative to the top clubs than at any time for at least fifty years.

The review needs to deliver a better balance between the various components of the game and recognise how Premier League spending distorts the whole game and doesn't fairly reward the value that the pyramid provides. Helpfully for future negotiations, although many of the proposals in Project Big Picture and the European Super League were designed to benefit the elite, there was a recognition that cross subsidy from rich to poor is an essential part of the game – the principle is now established. We need to build on this but change the proposed structure and associated governance to one that is in the interests of the whole game.

It is a huge task. Just as is the case across the whole of our economy and society, the exact scale and nature of the impact of COVID-19 is still unclear. There is though little doubt that football has been hit very hard. We have seen the huge losses racked up by clubs like Everton and Aston Villa, but all clubs have suffered. Richard Masters, Chief Executive of the Premier League has estimated that the competition might suffer a hit of £700 million in 2020/21.[32] Coming off the back of the published Premier League club financial results for 2019/20 suggesting a loss in the range of 5 per cent or more for that season alone. Other estimates are similarly bleak: Deloitte estimated that the twenty richest teams in Europe could lose €2 Billion over the two campaigns;[33] and Andrea Agnelli, Chair of the European Clubs' Association suggested the final loss for European football clubs due to the pandemic could be €8.5 billion.[34]

Whatever the final numbers, the shock will certainly be of such a scale that football will have to repair its balance sheet. And, if the predictions in this Chapter are accurate, it is unlikely football can bank on significantly higher incomes going forward – there is a good chance there will be less money in future than was previously expected.

An integrated strategy is required. The proposals for reform must aim to generate the maximum revenues possible consistent with the competitive balance we desire, while reducing expenditure, especially wages and transfer fees

Reform will not be easy, but without more effective leadership of football it will be impossible. An encouraging development during the pandemic was the publication of Saving the Beautiful Game by a number of individuals with experience in government, football governance and football and sport more generally.[35]

With several members having held positions in the FA, their call for an independent regulator for football told us how they perceived the FA. With a once-in-a-generation opportunity to reshape English football, the game needs to ensure it is in robust shape for what could be a rocky ride.

Hopefully, you are as convinced as I am that football is unique, on and off the pitch. And that it is both more than a game and more than a business. As a result, there should be no argument that the game has to be regulated to allow us to achieve the outcomes we desire. Four decades of light touch governance, leaving the game to the whims of the market has left us where we are today. Football is different, should be different and can be different. It's time to nail our colours to the mast.

11 BELIEVE IN BETTER

On 21 November 2019, Amazon launched its coverage of Premier League football in spectacular fashion. Subscribers to Amazon Prime, the company's premium service, were able to watch all ten games of the latest set of fixtures in the 2019/20 season live across three evenings. It was a true multimedia experience. Viewers could watch two games simultaneously on a split-screen and flick between games, rewinding to review incidents at the flip of a switch. My sons were watching the goals show on TV, switching to other games on their laptops while messaging their friends, some of whom were at the matches, on their mobiles. Four decades after the NFL's $2 billion TV deal alerted English investors to the potential value of football and Margaret Thatcher's policies sparked a transformation of the communications sector, the Premier League had arrived in the converged world.

From the sick man of European football in the 1980s, with crumbling and dangerous stadia, hooligans running wild, a blackout of televised football and falling attendances, the English game has transformed itself into the highest attended, most watched football competition in the world. On any given Saturday, players from all around the world compete in full stadia with their every move followed in all corners of the globe. Elite players and managers are handsomely rewarded, commercial sponsors want to be associated with the game and related industries such as broadcasting, gaming and gambling benefit from their links to football.

But the transformation has brought costs as well as benefits. It was the treatment of supporters that led me to question if the game had become unbalanced, I was right to be concerned: they have been pushed to the limit. Huge commercial success is only possible if someone is paying for it, and spending on football now consumes more than a three times greater share of supporters' income compared to when the Premier League started. Domestic sales of tickets, replica shirts and TV subscriptions make up much more than half of football's income and have been used to fund the expansion and improvement of stadia and underwrite soaring wage and transfer spending. Yet match-going supporters are taken for granted, their loyalty exploited, left to battle with Britain's unreliable public transport network at ever more inhospitable times to attend games. The desire to maximise income limits free-to-air coverage for young fans, while high prices and sold-out games in the Premier League make attending on a casual basis very difficult. Despite the sterling efforts of the Football Supporters' Association, the most valuable and important stakeholders still, as for over a century, have virtually no say in the governance of English football.

But the failures go beyond the exploitation and treatment of supporters. While the internationalisation of playing staffs, managers and owners has boosted the quality of English football, widened the competition's appeal and attracted new funding, it has diluted the identity of the national game and weakened the ties to local communities. With the revenues from international sponsors and TV rights becoming ever more important, the game is shifting ever further away from its base. As the incredibly ham-fisted attempts to create a European Super League demonstrated, major decisions are increasingly being made by people with limited knowledge of the traditions and culture of the English game.

What has shocked me most in my analysis of English football has been the state of the game's finances. Despite leading the world in revenue generation, in the last season before the pandemic hit, English professional football in total was loss-making. And that's only part of it – in total throughout the Premier League era, the game has been un-profitable. We have been told for so long to celebrate English football's much hyped commercial success, yet it is just that – hype.

Despite huge change in so many areas, football's fundamental challenges today are the ones that administrators have been battling with since the advent of professionalism: striking a balance between generating income, maintaining competition on the pitch and ensuring the financial stability of the game – stopping football destroying itself.

The imbalances begin at the top. With several of the largest clubs under the control of owners willing to pursue success with little apparent concern for the financial consequences, players, especially the elite group, have used their increased bargaining power to earn ever higher wages and inevitably, transfer spending has soared. Alongside owners chasing success are others focused on driving up revenues to allow them to spend to compete while generating profits. It is the worst of all worlds: greater disparities in revenues between the elite and the rest; and continuing increases in spending.

The Premier League distorts the whole of the pyramid. Seeking to compete with the world's richest clubs, the elite chase the world's top talent. Desperate to advance, ambitious Championship clubs pay higher wage levels to try to tempt players out of the Premier League, forcing other teams to stretch their budgets ever further. Pre-Covid, spending on wages was greater than income in the Championship, and at an uneconomic share of revenue across the pyramid. The problems at Bolton and Bury in the summer of 2019 are indicative of the financial challenges facing the whole of English professional football. This is now a dangerous and unstable model in all directions: Bolton's difficulties intensified as they slid down the pyramid, while Bury's pursuit of promotion contributed to their ultimate demise.

With the Football Association having ceded its position as the guardian of the game, there is no organisation able to provide overall leadership. The Premier League has been free to do pretty much as it pleases. Only a widespread outcry, such as over the thirty-ninth game, has forced it to amend its plans and even then, it is never clear if what is agreed is anything more than a temporary settlement. Decisions are made by negotiation rather than consultation leading to a bias towards tactical rather than strategic concerns. Youth development is a perfect example of a change made to benefit a few with little thought of the wider consequences. With young player development concentrated in elite clubs, exacerbated by a loan system that encourages hoarding of talent, EFL clubs are much less likely to be able to unearth new stars capable of boosting their fortunes either on the pitch as players, or off it through transfer fees. With smaller clubs starved of access to talent, financial and competitive imbalances increase. Sustaining a pyramid requires end to end management, but football's decision-making remains siloed and self-interested.

Covid-19 has now deepened the game's problems. English football today is: structurally and financially unbalanced; highly leveraged; facing a deteriorating commercial outlook; and handicapped by ineffective governance. Project Big Picture painted one future for us – offering greater financial redistribution in return for managed competition and more control of the whole game by the richest clubs. But it is just one option. And not a popular one. In a survey of over 5,000 of its subscribers, The Athletic magazine found 65 per cent of respondents opposed giving the Big 6 control of Premier League governance and 73 per cent were against ceding more control of TV income and rights to the elite group.[1]

Surely, the failed launch of the European Super League is the moment the tide turned? In less than seventy-two hours, all of football's issues were exposed to the world. The response was extraordinary. Unsurprisingly supporters moved quickly to express their outrage, but for the first time, a significant number of players and managers also broke cover to criticise the leadership of the game. Then the prime minister and other politicians made their views clear, going so far as to threaten legislative responses.[2] Even the broadcasters and pundits who have largely sat on the sidelines over the last three to four decades, nailed their colours to the mast.

In the early stages of this book, I highlighted just how unusual a business football is, indeed I questioned if it is a business at all. We can now be in no doubt; football is more than a business and more than a game – it is unique. How we run it must therefore reflect the game's position in society. This book is full of examples of the failure of previous attempts to create more balance between the interests of the game's stakeholders. Recent events have shifted the goalposts – football's vested interests have been weakened by their behaviour since the pandemic emerged, the support for change is now too strong to be ignored.

If we look back over history, change in football has generally been as a result of negotiations between different interests – with supporters not even at the table – rather than through consultation. If we have learnt anything, it is that solutions can't be imposed, we must seek a wide range of views and aim for consensus. With the threat of a break-away European League, forcing the Government to launch its long-promised 'fan-led review of governance', there is now a unique opportunity to come together around a new model.

We know what we don't want, but what do we want?

When I started this book, I envisaged building the case for re-turning to a game more like that when I was growing up. My view of football was formed in the 1970s and solidified in the 1980s and early 1990s. As I delved further into the issues, I realised just how much the game has changed, and hence I too have to change my objectives. How-ever, the reaction to recent events, especially to the proposed European Super League, means we should not hold back – the door is wide open.

The primary lesson from the experiences outlined in this book is unequivocal: agreement on the game's economic model is essential to reforming football. Since the emergence of professionalism, the battle between money and the game has dominated the management of English football. It is a common thread running through the game's history: the dispute over the minimum wage for players; the FA's re-strictions on paid Directors and dividends; sharing TV income; the creation of the Premier League; Project Big Picture; and the European Super League.

But we should also take comfort from the above events – they show us that the game will and should change – however, we can't solve every issue for ever. Our challenge is to allow the game to evolve in a managed fashion by defining clear principles and creating a framework that en-sures all interests are considered in decisions about change in future.

For me, given these requirements, the priorities to agree on are: the competitive structure in England and its relationship to the game be-yond our borders; a sustainable financial settlement consistent with the desired competitive model; governance of the game and stakeholder involvement at all levels; and support for communities and grass roots to help build a diverse and inclusive game. Happily, in no small part due to the impressive work of the Football Supporters' Association, all of these areas are included in the fan-led review of governance – we are heading in the right direction. Let's now consider each one in turn.

Competition wise, the options lie on a spectrum that stretches from the very restrictive NFL system in America to our current model, characterised by its ever-increasing instability and inequality. In between are myriad variants around either a strong, heavily regulated pyramid based on significant redistribution from rich to poor, or a hybrid model with a European (or global) Super League existing alongside the English structure. We now know that any solution offering reward irrespective of on the pitch performance is unacceptable to the football community.

As we have seen, on and off the field performance are closely linked: the financial settlement shapes the balance between the power of money and the interests of the game, on and off the pitch. The more balanced the competition we aspire to, the greater the redistribution and regulation required. English Football is a highly integrated sport, and addressing one issue in isolation, like parachute payments or salary levels in the lower leagues, typically creates other distortions.

What has become clear to me in writing this book is how important the relationship between owners and players is in determining the balance of the game. Faced with players exercising their market power, owners have shown themselves willing to squeeze supporters and take financial risks to secure the talent they want. If we can reduce the rate of increases in expenditure, then some of the need for redistribution will be reduced – if clubs are spending less, they will require smaller levels of financial support.

The events of the last four decades have demonstrated that constraints on owners alone will be insufficient to curb excess spending. Regulation of pay and conditions will be required to limit the more adverse consequences of player power, removing the temptation to excess from owners. Salary caps, the system of player development, transfer levels, caps on agents and standard contractual terms are some of the tools available.

The two other priorities are governance and its enforcement. In the aftermath of the failed attempt to launch a European Super League, there was a rush of solutions proposed for governance, such as those proposed in *Saving the Beautiful Game*, in which David Bernstein and others argue for an independent regulator, and calls for the adoption of the German model known as '50+1' of supporter representation.

I would hope independent regulation – meaning 'independent of clubs' – is something that could be agreed on: no representatives of individual clubs on a body tasked with balancing the interests of all stakeholders across the whole game from top to bottom. Certainly, supporters appear to be in favour: 86 per cent of respondents to the Athletic's post Project Big Picture survey felt the game would benefit from an independent regulator.[3]

However, we must be careful to avoid rushing to identify solutions for problems that are complex and long-standing. We need to be clear what these changes would mean in practice, mindful of the cultural and legal context in the UK into which they would need to fit. Does football really want to create a new, external body that would leave the game more exposed to party political shifts? I have been involved in the regulatory process in several industries in the UK and abroad. It is a complicated area that generally leads to an inflexible and legalistic environment. Do we want this for football? If we become buried in a bureaucratic process, we risk diverting attention from our desired outcomes: ensuring clear objectives; creating a structure to allow appropriate stakeholder representation; building in checks and balances; and giving the authorities the resources and competencies to carry out their remits.

To support the governance process, we need a licensing regime for clubs with clear rules on issues such as: the basis for approving owners and overseeing changes in ownership of clubs; management and protection of key assets; the regulation and monitoring of finances; and standards of behaviour in areas such as the treatment of supporters, commitment to increasing diversity and inclusion, and supplier relationships. This would also provide clarity on the division of responsibility between the regulator, clubs and other bodies. I have steered clear of the women's game in this book because I don't have sufficient knowledge for the depth of analysis it merits. Nevertheless, it is logical that a fundamental review of governance should extend to the women's game, assuming it wants to take part – staying at arms' length may be the prudent approach.

Alongside the professional game, a financial settlement needs to be agreed for community activities, grass roots and, to an extent to be defined, the women's game. The prime minister promised an investment in facilities; football should seize the opportunity and aim to secure the maximum possible amount of money.[4]

Finally, reform must ensure the authorities have the resources and skills to carry out their role, which will require regular access to financial information to allow them to use the powers to intervene as necessary. It is without question that more resources will be required to manage the game, partly to reflect its complexities and partly to ensure governance is improved.

It is an involved model.

That is the theory. Having asked you to follow me on the journey through this book, it is only fair I share my thoughts. What would I do? I share my thinking below. To help shape and test it, I have sought to understand and reflect what the largest stakeholder group – supporters – might want to happen. I have used the FSA's survey of supporters in 2017, the EFL's 2019 research and the Athletic's PBP research to inform my thinking.[5]

My starting point is to preserve the pyramid, because it captures the essence of the game: the opportunity to dream of success. Based on the public reaction to the proposed European Super League, I am not alone – football supporters everywhere want the same.

But I want a more balanced, open and sustainable pyramid that offers a realistic possibility to more clubs of promotion, and then a fighting chance of surviving at a higher level. We can achieve this by action in three areas: Firstly, a greater redistribution of income from rich to poor – both within the Premier League and across the whole pyramid – than today; second, reforms to curb wasteful expenditure and generate additional revenues, some of which will generate additional revenues to support redistribution and grassroots and community provision; and finally reforms to the labour market such as on player development and loans to enable football to help itself. The system established must have the capability to provide rigorous oversight to ensure clubs neither misuse the income they receive nor take risks that endanger their long-term sustainability.

My objectives rule out both a closed, elite model on the lines of the NFL and the current, unbalanced structure. I would establish a system of redistribution designed to reduce the financial cliff edges between divisions. Through its proposals to reduce the number of teams in the top division and replace parachute payments with effectively a withholding tax on promoted teams, Project Big Picture would have done exactly the opposite for Championship clubs earning promotion.[6]

Consistent with the research undertaken by Liverpool University[7], by creating a healthy battle for relegation places and dynamism throughout the Premier League, greater redistribution should be supportive for TV revenues over time. To maximise viewer interest across the EFL, as well as offering clubs a greater hope of advancing, I would retain three up and three down to the Premier League but increase promotion and relegation to four clubs in all other divisions and to the National League.

Turning to the financial settlement. Historically, a much greater proportion of the total revenues generated by football was redistributed within the pyramid. Allowing this percentage to fall when total income was rising explains why imbalances have risen to today's unsustainable levels. Revenue sharing does two things: first, as in horse racing, taking some money off the richest clubs acts as a handicap to limit their dominance; and second, the inflows to smaller clubs increase their financial resources, allowing them to plan with more certainty and security. However, revenue sharing alone can't solve football's financial challenges – in a market likely to be flat at best with balance sheets in need of repair – we also need to control expenditure.

Project Big Picture reportedly proposed sharing of around one fifth of forecast TV and associated income, around £750 million,[8] an increase on the roughly fifteen per cent in the existing approach but a long way short of the 50 per cent in the pre-1980s arrangement. An additional £180 million was offered to support the grass roots. As clubs in the EFL voted in favour of the proposals in Project Big Picture, we can assume the levels of redistribution offered are on the right lines. However, there were no alternatives on the table and with the financial pressure created by the pandemic high at the time, there may have been pressure to support a less than optimal outcome. Most importantly, presumably because of the need to keep the other 14 clubs in the top division on side, the proposals were relatively less generous in financial terms for clubs winning promotion to the Premier League. A more balanced approach offering a realisitic chance of survival is required.

A reasonable compromise, in my opinion, would be for a target of a third of total Premier League common income (TV and League sponsorship) to be redistributed to the wider football pyramid – roughly the midpoint of the current and pre-Premier League models. Applying this percentage to the 2018/19 numbers implies a reallocation of about £1 billion, about £250 million more than Project Big Picture implied, albeit significantly less than the £1.5 billion the historic 50/25/25 sharing formula of the 1980s would imply. Such is the financial strength of the richest clubs, the new level of redistribution would improve the competitive balance in the top divisions and across the pyramid, without seriously hampering the richest clubs. This would enhance competition and maintain the game's commercial appeal.

By setting the target as a share of income, the actual amounts shared will adjust as the game's finances change. This ensures balance is retained if revenues grow but also allows for adjustments if revenues are lower than previously forecast if economic conditions change. Let's not forget our aim is to create greater balance. To this end, if total income falls, provided the share that is redistributed remains the same, the impact on balance should be largely unchanged, every receiving club gets less income, every donating club loses a smaller amount. Provided the total revenue of the game does not collapse, the model works.

For now, let's use £1 billion as the base to identify what needs to change. We require an incremental amount of around £250 million to redistribute compared to the proposed sharing in Project Big Picture.

Based on the current TV deal rolling over, this could be achieved by reducing the payments to all clubs but mainly for clubs qualifying for Europe, that benefit twice under the current system, earning higher domestic payments plus European income. As this increase would come mainly from the most successful clubs and would dampen slightly the benefits of the additional revenues from European competition, it will also help balance the Premier League. If the negotiations over TV rights prove difficult, sharing a portion of gate receipts could be considered as a source of funds and a tool for helping create more competitive balance.

In the current environment, squeezing the richest clubs seems likely to be widely supported and we should take the opportunity to cap returns. By offsetting the impact of a tougher economic environment through more promotion and relegation struggles due to four up, four down and the greater excitement of a balanced competition, it seems reasonable to assume no fall in revenues from the next EFL TV deal.

Moving to the second theme. There are ways of improving the efficiency in current spending that could support the proposed higher levels of resources for grassroots without hurting the financial performance of Premier League clubs.

The stand out area is payments to agents, which have reached extreme levels. FIFA has already set out plans to regulate this area more tightly to reduce the money flowing out of the game.[9] As the highest spending competition on both transfers and agents' fees, the Premier League could take the lead. In 2018/19 payments to agents amounted to £318 million in the English game. Transfer market activity is likely to be subdued in the short to medium-term as clubs repair their finances post-pandemic in a more challenging global economic environment. This should provide additional leverage to improve the terms of business with agents. A 10 per cent levy on agents' fees should generate at least £25 million a year initially, even if transfer values remain below the peak levels of 2018/19.

Another measure that offers potential benefits for both income and expenditure levels is a levy on international transfers. Not only would this addition generate funds for redistribution, it would increase the incentive for clubs to do more domestic deals, offering the prospect of more income flowing around the English game – redistribution by another route. Again allowing for some reduction in the level of transfer market activity, a 5 per cent levy could generate £50 million or more annually.

A 1 per cent levy on Premier League player wages should not be too controversial. On a total wage bill of around £3 billion, this should raise an additional £30 million. In addition to £1 billion for redistribution in the pyramid, the levies on agents, transfers and player wages will provide an additional £90 to £100 million for grassroots and good causes, an increase of 50 per cent on the proposals in Project Big Picture. Let's now turn our attention to spending, especially wages.

An integrated system of salary caps, with levels set relative to the other divisions, should be introduced across the Premier League and Championship with the existing EFL's schemes incorporated into the model. (While this suggestion seems radical for the Premier League on first pass, both Project Big Picture and the European Super League proposals included salary caps of some form. With European leagues facing similar if not more challenging financial outlooks than the Premier League due to lower TV rights payments, pressure on wages to remain competitive is likely to ease. It is also the case that fans would be supportive of these moves: 70 per cent of those surveyed by the FSA were in favour of salary caps).[10]

The caps in the EFL should incorporate an element of flexibility by having links to income growth not just a simple spending cap, to reflect the greater revenue-generating potential of some clubs and incentivise commercial efficiency, but with clear spending limits. To ensure an integrated approach across the pyramid, a standard contractual framework that specifies a percentage reduction in salaries as players move divisions should smooth cliff edges between divisions and provide more protection for promoted clubs.

With wages accounting for £3 billion in the Premier League in 2018/19, a cap 10 per cent below this figure, would generate about £300 million of cost savings, offsetting the extra £250 million taken from TV rights. And post-pandemic, with the finances of European elite clubs suffering far more than those in the Premier League, there should be scope for even greater cost savings.

However, as the period under the Short-Run Cost Control model (SRCC) showed, design of any system is very important in determining the impact on competitive balance. The proposed levels of redistribution outlined above will create additional pressure on wages in the Premier League and, provided no changes are made to the rules around allowable losses, this should incentivise clubs to seek to reduce their wage levels. It seems highly likely, because TV revenues are relatively more important to clubs outside of the Big Six, that the proposed changes in revenue sharing will constrain salaries at the middle and lower end of the revenue distribution in the top division. Therefore, additional salary restrictions may be required on the highest earning, highest spending clubs. If needed, a requirement that clubs with wage bills in excess of £200 million (Only the Big Six excluding Tottenham Hotspur in 2018/19) must break-even on a pre-tax basis and those clubs with wage bills in excess of £300 million (only the two Manchester clubs and Liverpool in 2018/19) have to generate a pre-tax return equivalent to at least 10 per cent of their wage bill, would provide a robust check on wage levels. A transition period of four years should be introduced to allow the clubs to adjust over the typical contract life.

It is time for the PFA to play their part and bring their members on board – the highest earning players have to show solidarity with their fellow professionals and accept some restrictions on wages at the top end of the game. Players have found their voice now they need to back up their words with deeds. In the aftermath of the aborted European Super League proposals, The Times convened a panel of experts to provide ideas on the future of the game. The two players consulted, John Barnes and Graeme Le Saux, both ex-England internationals, identified the need for salary constraints[11] – the answers to football's problems are staring us in the face.

This greater level of redistribution will smooth the transition between divisions. Nevertheless, as we have seen, such is the scale of the move, the transition between the Championship and Premier League could still be challenging. Parachute payments attract a great deal of attention, mostly because they are believed to distort competition in the Championship. The evidence does not support this – wage levels are not a reliable predictor of outcomes in the Championship. However, the perceived effect is important, this does appear to cause clubs to take risks to compete with clubs believed to have an advantage from receiving these payments.

Whatever their impact, parachute payments are primarily a symptom of the massive difference in revenues between the Premier League and Championship. To provide promoted teams with a chance to survive in the Premier League without forcing them to take undue financial risks, therefore, some adjustment mechanism is required. If our ambition is more open competition and opportunity for all, and not just the clubs with wealthy backers, a more refined approach than parachute payments is required.

By reducing the gap between divisions, our overall proposals for greater total redistribution and cost control will help clubs promoted from the Championship, but this will not be equivalent in value to parachute payments. More flexibility in the fair play rules to permit additional losses that allow clubs to boost and restructure their finances using owner finance, at levels approved by the regulator, only available on promotion and relegation, should be considered. If clubs on relegation are incentivised, through favourable accounting rules and punitive future salary controls, to divest some of the players previously acquired on promotion, this should compensate for the absence of parachute payments, while at the same time satisfying other clubs concerned about the adverse impact on competition when teams return to the Championship.

Finally, to future-proof our model, we should consider how football can help itself over time. Young player development offers potential. Currently, the elite player performance programme (EPPP) has handed control of the development of the best young players in England to Premier League clubs, ever reducing the transfer income by Premier League clubs being recycled into the domestic game and letting them dominate the market using the loan system. Project Big Picture proposed a significant expansion of the loan system.

With more money available through revenue sharing, clubs outside the Premier League should be encouraged to invest more in youth development. This is likely to be popular: around four fifths of fans want to see local players in their team[12]. To create incentives for the Premier League not to hoard talent, we could consider linking the revenue-sharing target to the value of total transfer spending recycled within the English game, with potential to reduce the payments if targets are met. A reduction in the number of players that can be loaned would give all clubs greater access to talent. For competitive fairness, loans between teams in the same division should be prohibited.

In total, these proposals could support revenue sharing of £1 billion plus close to £300 million for grassroots, offer more balance between Premier League clubs and, by creating a framework for greater revenue generation by smaller clubs in future, provide a buffer to help withstand any future shocks – an achievable and fair settlement. This proposed model of revenue sharing and cost control, indexed to future revenue growth, is the minimum required for reasonable competitive balance and financial sustainability across the pyramid.

Momentum for change is strong and the Big Six are in a weaker position than for some time after the failed attempts at reform of Project Big Picture and the European Super League. Nevertheless, challenge is likely. In light of the prevailing mood, I expect clubs outside of the Big Six will be more open to change than previously, especially as the reforms do reduce some of the dominance of the richest clubs.

Finally on the competitive structure and financial settlement, the clubs should agree to abandon the proposed reform of the Champions' League that allows historic performance to influence future participation independent of performance in qualifying. As a quid pro quo, it may be necessary to accept exempting the top teams from the Carabao Cup, and moving forward with no replays in the FA Cup to ensure the teams competing in Europe have the proper time to rest and prepare.

These proposals would require significantly more regulation and oversight, but North American sports shows how complicated designing appropriate models is. It is a simple choice: if we want more balanced competition, we need more extensive regulation. The experience of the last four decades has proven beyond doubt that a free-for-all will lead to an unbalanced competition dominated by a few teams.

Let's turn to how we make this work. Football's challenges are complex and long-standing and likely to change in future. We cannot create a permanent solution today. Alongside the proposals for re-shaping the game's economics, we need to establish a governance structure we are confident can guide and protect the game over time. Despite the support for an independent regulator and the German 50+1 model, there are no simple panaceas, we need to establish a *system* not rely on a single body – a structure that incorporates power sharing, ensures representation of stakeholders, especially supporters and communities, and encourages consensus-based decision-making.

Regulation must be independent of clubs. Armed with their knowledge of working within the Football Association, the authors of *Saving the Beautiful Game* believe the best option would be for the government to establish an independent football regulator. Although they do suggest this could be temporary until the FA has completed its restructuring.

I am not so sure. Having designed regulatory bodies, worked for them and for companies dealing with them, we should be careful what you wish for. Inevitably the remit expands – sometimes necessarily, sometimes accidentally. No-one involved in the UK's privatisation programme ever envisaged that the regulatory bodies established at that time would develop into the large, complex institutions they are today. One of the main reasons is the inevitable increase in legal process and awareness created by statutory bodies. This creates a culture of risk which drives more intervention, increasing the burden and costs of regulation.

There is also the issue of resources. Where would the staff of the new body come from? Without doubt, there is a need to recruit more specialists into football, especially in finance and stakeholder engagement, but, unlike most new regulators, there is not a body of staff to transfer from elsewhere in the public sector. As it seems the majority of the resources would have to be recruited from the FA, Premier League or EFL, how practical would it be to move people into the civil service? Does setting up a new body merit the disruption?

For me, the Football Association is the obvious candidate to manage the overall pyramid, minimising disruption, and maximising the chances of successful reform. The concern is its ability to take on the role? It is not fit for purpose as currently managed and constituted. It needs new people, restructuring and a reshaping of its relationships with the rest of football. However, we shouldn't judge the future by the past. Having lost the political battle when the Premier League was created, the FA sought to redefine its role, opting out of aspiring to lead the English game. We can change this.

There is so much knowledge of all aspects of the management and regulation of football within the FA that I am loath to put at risk. It is also important that the English game rebuild its reputation and influence in European and world football, which the FA is best placed to do. My preference would be to make the FA the regulator, with responsibility located in a dedicated unit in the organisation outside the main body of the organisation. Leadership would be vested in a board with members from the Premier League and EFL (not their clubs), alongside supporters, players and representatives of the game across the country and truly independent voices to ensure the board is representative of society as well as the mix of people in the game. Work to reform the FA could continue in parallel to the operation of this new entity with the aim of strengthening governance of the wider game.

I believe that the concentration of power in a small group has contributed to football's problems today. Football is a national asset, but its impact is felt locally. We should not expect a national regulator alone to lead the game; more authority and responsibility should be devolved to supporters and communities. Our aim should be to build additional layers of checks and balances into the governance structure to temper extreme or narrow decision-making and to ensure the game's values are front and centre at all times.

Supporters are the largest stakeholder group in English football and responsible for more than thirty-two million appearances at professional grounds in a typical season. They are also the group with the least formal representation in the game's decision-making, a stark contrast to Germany, where most ownership models have a role for supporters built in. Ninety per cent of fans surveyed by the FSA in 2017 were in favour of supporters having seats on club boards.[13]

Suggestions that a version of Germany's 50+1 role could be adopted in England were prominent in the response to the proposed European Super League. While it is an appealing idea, it seems a huge ask. On a practical level, Germany moved from a membership owned model to this approach in 1998, the opposite direction to what is now being proposed in England. It is more difficult to shift from a privately owned model to a collective one, especially as the UK's cultural and legal business environment is so different to the one in Germany.

There are other potential barriers to change. It seems unlikely supporters could raise the funds to buy a majority share in most Premier league clubs and maybe others. This suggests an approach to transfer control without equity would be required. As a member of the Government's Trade Advisory group on investment, I am aware how sensitive foreign investors are to changes in the regulation of their assets. Control attracts a premium so losing control of a valuable investment could potentially reduce the value of the business. I doubt the owners would go quietly. Would the UK really want to risk jeopardising its global relationships, at a time after Brexit when our bargaining strength is relatively low, for football, popular yes but still a small industry?

How best then to ensure decisions take into account the values of the game as well as financial and business considerations? My preference would be for the creation of football boards with majority community and supporter control (a 'golden share', in effect), separate from the main corporate board. The responsibilities of this new entity would be the major footballing issues impacting supporters and communities and financial scrutiny and oversight. By defining the responsibilities in conjunction with those for the overall regulatory body, this would provide an additional source of checks and balances on club owners and management, make day-to-day decision-making reflective of stakeholder interests, and provide an early-warning system allowing crises such as those at Bury and Bolton to be dealt with before they become critical.

Alongside these changes, there should be a mandatory requirement for independent supporter non-executive directors on the main club board. More work is required to identify how legally to best allow these people to speak on behalf of supporters not just as individuals as this will be an unusual model for UK corporate governance – initially it may be as an observer. Clubs would have the option of offering ownership to supporters, but this would not be a requirement. When filling the positions on the new boards, clubs should be obliged to consider the composition in terms of their diversity and inclusiveness.

To maximise further the likelihood of the game's values being reflected in decision-making, the Owners and Directors test should be revised. Currently, in its various forms, scrutiny of potential new owners and officials focuses on a narrow set of financial commercial criteria. We should take the opportunity to broaden the remit to allow for consideration of attitudes to the game and broader social responsibility. The people in positions of authority in the English game should be 'fit and proper' across the board.

To provide further protection for supporters, the role of the Independent Football Supporters Ombudsman should be broadened and strengthened from one of review to a more pro-active stance within the formal regulatory authority. As things currently stand, supporters can initiate a dispute process after an event, but have no ability to influence decisions on ticketing, match scheduling or merchandising strategy. The new body would have the power to review decisions on ticketing prices, such as hikes in prices for specific games and the timing and reasonableness of TV kick-off times, in the event a club's own governance was unable to reach a satisfactory outcome.

The investment in community activities is one of the true success stories of the English game, and the more resources they can be given the better. Now seems appropriate to review the 5 per cent indicative figure. The Project Big Picture proposal of an initial fund of £180 million can be increased by around 50 per cent based on the proposals for revenue sharing outlined above. Within the regulator, a new community board should oversee distributions and monitor and quantify impact on an annual basis. With government having promised support for building new facilities, the board should be responsible for distribution and monitoring this fund.

The Premier League should be required to broaden access to the game for low-income groups and young supporters. This should be a threefold approach: two live games per season featuring each club in the Premier League to be made available on free-to-air TV channels; an open ticketing model that keeps a percentage of tickets for each club available once or twice a season for young supporters or people on minimum wage (or a similar measure of low income) to purchase at discounted rates.

Finally, what of the England team? I have always been supportive of the FA's desire to improve the team's fortunes. As Russia 2018 and Euro 2020 reminded us, when England do well in a major tournament the mood of the whole nation improves, and the TV viewing figures confirm this is the case. I am convinced by the arguments that players should be adequately rested for summer tournaments. A mid-season break of four weeks should therefore be introduced in the Premier League, after the Christmas period. Not only would this allow elite players to rest, but it would also provide a window for the EFL to show-case itself.

Such a proposal is likely to be met with criticism. To head this off, the FA should be tasked with building a consensus for reform of the international fixture schedule. Since the fall of the Berlin Wall, the increase in the number of nations entering World Cup and European Championship qualifying has increased. There has been little sign of the smaller nations improving their on the pitch performance despite greater exposure.[14] Now is the time to push for a more segmented international regime similar to the European Nations' League model with countries tiered based on their performance in the previous qualifying round. The countries with the worst record will have to qualify to move back into the main qualifying competition, possibly with a small number of wild card slots for each tournament for countries not in the main groups. This would be similar to how tennis has historically organised the Davis Cup. The reduction in fixtures would limit any disruption of a mid-season break.

After two successful tournaments, how best to ensure the continuing success of the national team? I believe increased investment in player, manager and coach development is the best route forward. If we have the best talent, developed and recruited in a totally diverse and inclusive fashion, we should have the best possible chances of success. A share of the money redistributed should be ear-marked for youth development and the current regime adjusted to give clubs outside of the elite more ability to recruit and develop talent.

With the UK having left the European Union, there is an opportunity to change the current rules on quotas and work permits. I would propose that twelve players in every Premier League squad, up from eight but still less than half of the twenty-five, have to be England-qualified, not home-grown as currently stipulated by 2024/25. Alongside the proposed changes to youth development this will provide an additional incentive to help boost the pipeline of English talent.

Alongside changes to the rules governing international players, the criteria for granting work permits to international managers and coaches should be reviewed to give the next Gareth Southgate the best possible chance of rising to the top. Accompanying this with a commitment of increased resources to support the personal and professional development of English coaches and managers should create more opportunities for domestic managers to gain top-flight experience and build a stronger network from which future England staff can be recruited. Change in this area offers other benefits. If we are serious about increasing diversity in all aspects of the game, applying objective criteria to recruitment offers a way to make management and coaching reflect the society the game is based in.

When I started thinking about the future, I thought that to set a focal point for the reform programme, the FA should look to lead a bid for the 2030 World Cup, setting a target for the transformed English game to showcase itself to the world. As I learnt more about the failings in the governance of the game, I realised this was too ambitious, and I was in danger of making the same mistakes the FA has made.

However, with the new mood around the game and with the prime minister having signalled his backing for a 2030 World Cup bid, maybe there is an option? In addition to reforming its approach to managing the domestic game, the proposals set out above do require the English game to co-ordinate and influence opinion across Europe – a salary cap will be more effective if it is applied broadly consistently across Europe.

Securing change in the international fixture list is one example, but other initiatives such as better regulation of agents and a transfer levy will be more effective if other countries adopt similar approaches. We do need the FA and the Government to be more engaged in the management of the international game

Our overriding aim in 2030 should be a sustainable national game but an aspirational target may be the way to engage and enthuse everyone behind the reform. It will require adequate resourcing and extensive support to the FA but setting out to hold the most diverse and inclusive World Cup in 2030 could be the way to make the reform programme relevant to all.

Covid-19 has reset the dial. There is a chance to reshape the English game in the way we choose. It is not a nice-to-have; it is essential. Failing to act will see many clubs disappear and the game become ever more dominated by a few teams. Football is more than a game – now is the time for us to reclaim it and save it from itself.

FURTHER READING

Writing on football has tended to lag behind that for other sports such as cricket and boxing. This has started to change in recent years following Nick Hornby's pioneering. Understandably, football has led the way in stimulating books analysing the economics, finances and politics of the game. Here are some of the works I have relied on in this book together with others that capture key elements of the reasons why we love the game.

For more detail in chronological order of the history of the Premier League and its consequences, the following books are invaluable. To keep up to date, David Conn continues to unpick and chronicle the financial manoeuvring of the game in his articles in the *Guardian*.

Alex Fynn and Lynton Guest, *Out of Time,* (Simon & Schuster, 1994).
Tom Bower, *Broken Dreams,* (Simon & Schuster, 2003).
David Conn, *The Beautiful Game,* (Yellow Jersey Press, 2005).
Mihir Bose, *Game Changers,* (Marshall Cavendish Business, 2012).
David Goldblatt, *The Game of our Lives,* (Penguin Viking, 2014).
Adrian Tempany, *And the Sun Shines Now* (Faber & Faber, 2016).
James Montague, *The Billionaires Club,* (Bloomsbury, 2017).
Joshua Robinson and Jonathan Clegg (2019), *The Club,* (John Murray, 2019).
David Conn, *Richer than God,* (Quercus, 2019).

For a slightly different angle, placing the economic and financial activities in a broader context, try,

The English Premier League: A Socio-Cultural Analysis, edited by Richard Elliot, 2017, Routledge.

As introductions to more rigorous economic analysis of football, these two books are a great place to start,

Stephen Dobson and John Goddard, *The Economics of Football,* (Cambridge University Press, 1999).

Simon Kuper and Stefan Syzmanski, *Soccernomics* (Harper Collins, 2012).

If you want to explore how on the field events have developed, I recommend,

Jonathan Wilson, *Inverting the Pyramid,* (Orion Books, 2008), and

Michael Cox, *The Mixer,* (Harper Collins, 2017).

To remind yourself of why people love the game, I would turn to,

Nick Hornby, *Fever Pitch,* (Victor Gollancz, 1992),

Colin Schindler, *Fathers, Sons and Football,* (Headline, 2002), and

Jim White, *You'll Win Nothing With Kids,* (Little, Brown, 2007) – like looking in a mirror for anyone who has coached their children.

And to go deeper into specific topics,

David Conn, *The Fall of the House of FIFA,* (Yellow Jersey Press, 2017),

Chris Porter, *Supporter Ownership in English Football,* (Palgrave Macmillan, 2019), and

Daniel Geey, *Done Deal,* (Bloomsbury, 2019), an inside view on transfers and agents.

ACKNOWLEDGEMENTS

As I'm well into my fourth decade as a business economist, I know forecasting is never easy and it is always good to be prepared for any outcome. Nevertheless, when I started working on this book in December 2018, no one could have foreseen what was coming. *One* unexpected development, perhaps, but the Covid-19 pandemic, the failed launch of the European Super League and the UK Government's rediscovery of football each had a significant enough impact on the English game to require inclusion.

With the publication date continually moving into the future, what started out as an exciting journey for me and a minor distraction at home became an ongoing burden on my wife Jax – the kitchen table often resembling a crime scene as I fumbled around for the right quote or piece of data to update my analysis. Despite her apparent disinterest in football – I say 'apparent' as she is not averse to providing a key statistic out of the blue – she stuck with me, her interventions improving the book just as they do daily in my life, for which I remain both surprised and eternally grateful. Similarly, my three adult children (I can't bring myself to view them as real 'adults'), Joe, Ben and Molly, never showed their frustration despite the likelihood of them ever having something tangible to show their friends seeming to decline every day. Their faith in their dad is humbling and deeply appreciated.

On the days when it was unclear if there would be a traditional game to save, it was the encouragement I had received when I first floated the idea of writing a book that kept me going. That publishing industry heavyweights Susan Sandon and Richard Cable thought my idea was worth pursuing was a massive boost, as was the very positive reaction to my initial ideas from Tim Broughton. Once committed, the ongoing interest and support from colleagues, clients and friends – the regular, extensive and heated debates on the future of the game at the end of the EY Business Dinners hosted by Sam Woodward in Manchester a prime example – was a huge and much appreciated motivation.

As to the book itself, I was extremely fortunate to be able to draw on the works of the writers set out in the Additional Reading section to plot a course through the history of the English game, allowing me to focus my attention on recent events and developments.

For up-to-date information, I relied on: Deloitte's work (presented in their Annual Review of Football Finance and accompanying Databook) as the go-to source for financial information on the English and European game; the regular analysis provided by Swiss Ramble (his description of himself as a football blogger fails to do justice to the insight he provides on the financial structure of the English and European games – if you have a question, he will usually have already answered it); and *Off The Pitch*, an online football newsletter that provides daily insight into what is happening in the business side of football. For media-related data and analysis, Enders Analysis are the gold standard.

To challenge the narrative of the professional game, I have relied extensively on the high-quality research produced by the Football Supporters Association – an incredibly valuable voice for the game's loyal followers. Their work and advocacy across a wide range of issues such as ticket pricing, financial regulation and supporter ownership of clubs has provided the only protection for fans from the increasing commercialisation of the English game. It is vital the 'fan-led review' rightly recognises their expertise and knowledge.

The back cover wording references lyrics from 'Three Lions' written by David Baddiel, Frank Skinner and The Lightning Seeds.

A big thank-you is also due to the teams I have worked with at EY in the sports business. Peter Arnold and Colin Edwards for their insight on the economics; financial experts, Andy Williams and Mike Timmins; Tom Kingsley across all sports; and Matt Corkery – a proper economist and supporter who was the perfect sounding-board, often without him knowing, as we spent hours talking about the game in general, Stoke City, QPR, England and much more. The time spent working through the data, challenging and revising conclusions has been hugely important in shaping my thinking.

Last but certainly not least, the people who did the work. Joe Pickering and his team at Yellow Jersey for their patience with a novice author, always ready to take the time to offer support and guide me through each step of the process. And Binita Shah, my long-suffering right hand, who worked tirelessly to manage my diary to create slots to allow me the time to write uninterrupted. At the height of the pandemic, this was an almost impossible task, but one she pulled off in her inimitable style.

This book is for everyone I have played with and against (especially the Manchester University AFC team of the early '80s and the Saturday morning dads), the players I have coached as best I could, those I have watched or talked football with, and all those people who love football and who recognise the mix of hope, anticipation, anxiety and dread when they wake up on a Saturday morning. My hope is that it contributes to a move to a better game, one run for the benefit of all stakeholders. The more the content is used the better, but the responsibility for the ideas, analysis and conclusions, as well as any omissions or errors, are mine and mine alone.

NOTES

1 What is the point of Stoke City?

1 Nick Lustig and Paul Gilmour, 'Marco Arnautovic labels West Ham "a bigger and more ambitious club than Stoke",' www.skysports.com, 27 July 2017.

2 Graham Hill, 'We're disappointed in him,' *Sun*, 26 July 2017.

3 Statista.com, Q1 20202. Radio stations ranked by weekly reach in the United Kingdom (UK) as of 1st quarter 2020 (in 1,000 listeners).

4 Tom Bower, *Broken Dreams,* (Simon & Schuster, 2003).

5 EY reports available at www.ey.com. Including: *NFL2016 Mexico Game: The Economic Impact, Final Report February 2017*; and *The Economic Impact of Rugby World cup 2015. Post-event Study (2016)*.

6 EY and the Premier League, *The Economic Impact of the Premier League,* (2015).

7 *Sport and Business: A Winning Combination* (Department for Business, Innovation & Skills, Department for Digital, Culture, Media and Sport, the Rt Hon. Sajid Javid MP, 18 November 2015).

8 EY and Premier League, *Stoke City Football Club: Economic and Social Impact Assessment* September 2017). *Social Return on Investment in Sport – A participation model for England* (Sheffield Hallam, 2016).

9 Throughout this book, I use 'Big Six' to refer to Arsenal, Chelsea, Liverpool, Manchester City, Manchester United and Tottenham Hotspur. It should not be viewed as any support for such a grouping.

10 Stoke City Football Club Limited, Report and Accounts 2016/17, 31 May 2017.

11 'Premier League global audience climbs to 3.2 billion for 2018/19 season.', Sam Carp, Sportspromedia for the Premier League, 17 July

2019. 'La Liga sees 2019/20 audience surge to 2.8 billion global viewers.', Steve Impey for Sportspromedia, 2 September 2020.

12   Deloitte, *Home Truths*: Annual Review of Football Finance (2020).

13   Sami Mokbel and Laurie Whitwell, 'Arsenal v Liverpool will not be played on Christmas Eve.', *Daily Mail*, 19 October 2017.

14   Lizzie Dearden, 'Barry Bennell: football coach jailed for 31 years for sexually abusing young boys,' *Independent*, 19 February 2018. Sonny Cohen, 'Discrimination in football like "wild west" at grass roots level', *Guardian*, 24 July 2019. Dan Kilpatrick, 'Grassroots football in crisis', *Daily Telegraph*, 14 December 2018.

15   *Home Truths*, op. cit., Databook, June 2020. Stephen Dobson and John Goddard, *The Economics of Football*, (Cambridge University Press, 1999) p.71. Figures quoted after adjusting for revenue sharing.

16   Deloitte, op.cit.

17   Enders Analysis, *Peak football revenues and boom scenarios*, 25 October 2019.

18   All 3 national UK political parties included plans for a review of football in their manifestos. *Our Plan*. Conservative Manifesto 2019, conservatives.com. *Its time for change; The Labour Party Manifesto 2019*.www.labour.org.uk. *Plan for Britain's Future*. www. libdems.org.uk.

19   BT Group, www.Forbes.com, 12 May 2020.

20   GDP First quarterly estimate, UK: April to June 2020, ONS.

21   Matt Slater, 'Explained: Project Big Picture – The winners and losers', *Athletic*, 12 October 2020.

22   Dom Farrell, 'Project Big Picture unanimously rejected by Premier League.', www.goal.com, 14 October 2020.

23   For a summary see Super League Special Report, *Off the Pitch*, 20 April 2021.

24   *Our Plan*. Conservative Manifesto 2019, conservatives.com..

2 A Whole New Ball Game

1   Nick Davies, 'The Anatomy of a Soccer Slaying, *Guardian*, 8 August 1983.

2 Urban75.org, 'After the act? The (re) construction and regulation of football fandom'. Retrieved via Wikipedia.

3 For more details see Urban75.org, op. cit., Mihir Bose, *Game Changers,* (Marshall Cavendish Business, 2012), and Simon Brunton, 'Quarantine: Our sad, sick game.', *The Guardian,* 2 June 2020.

4 *'History of English Football'*, www.european-football-statistics. co.uk, with thanks to Kevin Brandsatter and Paul Merkens

5 There are many excellent books that cover the Hillsborough tragedy and its consequences over the next three decades. *And the Sun Shines Now* by Adrian Tempany (Faber & Faber, 2016) is a forensic analysis.

6 Deloitte, op. cit.

7 Ibid. *'History of English Football'* op.cit., and Sportspromedia, op. cit.

8 See suggested list of further reading.

9 David Edgerton, *The Rise and Fall of the British Nation* (Allen Lane, 2018), p.389–394.

10 *'History of English Football'*, www.european-football-statistics. co.uk, op.cit.

11 William Keegan, *Mrs Thatcher's Economic Experiment* (Allen Lane, 1984).

12 'The Thatcher Years in Statistics', www.bbc.co.uk, 9 April 2013.

13 Department of Employment, *Employment Gazette, 1980–84* (HMSO).

14 Margaret Thatcher, *Margaret Thatcher: The Downing Street Years,* (Harper Collins, 1993), p.626.

15 Peter Riddell, *The Thatcher Decade,* (Blackwell, 1989), p.81–82.

16 Rana Foroohar, *Makers and Takers,* (Crown Business, 2016), p.5.

17 See David Conn, *The Beautiful Game,* (Yellow Jersey Press, 2005) Chapter 5 for details of the shifts in ownership. MMC intervention is discussed in Chapter 2 of *The Economics of Football*, Stephen Dobson and John Goddard, (Cambridge University Press, 1999) and Tempany, op.cit, p.110.

18 Nigel Lawson, *The View from No. 11* (Bantam Press, 1992), p.722.

19 Quoted in Tempany, op. cit., p.99, 'Mr Murdoch for you, Prime Minister'.

20 Conn, op.cit., p.47.

21 Tempany, op. cit., Chapter 4 provides a detailed history and analysis of the process by which of BskyB, later Sky, was formed.

22 Ibid., p.109.

23 For a history, see Regulator Archives, www.ofcom.org.uk. and David Parker, *The Official History of Privatisation Volume 1 (Routledge, 2008)*.

24 Margaret Thatcher, *The Downing Street Years* (Harper Collins, 1993).

25 Nigel Lawson, op. cit., and Michael Heseltine, *Life in the Jungle* (Hodder & Stoughton, 2000).

26 *Popplewell Inquiry into Crowd Safety at Sports Grounds* (HMSO, January 1986).

27 See Conn, op.cit., p.95–7, David Goldblatt, *The Game of our Lives*, (Penguin Viking, 2014), p.14–15, Alex Fynn and Lynton Guest, *Out of Time*, (Simon & Schuster, 1994), Chapter 2, 'Blueprint for Chaos', for more detail on events in this period.

28 This section draws on *The Hillsborough Stadium Tragedy*, the Inquiry by the Rt Hon. Lord Justice Taylor, Final Report, January 1990 (HMSO).

29 Taylor Report, op.cit., paragraph 117.

30 Taylor Report, op. cit., paragraph 72.

31 Taylor Report, op.cit, paragraph 53

32 Taylor Report, op.cit., paragraph 51

33 Taylor Report, op.cit., paragraph 118, identified a cost of £130 million. Tempany, op.cit, suggests a figure of £500 million was the revised estimate, pages 51–52

34 Taylor Report, op.cit., paragraphs 104–117.

35 Moments in Football History: The Bosman Ruling, 26th May 2020, www.bloomsburyfootball.com. Stephen Dobson and John Goddard (2004),

36 Taylor Report, op.cit., paragraph 117.

37 Mihir Bose, op.cit., p. 60.

38 History of the 5 clubs.

39 For more details see Conn (2005), op. cit., p.41–42 and 'Follow the Money', *London Review of Books*, 30 August 2012.

40   Alex Fynn and Lynton Guest, *op.cit.*, p.26 to 29 and *'The History of Football'*,op.cit., for a detailed history.

41   Fynn and Guest, op.cit, p.31, p.197–198.

42   See Conn (2005) op.cit. p.40–42, and Goldblatt, op.cit., p.11 for more details on events in this period.

43   '$2 Billion deal for NFL', *New York Times*, 23 March 1982.

44   David Conn (2005)., op.cit., p.40.

45   Joshua Robinson and Jonathan Clegg (2019), *The Club*, (John Murray, 2019), p.23–28.

46   Simon Inglis quoted in David Goldblatt, (2014), op.cit., p. x.

47   For a detailed discussion see Goldblatt, op. cit., Chapter 1.

48   *'History of English Football'*, www.european-football-statistics. co.uk. Statistic refers to Premier League attendances.

49   *'A History of Football on TV'*, www.live-footballontv.com.

50   Martin Kelner, *'Sit Down and Cheer'*, Wisden Sports Writing, 2012.

51   Ibid.

52   Conn (2005), op. cit., p.47. Deal was inflation linked.

53   Fynn and Guest, op.cit., p.26.

54   *One Game, One Team, One Voice: Football's Future* (Football League, 1989).

55   Fynn and Guest, op. cit., p. 30, p.36.

56   Ibid, p.25–26. Chapter 2 provides a fascinating participant's view of this period.

57   Football Association, *The Blueprint for the Future of Football*, (1991).

58   Fynn and Guest, op.cit., p.40.

59   Fynn and Guest, op.cit. p.55.

60   'Explained: Project Big Picture – The winners and losers', Matt Slater, *Athletic*, 12 October 2020.

61   For a detailed history see Fynn and Guest, Conn, Tempany, op. cit.

62   Alan Sugar, *What You See is What You Get p.385,* (Macmillan, 2011).

63   Ibid., p.385–6.

64   Goldblatt (2014), op. cit., p.18.

65   Tempany, op. cit., p104., Bose op.cit., p.76, www.skyuser.co.uk, *Sky at 20 – Time Line,* (2009) and www.skygroup.com.

66 Moments in Football History: The Bosman Ruling, 26th May 2020, www.bloomsburyfootball.com. Stephen Dobson and John Goddard (2004), op.cit., p.95–98.

67 'There were only 13 foreign players when the Premier League began in 1992' Joe Bernstein, *MailOnline*, 9 August 2017.

68 Transfermarkt.com

69 Conn, op. cit., p.289.

70 For a fuller discussion of a complicated process see Bower, op. cit., Chapter 5; Conn, op. cit., Chapter 6; Tempany, op. cit., Chapter 8.

71 The economic arguments in the RPC case are discussed in Chapter 2 of *The Economics of Football*, Stephen Dobson and John Goddard, (Cambridge University Press, 1999)

72 For a fuller discussion of a complicated process see Bower, op. cit., Chapter 5; Conn, op. cit., Chapter 6; Tempany, op. cit., Chapter 8.

73 'NTL pull plug on Premier League deal,' BBC Sport website, 18 October 2000.

74 Ibid.

75 When ITV Digital collapsed: the deal that almost took down the Football League, Jack Pitt-Brooke, *The Athletic*, 28 April 2020.

76 Conn (2005), op. cit., p.289.

77 *Disruption in Premier League Football: 2018 Auction finally over?*, Julian Aquilina, Enders Analysis, 8 June 2018. TV rights quoted include all broadcasters not just pay-TV payments.

78 Joshua Robinson and Jonathan Clegg (2019), op.cit., p.231.

79 Jane Martinson, 'EU moves to end TV soccer monopoly', *Guardian*, 15 August 2005.

80 Enders Analysis (2018), op. cit.

81 Ibid.

82 Ofcom, *Pay TV Statement*, 31 March 2010, www.ofcom.org.

83 M. Michalis and P. Smith, 'The relation between content providers and distributors: Lessons from the regulation of television distribution in the United Kingdom', *Telematics and Informatics*, 33(2), 665–673, www.Westminster.ac.uk, 2016, provides a detailed discussion of the various regulatory interventions.

84 Robinson and Clegg, op.cit., p.109.

85   See Conn, op.cit., p.109–113, Goldblatt, op.cit., p.35–36, and Bower, op.cit., p.138 for more details on owner sales.

86   James Montague, *The Billionaires Club,* (Bloomsbury, 2017) and Robinson and Clegg, op.cit., provide more details on the history of foreign ownership.

87   Daily Telegraph, op.cit., Robinson and Clegg, op.cit., p.95.

88   Robinson and Clegg, op.cit., p.109–112.

89   'Debt £511 million but dividends galore: The Glazers' legacy at Manchester United', David Conn, *Guardian*, 17 October 2019.

90   Swiss Ramble, Twitter, 14 September 2020.

91   My analysis of club data.

92   James Montague, *The Billionaires' Club,* (Bloomsbury, 2017) and Joshua Robinson and Joanthan Clegg (2019) op.cit., provide more details on the development of foreign ownership.

93   David Conn, *Richer than God,* (Quercus, 2019) is an insightful analysis of the ownership of Manchester City with a fan's perspective.

94   My analysis of club data and Kasper Kronenberg, 'New Burnley owners could lead the way for future Private Equity takeovers', *Off the Pitch*, 28 January 2021.

95   *Premier League Consumer Research*, Ofcom, 5 February 2016, www.ofcom.org.

96   Enders Analysis, op. cit.

97   Ibid.

98   Ibid.

99   Robinson and Clegg op.cit., Chapters 28 and 29.

100   Discussed in Chapter 1 and in more detail in Chapters 8 and 9.

101   Deloitte, op.cit.

102   Matt Slater, 'Explained: Project Big Picture – The winners and losers', *Athletic,* 12 October 2020.

3 Show Me the Money

1   Deloitte,op.cit., Office of National Statistics.

2   Kantarmedia.com, 16 August 2019.

3   Deloitte, *Home Truths: Annual Review of Football Finance,* 2020.

4 Deloitte, op.cit., net transfer spend. Manchester United plc., 2020 Annual Report, (wages exclude £20 million of severance payments), AFC Bournemouth, Annual Report and Financial Statements for the year ended 30 June 2019.

5 Deloitte, op.cit.

6 My analysis of Deloitte, worldmeters.info and IMF data.

7 Enders Analysis, *Peak Football Revenues and post-boom scenarios.*, 25 October 2019. Swiss Ramble, Twitter, 3 September 2019.

8 Enders Analysis, op. cit., Robinson and Clegg, op.cit.

9 EY and the Premier League, *The Economic Impact of the Premier League*, 2015, www.ey.com., Sportspromedia, op.cit..

10 Deloitte, op. cit.

11 Ibid.

12 Robinson and Clegg, op.cit., p.285.

13 EY and the Premier League (2015), op. cit.

14 Swiss Ramble, Twitter, 2 September 2019.

15 Swiss Ramble, Twitter, 23 June 2020.

16 Deloitte, op. cit.

17 Swiss Ramble, Twitter, 23 June 2020, op. cit., Deloitte, op. cit.

18 Ibid.

19 'Netting profits without trophies', Murad Ahmed, *Financial Times*, 4 March 2019.

20 Ibid.

21 Ibid.

22 'Manchester United unveil tech company as Chevrolet shirt sponsor replacement.', Emil Gjerding Nielson, *Off the Pitch*, 19 March 2021.

23 Swiss Ramble, Twitter, 23 June 2020.

24 My calculations based on Deloitte (2020), op.cit., 'Football clubs power past recession as investment soars.' Stephen Jepson and Mark Roberts, *Construction News*, 26 September 2013, and 'Tottenham's new stadium', Miguel Delaney, *Independent*, 2 April 2019.

25 'Tottenham's new stadium', Miguel Delaney, *Independent*, 2 April 2019.

26 David Hytner, 'Tottenham take £175m Bank of England loan to ease coronavirus impact.' *Guardian*, 4 June 2020.

27   Deloitte (2020), op.cit, and analysis of club annual reports 1998, 4 clubs are Manchester United, Arsenal, Tottenham Hotspur and West Ham United.

28   *'Everton stadium plans given green light.'* 26 March 2021, Evertonfc. com.

29   Jose Ignacio Gregorio Santos, 'The economic geography of football success: empirical evidence from European cities', *Rivista di dritto ed economia dello sport*, 2007.

30   Deloitte (2020), op.cit.

31   Swiss Ramble, 23 June 2020.

32   Deloitte, op.cit., and *'Revenue figures of German football clubs.'*, Christian Ott, www.chritianott.com, 25 May 2020.

33   Dan Roan, Twitter, 20 April 2021.

34   Deloitte, op. cit. The reported value of transfers was £1.8 billion, but this will typically be paid over several seasons; £1.3 billion is the amortisation in the accounts. This is the annual charge clubs estimate by dividing transfer payments over the length of player contracts, and is the measure used for financial regulation.

35   'Taking stock on pay', www.newfinancial.org, William Wright, February 2016.

36   Moments in Football History: The Bosman Ruling, 26th May 2020, www.bloomsburyfootball.com, op.cit.

37   Wages and success, see for example: Stefan Szymanski, *'The business of football'* open.edu, 11 April 2016; I. G. McHale, Fiona Carmichael and Dennis Thomas, 'Maintaining market position: Team performance, revenue and wage expenditure in the English Premier League', *Bulletin of Economic Research*, 2011.

38   Michael Lewis, *Moneyball: The Art of Winning An Unfair Game* (W. W. Norton, 2002).

39   'Why does Jim White wear a yellow tie on transfer deadline day?' *Sun*, 30 January 2018.

40   www.transfermarkt.co.uk., 'On this day: Alan Shearer joins Blackburn Rovers for British record fee.', www.sportsmole,com, 19 July 2020. Refers to moves between British clubs only.

41   Deloitte, *Annual Review of Football Finance 2002*.

42 Ibid.

43 Deloitte (2020), op.cit., and Mihir Bose (2012), op.cit.

44 'Bates sells Chelsea control to Russia.' *Irish Times,* 2 July 2003.

45 Data in this section derived from Deloitte, *Annual Review of Football Finance,* 2003 to 2020, and 'Premier League Wage Data 2000/1 to 2013/14', *Daily Telegraph,* www.telegraph.co.uk.

46 Nick Miller, 'Quote, unquote: Jose Mourinho's "Special One"', Football365.com, 28 July 2016., Deloitte, op.cit., Robinson and Clegg, op.cit., p.95.

47 Robinson and Clegg, op. cit., p.93–94, and *Daily Telegraph,* op.cit.

48 *'Premier League clubs spend £430 million in January transfer window.'* Deloitte Press Release, 1 February 2018. Note values quoted are Gross spend ie do not take account of receipts from selling players.

49 *Daily Telegraph,* op.cit.

50 Swiss Ramble, op.cit., 23 June 2020.

51 Deloitte, (2020), op.cit.

52 'EU finds that Barcelona and Real Madrid benefitted from illegal state aid in Spain for three decades.', Sam Wallace, *The Telegraph,* 4 March 2021.

53 'Timeline of Manchester City FFP case as their two-year European ban is lifted', PA Staff, fourfourtwo.com, 13 July 2020.

54 Deloitte (2020), op. cit.

55 'Premier League unveils cost control measures.', *Soccerex,* 8 February 2013.

56 Deloitte, op. cit.

57 My analysis of Deloitte (2020), op.cit.

58 'Everton make annual loss of £139 million as COVID-19 takes toll.', Andy Hunter, *The Guardian,* 11 December 2020. *'Aston Villa publish 2019/20 Year End Accounts.',* www.avfc.co.uk, 9 April 2021.

59 John Sinnott, 'Qatari takeover heralds new dawn for Paris Saint-Germain.', www,bbcsport,co.uk, 3 August 2011.

60 'Spanish clubs sold just 9 per cent of their tickets for the Super Cup in Saudi Arabia.' Emil Gjerding Nielsen, *Off the Pitch,* 8 January 2020.

61 For discussion of private equity interest in Italy and the potential sale of La Liga's tech unit see 'Potential for optimising stadium and commercial infrastructure will retain Serie A interest even if Private Equity sale breaks down.', *Off the Pitch*, 26 February 2021.

62 Swiss Ramble, 29 September 2019.

63 Joshua Robinson and Jonathan Clegg, op. cit., Chapter 28.

64 Joshua Robinson and Jonathan Clegg, (2019), op.cit. p.291 and Chapter 29.

65 Glenn Moore, *Football: A game in search of its soul. The Independent*, 14 April 1999.

66 www.premierleague.com, *Clubs agree new share of international television revenue.* 7 June 2018.

67 'Premier League: Significant concerns over European Super League.', James Corbett, *Off the Pitch*, 5 April 2019.

68 Deloitte, Money League 2021, *Testing Times'*, January 2021. 'Agnelli forecasts loss of up to €8.5 billion for European football clubs due to pandemic.', Emil Gjerding Nielsen, *Off the Pitch*, 27 January 2021.

69 Matt Slater (2020), *The Athletic* op. cit.

70 'Aleksander Ceferin and the battle to save European football from itself.', James Corbett, *Off the Pitch*, 7 December 2020.

4 The Best League in the World?

1 'The Canal', www.wedgewoodmuseum.org.

2 Goal.com, 31 January 2018.

3 'Incredible stat shows that ball was in play for less than 45 minutes in Stoke v time-wasting Watford,' Peter Smith, *Evening Sentinel*, 1 February 2018.

4 www.brainyquote.com, Mezit Ozil. Tony Pulis, Ilkay Gundogan, Danny Ings, David Luiz, Luka Modric and Emre Can amongst others are quoted describing the Premier League in these terms.

5 Shamoon Hafez, 'Calciopoli: The Scandal that rocked Italy and left Juventus in Serie B.', www.bbc.sport.co.uk, 5 October 2019.

6   EY and Premier League, *Premier League: Economic and Social Impact*, January 2019.

7   FIFA.com.

8   'List of Ballon d'Or winners', www.topendsports.com.

9   Fynn and Guest, op.cit., p.29.

10 Liam Apiella, 'On this day: UEFA bans British clubs from Europe.', BBC Sport, 4 June 2016.

11 BBC Sport, 28 May 2011.

12 'Barcelona legend Xavi reveals what Wayne Rooney said to him at end of 2011 Champions League Final,' Ollie Knight, www.90min. com, 17 November 2016.

13 UEFA.com, coefficients 2015/16 to 2020/21.

14 Robinson and Clegg, op. cit. p. 293.

15 For a summary of the literature see Selouko Zaydin and Murat Dondurian, An Empirical Study of Revenue Generation and Competitive Balance in European Football, *European Journal of Business Economics*, 12(24), 17–44, 2019.

16 Kjetil K. Haugen and Knut P. Heen, 'The competitive evolution of European top football – signs of danger', *European Journal of Sports Studies*, 2018.

17 *Daily Telegraph*, op. cit.

18 Kevin Keegan, quoted in Simon Kuper and Stefan Syzmanski, *Soccernomics* (Harper Collins, 2012), p.200.

19 Bose, op.cit., p.293. David Conn, Premier League Accounts show Sheik Mansour has put £1.3 Billion into club, *The Guardian*, 13 September 2018.

20 My analysis of league tables.

21 Paul Kelso, 'Premier League boss: Leicester give hope to all.', Sky Sports, 3 May 2016.

22 Rob Tanner, *5000–1. The Leicester City story: How we beat the odds to become Premier League Champions* (Allen & Unwin, 2016).

23 Transfermarkt.com.

24 Transfermarkt.com., values calculated at 1st September each season.

25 'Premier League agrees new financial regulations.', www.bbc. co.uk, 8 December 2013.

26 Swiss Ramble, 23 June 2020.

27 Swiss Ramble 28 May 2020

28 Crystal Palace Report and Accounts, 2017/18., Deloitte, op.cit.

29 Swiss Ramble, 28 May 2020.

30 Ibid.

31 Deloitte, op. cit.

32 Opta statistics.

33 Jonathan Wilson, *Inverting the Pyramid,* (Orion Books, 2008).

34 Jonathan Wilson, Premier League 2019–20 Review: What we learnt technically from the season. 28 July 2020, *Guardian.*

35 *'Armchair Fans: Modelling Audience Size for Televised Football Matches',* Centre for Sports Business, University of Liverpool Management School, 2020.

36 Global rankings, see for example www.soccerex.com, www.ispo.com.

37 Enders Analysis, *'Analysing UK Sports Rights.',* 20 January 2021. BARB 2016/17, 2018/19.

38 *Fan Attendance Report,* European Professional Football Leagues, 2018., Deloitte, op.cit.

39 Sean Ingle, 'Unpublished documents justify breakaway.', *Guardian,* 20 April 2021.

40 James Corbett, 'Premier League concerns on Champions League revamp.', *Off the Pitch,* 16 February 2021.

41 Ibid.

42 Tom Bassam, 'European Super League less valuable to broadcasters: BT Sports Simon Green.', www.sportspromedia.com, 18 February 2021.

43 James Corbett, 'Premier League concerns on Champions League revamp.', *Off the Pitch,* 16 February 2021.

5 We Shall Not Be Moved

1 'Huddersfield Town head for EPL after "football's richest game" win,' www.en.as.com, 29 May 2017.

2 'Why the Championship play-off is the richest game in soccer,' Matt Scott, www.espn.com, 29 May 2018.

3 Deloitte, *Annual Review of Football Finance*, 2002.

4 Deloitte (2020), op.cit., Huddersfield Town AFC Ltd., Group Strategic Report for the year ended June 2018.

5 Deloitte (2002), op.cit.

6 ONS.

7 Conn, op.cit., p.45.

8 Deloitte (2020), op. cit.

9 Swiss Ramble, op. cit., www.avfc.co.uk.

10 www.avfc.co.uk., op.cit.

11 Deloitte, op. cit.

12 DCMS Select Committee (2020), *Written evidence submitted by David Cockayne, Kieran Maguire and Professor Sue Bridgewater*, Centre for Sports Business, University of Liverpool Management School.

13 Deloitte (2020), op. cit.

14 Deloitte (2020), op. cit., payments in League 1 includes parachute payments to Sunderland.

15 Ibid.

16 Ibid.

17 Ibid.

18 Birmingham City deducted nine points for EFL Profit and Sustainability rule breaches, www.bbc.co.uk, 22 March 2019.

19 Mark Bisson, 'Q&A football finance experts', *Off the Pitch*, 9 September 2019.

20 Christian Fomsgarrd Jensen, 'Middlesbrough Chairman urges EFL to probe rivals over conduct,' *Off the Pitch*, 16 April 2019.

21 James Corbett, 'Behind the scenes at Bury and Bolton – seven days that shook the football world, *Off the Pitch*, 6 September 2019. DMCS Committee 2019, op. cit.

22 Ibid.

23 'Back from the brink', Football Daily, BBC Radio 5 Live, 28 August 2019.

24 DCMS, *Inquiry into the Administration of Football Clubs*, evidence session, 21 October 2019.

25 *Our Plan*. Conservative Manifesto 2019, conservatives.com. *It's time for change; The labour Party Manifesto 2019*.www.labour.org. uk. *Plan for Britain's Future*. www.libdems.org.uk.

26 Deloitte (2020), op.cit.

27 Adrian Goldberg, 'A major global scandal: the collapse of Wigan Athletic', www.bylinetimes.com, 6 July 2020.

28 Matt Slater, op.cit.

29 Centre for Sports Business, University of Liverpool Management School, 2020, op.cit.

30 Mark Palios, quoted on 'How to run a Football League club', Football Daily, BBC Radio 5 Live, 16 October 2019.

31 'Premier League is destroying the game while EFL is starving, says Accrington Chairman,' PA, *Guardian,* 9 May 2017.

32 Jonathan Dyson, 'Mind the Gap', *FC Business*, July 2019.

33 Michael Benson, 'Sheffield Wednesday have 12-point deduction halved to 6 points after breaching Profit and Sustainability rules,' talkSPORT, 4 November 2020.

34 'Mourinho: English prices are crazy.', www.thestar.com.my, 22 July 2005. 'Pep Guardiola bemoans high cost of English players.', www.independent.ie, 7 March 2017.

35 Deloitte, op. cit.

36 Dobson and Goddard, op.cit.

37 Deloitte (2020), op.cit.

38 Bryan Kelly, 'Why FIFA sanctioned Blues and what the appeal process is.', www.goal.com, 28 October 2019.Chelsea transfer ban

39 Murad Ahmed and John Burn-Murdoch, 'How player loans are reshaping Europe's transfer market.', *Financial Times,* 30 August 2019. Transfermarkt.com.

40 Graham Hill, 'Mark Hughes reckons Kurt Zouma is worth £40 million – and his £7 million Stoke loan is a bargain.' *The Sun, 30 September 2017.*

41 Transfermarkt.com.

42 www.efl.com.

6 We'll Support You Ever More

1 BT Sport, Champions' League Final broadcast, 23 August 2020.

2 Football Supporters' Federation, www.fsa.org.

3 Football Supporters' Federation, *National Supporters Survey 2017*, www.fsa.org.

4 Kevin Brandstatter and Paul Mertens, www.european-football-statistics.co.uk.

5 Ibid.

6 Andrew Aloia, '11 out of 20 Premier League clubs could have made profits in 2016–17 without fans at games.', www.bbc.co.uk, 13 August 2018.

7 Nick Hornby, *Fever Pitch* (Penguin, 1992), p.135.

8 EFL, *Supporters Survey 2019*.

9 The Hillsborough Stadium Inquiry, Final Report by the Rt Hon. Lord Justice Taylor, presented to Parliament January 1990.

10 Andy Kelly, 'History of Arsenal Ticket Prices since 1980', www.arsenalhistory.com.

11 *Annual Survey of Hours and Earnings*, (ASHE 2019), ONS.

12 'Premier League tickets cost £31 on average in season 2018/19.', Premier League Ticketing Study, Premier league Press Release, 6 November 2018. prices

13 Dobson and Goddard, op.cit.

14 Sam France, 'Premier League 2019–20 season tickets: How much does it cost for each club?', www.goal.com, 10 July 2019.

15 Nick Baker, 'What's the cheapest way to watch football on TV?', www.uswitch.com, 31 March 2021.

16 C. B. Stride, N. Catley and J. Headland, 'Shirt tales: how adults adopted the replica football kit', *Sport in History*, 2019.

17 EY and Premier League, *Stoke City Football Club: Economic and Social Impact Assessment*, September 2017.

18 Blake Welton and David Dubas-Fisher, 'REVEALED: How often Premier League clubs use their change kits during a season', *Yorkshire Live*, 17 July 2017.

19 Charli Casey, 'Premier League kit sales: Every club ranked by average global shirt sales per year from 2011/12 to 2015/16 – from lowest to highest', www.talksport.com, 18 October 2016.

20 *Lancs.Live*, 'Premier League kits: Burnley's the cheapest – Tottenham, Chelsea and Liverpool most expensive.' Douglas Dubas-Fisher and Alex James, 17 August 2020.

21 'Chelsea's new shirt deal shows sponsors are re-evaluating their potential ROI in football.', Emil Gjerding Nielson, *Off the Pitch*, 2 February 2020.

22 eToro Fan Financial Statement; research carried out in association with KPMG Football Benchmark, 26 November 2019, www.etoro.com.

23 *Inflation Calculator*, Bank of England. Wages from Kelly, op.cit. and ASHE, ONS, op.cit.

24 Office for National Statistics, *Family Spending in the UK: April 2018 to March 2019.*

25 Dan Roan, Twitter, 19 April 2021.

26 FSA research, www.fsa.com.

27 Enders Analysis, *Peak Football Revenues and post-boom scenarios.*, 25 October 2019.

28 Robinson and Clegg, op. cit., p. 297.

29 Ibid.

30 See for example, 'pre-season tours' Mark Bisson, *Off the Pitch*, 17 June 2019.

31 Summary of bond schemes in Fynn and Guest, op.cit., p.100–112.

32 'Liverpool fans' walkout protest', PA, *Guardian*, 6 February 2016.

33 Andy Hunter, 'Liverpool owner backs down on ticket prices and apologises to fans,' *Guardian*, 10 February 2016.

34 BBC, Cost of Football Study 2015, www.bbc.com.

35 FSA Statement on 'Twenty's Plenty', www.fsa.com, October 2015.

36 'Two of the wealthiest clubs in the Premier league were shamed into reversing cuts to staff wages amid the coronavirus pandemic.', Barney Lane, 14 April 2020, www.insider.com.

37 Conor Pope, 'Premier League fans raise hundreds of pounds for food banks in pay-per-view boycott.', *Four Four Two,* 29 October 2020.

38 For details see among others, *Guardian, Financial Times off The Pitch,* 19, 20 and 21 April 2021.

39 Paul MacInnes, 'Premier League's pay-per-view deal under fire from furious fans.' *Guardian,* 10 October 2020.

40 Enders Analysis, *Peak Football Revenues and Post-boom Scenarios,* 25 October 2019.

41 'Back from the Brink', Football Daily, Radio 5 Live, 28 August 2019..

42 Adrian Tempany, 'Has football lost touch with its young fans?' *Guardian,* 8 March 2014.

43 David Conn, 'The Premier League has priced out fans, young and old.', *Guardian,* 16 August 2011.

44 David Conn, 'The Premier League has priced out fans, young and old.', *Guardian,* 16 August 2011.

45 Premier League in conjunction with EY, *Premier League Ticket Research 2019/20,* 18 December 2019.

46 BBC Cost of Football Study 2017, op. cit.

47 FSA, www.fsa.org.uk, 29 November 2016.

48 From 'Fever Pitch and the rise of middle class football', Eamonn Walsh, BBC News, 6 March 2012.

49 Vincent Kompany, Executive Summary, MBA Final Project, www,newsroom.roulata.be., and Vikas Shah, www.thoughteconomics, 1 April 2018.

50 Alex Bryson, Peter Dolton, J. James Reade, Dominik Schreyer and Carl Singleton, *'Experimental Effects of an Absent Crowd on Performances and Refereeing Decisions during COVID-19',* IZA DP No. 13578, August 2020.

51 Bill Edgar, *The Times* 9 March 2021, to be updated at season end.

52 'Football Daily: Bury FC expelled from the Football League', BBC 5 Live, 28 August 2019.

53 DCMS, *Inquiry into the Administration of Football Clubs,* evidence session, 21 October 2019.

54 Chris Porter, *Supporter Ownership in English Football* (Palgrave Macmillan, 2019), p.186.

55 Ibid.

56 Adam Shergold, 'The scandal of Premier League ticket prices as €104 buys you a Bayern Munich season ticket!', *Daily Mail, 2 May 2013*.

57 Adam Crafton and more, 'European Super League explained', *The Athletic*, 18 April 2021.

58 'German soccer rules: 50+1 explained.', www.bundesliga.com, 2018.

59 Deloitte, op.cit.

60 https://www.gov.uk/government/news/government-announces-terms-of-reference-for-fan-led-review-of-football

61 Jasper Jolly, JP Morgan given lower sustainability rating after funding failed European Super League, *Guardian*, 21 April 2021.

7 You'll Never Walk Alone

1 EY and Premier League, *West Ham United Players' Project: Economic and Social Impact.'*, 6 November 2019.

2 EY and Premier League (2019), op.cit., Marks & Spencer plc., Annual Report 2019.

3 Tempany, Goldblatt, Conn (2005), Hornby, op. cit.

4 EY and Premier League, *'Newcastle United Football Club and Newcastle United Foundation: Economic and Social Impact.'*, February 2019.

5 EY and Premier League (2015), op.cit.

6 EY and Premier League (2019), op.cit.

7 Ibid.

8 EY and Premier League (2015), op.cit.

9 EY and Premier League (2017), op.cit.

10 Deloitte, *'Liverpool boosts Liverpool City Region.'*, 21/2/19, www.liverpoolfc.com.

11 EY and Premier League, *'Newcastle United Football Club and Newcastle United Foundation: Economic and Social Impact.'*, February 2019.

12 Crystal Palace for Life Foundation, Report of the Trustees and Financial Statements for year ended 30 June 2018.

13 The Premier League Charitable Foundation, Report and Financial Statements for year ended 31 July 2017.

14 EY and Premier League (2019), op.cit.

15 EY and Premier League (2017), op.cit.

16 EY and Premier League, 'Newcastle United Football Club and Newcastle United Foundation: Economic and Social Impact.', February 2019.

17 EY and Premier League (2017), op.cit.

18 EY and Premier League, 'Newcastle United Football Club and Newcastle United Foundation: Economic and Social Impact.', February 2019.

19 Sheffield Hallam (2016), op.cit.

20 www.thehubbfoundation.com

21 www.Footballfoundation.com

22 CEBR, 'Economic Impact of Football', 2 October 2012.

23 Dan Kilpatrick, 'Grassroots football in crisis.', Evening Standard, 14 December 2018.

24 Jeremy Wilson, 'Save our game.', Daily Telegraph, 18 October 2018.

25 www.Gothiacup.se.

26 Daily Telegraph (2018), op.cit.

27 Ibid.

28 Bernstein et al, Saving the Beautiful Game: A manifesto for change, October 2020.

29 'Letter from the Chairman.', www.wsyl.org.uk, April 2016.

30 The FA Limited, Annual Report and Financial Statements, Year ended 31st July 2018.

31 'GE 2019: Tories pledge £550 million for grassroots football.', www.bbc.co.uk, 7 December 2019.

32 Matt Slater (2020), op.cit.

33 PL Report and Accounts, year ending 31 July 2019.

34 David Conn, 'Football's crisis shines merciless light on game's inequalities.', Guardian, May 2021

35 Deloitte, op.cit.

8 It's Coming Home

1 Alex Fynn and Lynton Guest, *Out of Time* (Simon & Schuster, 1994), p. 51.

2 Joe Lovejoy, Norway destroy Taylor's England: Calamity in Oslo as a revamped team collapses in the face of Scandinavian skill. *The Independent*, 2 June 1993.

3 FIFA/Coca-Cola World Rankings, www.fifa.com, 7 June 2018.

4 I used ELO rankings (a categorisation developed initially by the Hungarian-American mathematician Arpad Elo and applied to Chess and Go, adapted for football by Bob Runyan and now published by elorankings.net) since 1966, switching to use the FIFA World Rankings from 1992 onwards.

5 Kuper and Szymanski, op. cit., p.309–11.

6 Rob Maul, 'Sweet comeback: David Beckham's pain at being constantly abused by fans while at Manchester United for England red card.', *The Sun,* 24 May 2019.

7 2018 World Cup squads, www.fifa.com.

8 Kuper and Syzmanski, op.cit., p.316.

9 Centre for Sports Business, University of Liverpool Management School, 2020, op. cit.

10 Football Supporters' Association Survey, www.thefsa.org.uk, 2017.

11 Kuper and Syzmanski, op.cit., p.317.

12 Joe Bernstein, *Daily Mail Online*, "there were only 13 foreign players when the Premier League began in 1992. So, how many do you remember?". 9 August 2017.

13 Robinson and Clegg, op.cit., p.85, 'Arsenal 5–1 Crystal Palace.', www.bbcsport.co.uk, 14 February 2005.

14 'England players starting Premier League games reaches record low,' www.bbcsport.com, 3 December 2018.

15 Transfermarkt.com.

16 Stephen Clarke, 'A Brave New World.', *Resolution Foundation Briefing,* August 2016, p.20.

17 Goldblatt, op.cit., p.187.

18   'Gareth Southgate warns Premier League could soon be only 15 per cent English,' *Guardian*, 18 May 2019.

19   Kuper and Syzmanski, op.cit., p335-348.

20   My analysis of club records on managers.

21   Barney Ronay, 'Marco Silva appears to be done in England – but he remains a managerial mystery,' *Guardian*, 5 December 2019.

22   Press Association, 'Frank Lampard will not allow himself to be the standard bearer for English managers.', www.btsport.com, 27 October 2020.

23   'England managers' results and statistics 1872–2020', www.myfootballfacts.com.

24   Graham Hunter, Spain: The Inside Story of La Roja's Historic Treble, quoted in Nathan Bliss, The revolution that changed Spain and has yet to arrive in England, www.thesefootballtimes, 11 May 2018.

25   Jonathan Wilson, 'Pioneering reds to the Reds: Why Jürgen Klopp's pressing is a perfect fit for the age,' *Guardian*, 1 February 2020.

26   Jonathan Wilson, *Inverting the Pyramid* (Orion, 2008).

27   Karan Twejani, 'Clairefontaine: the dream factory that changed French football for ever.', www.thesefootballtimes.com, 24 August 2018.

28   Matt Scott, 'FA takes control of coaching from Trevor Brooking,' *Guardian*, 29 September 2010.

29   'Long-term strategy developed to advance premier league youth development.', www.premierleague.com/youth/EPPP.

30   'The English DNA.', www.thebootroom.thefa.com, 10 October 2018.

31   Nathan Bliss, 'The revolution that changed Spain and the one yet to arrive in England', *These Football Times*, 17 May 2018.

32   Football Supporters' Association Survey, www.thefsa.org.uk, 2017. EFL, Supporters Survey 2019.

9 You Don't Know What You're Doing

1   DCMS, *Inquiry into the Administration of Football Clubs*, oral evidence, 21 October 2019.

2   Fynn and Guest, op. cit., p.26

3   For details see Conn (2005) op.cit., Goldblatt, op.cit.

4   Fynn and Guest, op. cit., p.37.

5   David Conn, 'How the FA betrayed their own game.', *Guardian*, 14 November 2004.

6   Wembley Stadium (1923), www.stadiumguide.com.

7   White City Stadium (1923), www.stadiumguide.com.

8   Bower, op. cit., Chapters 7 and 8.

9   'Stadium: The Facts and Features', www.wembleystadium.com.

10   'Rednapp and Grant: Wembley Pitch a disgrace', www.fourfourtwo. com, 11 April 2010.

11   Bower, op.cit., Chapters 7 and 8.

12   Conn, *The Beautiful Game?*, op. cit., p.294. Bose, op.cit., p186-7.

13   David Conn, *The Fall of the House of FIFA* (Yellow Jersey, 2017).

14   Insight Team, 'World Cup votes for sale', *Sunday Times*, 17 October 2010.

15   'FIFA's Dirty Secrets', *Panorama*, 10 December 2010, www.bbc. com.

16   Michael Seamark and Tim Shipman, 'World Cup "shamed": Four FIFA officials "wanted bribes", says ex-FA chief', *Daily Mail*, 11 May 2011.

17   FA, Strategic Plan 2016–20, www.thefa.com.

18   Daniel Taylor, 'Six come forward after Andy Woodward's allegations of abuse at Crewe,' *Guardian*, 21 November 2016.

19   Daniel Taylor, 'FA sets up review into child sex abuse in football after Barry Bennell claims,' *Guardian*, 27 November 2016.

20   'Southampton "abuser" still working in football', BBC News, 3 December 2016.

21   Jacob Steinberg, 'FA sexual abuse inquiry head ready to investigate any clubs who fail to co-operate', *Guardian*, 28 March 2018.

22   Daniel Taylor, 'FA sexual abuse inquiry finds no evidence of institutional cover-up,' *Guardian*, 26 July 2018.

23   'Child abuse inquiry accuses FA of "institutional failings"', Daniel Taylor and Luke Brown, *The Athletic*, 17 March 2021.

24   Daniel Taylor, 'Eni Aluko "hush-money" case: FA bows to pressure and reveals findings,' *Guardian*, 17 August 2017.

25   Eni Aluko: 'we all have moments in life when our morals are called into question.' Simon Hattenstone, *Guardian,* 24 August 2019.

26   Ibid.

27   'Mark Sampson: FA sorry over race remarks to Eniola Aluko and Drew Spence', www.bbc.co.uk, 18 October 2017.

28   Dr Steven Bradbury (Loughborough University), *'Levels of BAME Coaches in Football: 1ˢᵗ annual follow up report.'* On behalf of Sports People's Trust, October 2015.

29   Jonathan Liew, 'Football must face up to an indisputable truth: black managers do not get the same chances as white managers.', *Independent,* 4 June 2018.

30   Football Association, Annual Report 2018.

31   The FA Limited, Annual Report and Financial Statements, Year ended 31ˢᵗ July 2018.

32   BARB, 'Top 10 most watched UK TV programmes countdown.' Anthony Lane, www.showtimephotobooth.co.uk, 11 November 2015.

33   'FA cup Final on BBC sets viewing record for 2019–20 season.' www.bbc.co.uk, 2 August 2020.

34   'Wembley Stadium sale plan "ridiculous", says Gary Neville,' www. bbcsport.com, 18 July 2018.

35   'Wembley: Shahid Khan withdraws "divisive" offer to buy national stadium from FA,' 17 October 2018, www.bbc.com.

36   Sonny Cohen, 'Discrimination in football like "wild west" at grass roots level', *Guardian,* 24 July 2019.

37   Guy Davies, 'Racism in soccer an "epidemic" that mirrors disturbing trends in Europe', abcnews.com, 1 February 2020.

38   Kick It Out reveals 'shocking' rise in reports of racism in football.', Sean Ingle, *The Guardian,* 3 September 2020.

39   www.efl.com.

40   Lawrie Holmes, 'Powerful Championship clubs at war with EFL over Sky deal', *Off the Pitch,* 17 September 2019.

41   Kuper and Syzmanski, op. cit., p.81.

42   DCMS, op. cit.

43   DCMS Inquiry, op.cit., Q11.

44   DCMS Inquiry, op.cit., Q72.

45 DCMS Inquiry, op.cit., Q74.

46 DCMS Inquiry, op.cit., Q82, Q104, Q109.

47 DCMS Inquiry, op.cit., Q82.

48 DCMS Inquiry, op.cit., Q118.

49 David Bond, '99 per cent vote to strike in TV row.', *Evening Standard*, 13 April 2012.

50 David Conn, 'Gordon Taylor is paid four times sum of benevolent grants to former players,' *Guardian*, 16 February 2018.

51 PFA AGM: *Proposal for the Future of the PFA*, www.pfa.com.

52 'Back from the brink', *Football Daily*, Radio 5 Live, 28 August 2019.

53 Jack Gaughan, 'Ilkay Gundogan hits out at UEFA over Champions' League reforms.', *Daily Mail*, 22 April 2021.

54 Fynn, op. cit., p.28.

55 Quoted by Glenn Moore, 'Football: A game in search of its soul', *Independent*, 14 April 1999.

56 Bernstein et al, *Saving the Beautiful Game: A manifesto for change*, October 2020.

57 'Former Football Association executives urge reform of FA governance,' www.committees.parliament.uk, 12 December 2016.

58 FA Annual Review 2017.

59 Alyson Rudd, '"We're not trusted by the public," says FA Chief Greg Clarke,' *The Times*, 27 October 2017.

60 Paul Macinnes, 'FA Chairman Greg Clarke resigns after "unacceptable" comments,' *Guardian*, 10 November 2020.

61 'Debbie Hewitt MBE nominated as new FA non-executive chair'. www.thefa.com, 8 June 2021.

62 James Corbett, 'Premier League concerns on Champions League revamp.', *Off the Pitch*, 16 February 2021.

63 https://www.gov.uk/government/news/government-announces-terms-of-reference-for-fan-led-review-of-football

10 World in Motion

1 James Reade, Matthew Olczak and Matthew Yeo, 'The spread of Covid-19 and attending football matches in England', www.voxeu.org,

30 November 2020. Chris Bengel, 'Coronavirus: How a Champions' League match contributed to Italy's COVID-19 outbreak', CBSsports. com, 25 March 2020

2 Sam Wallace, 'World exclusive – Manchester United and Liverpool driving Project Big Picture, football's biggest shake-up in a generation', *Daily Telegraph*, 11 October 2020.

3 Phil Dawke, 'The 1970 FA Cup Final:The most brutal game in English football history.'www.bbcsport.co.uk, 27 April 2020.

4 Deloitte 2020, op. cit.

5 Alex Fynn quoted in the Foreword of *The English Premier League: A Socio-Cultural Analysis,* edited by Richard Elliot, 2017, Routledge.

6 *Disruption in Premier League Football: 2018 Auction finally over?,* Julian Aquilina, Enders Analysis, 8 June 2018.

7 Ibid.

8 Ibid.

9 Enders Analysis, *Amazon's Premier League performance. No challenge for premium packages,* 20 March 2020.

10 Enders Analysis, *'Champions' League senses end of growth cycle.',* 26 November 2019.

11 Enders Analysis, *'Peak football and post-boom scenarios.',* 26 October 2019.

12 Enders Analysis, *'Premier League Auction: Not ripe for GAFAN disruption.',* 9 February 2018.

13 Enders Analysis, *'Peak football and post-boom scenarios.',* 26 October 2019.

14 'BT confirms talks over the future of its sports business.", www. bbc.co.uk, 29 April 2021.

15 Enders (2021), op.cit.

16 Jim O'Neill, *'Building Better Global Economics BRICs.',* Global Economics Paper No:66, Goldman Sachs, 30 November 2001.

17 Robinson and Clegg, op.cit., p.231.

18 'Betting advertisements absent among football's biggest brands', Henrik Lonne, *Off the Pitch,* 12 June 2019.

19 'Asian shirt sponsors may overpay due to naivety', Alex Miller, *Off the Pitch,* 3 November 2019.

20 'Bet365 reported 80 per cent of all sports betting revenue derived in-play', Jackson L., Live Betting at Bet365, www.online-betting. me.uk, 2015.

21 "Children 'bombarded' with betting adverts during World Cup", Pamela Duncan, Rob Davies and Mark Sweeney, *Guardian*, 15 July 2018.

22 Premier League shirt sponsors facilitate 'illegal' gambling.', Joey d'Urso, *The Athletic,* 2 February 2021.

23 'Its not a coincidence', Emil Gjerding Nielsen and Kasper Kronenburg, *Off the Pitch*, 10 February 2021.

24 'China appears to demote Premier League football broadcasts', Helen Davidson, 23 July 2020, *Guardian*.

25 'Premier League terminates deal with Chinese broadcaster', Emil Gjerding Nielson, *Off the Pitch*

26 David Conn, *The fall of the house of FIFA*, Yellow Jersey Press, 2017. 'Inside Russia's plot to buy the World Cup, James Corbett, *Off the Pitch*, 6 November 2019.

27 'Why the Gulf States are betting on sport', Murad Ahmed, *Financial Times*, 27 November 2019

28 'Broadcast giant seeks to claw back millions after piracy scandal', James Corbett, *Off the Pitch,* 14 September 2020.

29 Jasper Jolly, JP Morgan given lower sustainability rating after funding failed European Super League, *Guardian*, 21 April 2021.

30 'Nike's disappearing boot deals', Adam Crafton, The Athletic, 4 February 2021.

31 Chris Dillow, 'Capitalists against competition.', *Stumbling and Mumbling,* 19 April 2021.

32 Emma Smith, " 'Absolutely critical' that fans return as soon as possible.', says Premier League chief Masters.", www.goal.com, 10 September 2020.

33 Deloitte, Money League 2021, *'Testing Times.'*

34 'Agnelli forecasts loss of up to €8.5 billion for European football clubs due to pandemic.', Emil Gjerding Nielsen, *Off the Pitch,* 27 January 2021.

35 *'The Beautiful Game.',* op.cit.

11 Believe in Better

1 Survey results: Drop League Cup, block Big Six, little faith in FA and EFL', Staff, *The Athletic,* 31 October 2020.

2 For details see among others, *Guardian, Financial Times, Off The Pitch,* 19, 20 and 21 April 2021.

3 Survey results: Drop League Cup, block Big Six, little faith in FA and EFL', Staff, *The Athletic,* 31 October 2020.

4 *Our Plan.* Conservative Manifesto 2019, conservatives.com.

5 FSA, EFL and Athletic surveys, all op.cit.

6 Matt Smith (2020), op.cit.

7 Liverpool University, op.cit.

8 Matt Slater, op.cit.

9 Paul MacInnes, 'FIFA takes aim at super-agent influence with regulations and fee restriction.' *Guardian,* 5 November 2020.

10 FSA Supporter Survey op.cit. Total revenues include all TV and sponsorship income for the Premier League and EFL.

11 'European Super League: Give fans a voice, support the pyramid and create a regulator – how to fix football.', *The Times,* 24 April 2021.

12 Ibid.

13 Ibid.

14 Luke Bosher, 'North Macedonia, Luxembourg – are Europe's smaller nations catching up or is this a blip?, *The Athletic,* 1 April 2021.